HITLER'S GOLD

HITLER'S GOLD

THE NAZI LOOT AND HOW IT WAS
LAUNDERED AND LOST

NORMAN RIDLEY

FRONTLINE
BOOKS

First published in Great Britain in 2023 by
Pen & Sword Frontline Books
An imprint of
Pen & Sword Books Ltd
Yorkshire – Philadelphia

Copyright © Norman Ridley 2023

ISBN 978-1-39905-260-3

The right of Norman Ridley to be identified as the author of this work has been asserted by him in accordance with the Copyright, Designs and Patents Act 1988.

A CIP catalogue record for this book is
available from the British Library.

All rights reserved. No part of this book may be reproduced or transmitted in any form or by any means, electronic or mechanical, including photocopying, recording or by any information storage and retrieval system, without permission from the Publisher in writing.

Typeset by Lapiz Digital
Printed and bound by CPI UK

Pen & Sword Books Limited incorporates the imprints of Atlas, Archaeology, Aviation, Discovery, Family History, Fiction, History, Maritime, Military, Military Classics, Politics, Select, Transport, True Crime, Air World, Frontline Books, Leo Cooper, Remember When, Seaforth Publishing, The Praetorian Press, Wharncliffe Local History, Wharncliffe Transport, Wharncliffe True Crime, White Owl and After the Battle.

For a complete list of Pen & Sword titles please contact:

PEN & SWORD BOOKS LIMITED
47 Church Street, Barnsley, South Yorkshire, S70 2AS, England
E-mail: enquiries@pen-and-sword.co.uk
Website: www.pen-and-sword.co.uk

or

PEN AND SWORD BOOKS
1950 Lawrence Rd, Havertown, PA 19083, USA
E-mail: Uspen-and-sword@casematepublishers.com
Website: www.penandswordbooks.com

CONTENTS

Author's Note vii

Chapter 1 The Financing of Warfare 1
Chapter 2 Nazi Plunder of European Monetary Gold 10
  Austria. 11
  Czechoslovakia 14
  Poland 20
  Denmark 22
  Norway 22
  The Netherlands 23
  Belgium. 25
  France 33
  Greece 34
  Albania 34
  Italy 35
Chapter 3 Trading with the Third Reich. 40
  Sweden 42
  Turkey 44
  Spain 47
  Portugal. 49
  Switzerland. 52
Chapter 4 The Swiss Banks. 53
Chapter 5 The Bank for International Settlements. 60
Chapter 6 Ustaše Gold and the Vatican. 67
Chapter 7 Safehaven. 71
Chapter 8 The Red House Document 76
Chapter 9 The Merkers Mine and the Foreign Exchange
    Depository 82

Chapter 10	Melmer Gold	91
Chapter 11	Degussa	100
Chapter 12	Hungarian Gold Trains	104
Chapter 13	Eagle and Jackdaw	108
Chapter 14	The Gold Pot and the Paris Reparations Conference	112
Chapter 15	The Tripartite Gold Commission	122
Chapter 16	Allied Negotiations with Neutral Countries	130
	Sweden	130
	Portugal	131
	Spain	133
	Turkey	135
	Argentina	137
Chapter 17	Ratlines	138
Chapter 18	The Argentine Connection	142
Chapter 19	Martin Bormann: Casualty or Fugitive?	148
Chapter 20	The London Conference of 1997	164
Chapter 21	Treasure Hunters	169
	Globocnik and the Wassensee Horde	169
	The Walbrzych Gold Train	173
	Minkowskie Palace	174
	Hochberg Palace	175
	Secrets hidden in a Music Score?	176
	Hans Glueck and the Arrach Treasure	177

Postscript *180*
Appendix 1 US Military Intelligence report EW-Pa 128 .... *182*
Appendix 2 Part III of the Paris Reparations Agreement *186*
Sources *189*
Notes *194*
Index *202*

AUTHOR'S NOTE

In the context of this book, gold falls into five categories based on its origin.

1. Gold which came under the control of the Reichsbank through the actions of the Third Reich, which included extortion by tax laws and foreign currency regulations. Previous owners could be of German Jewish or non-Jewish origin, as well as other disenfranchised persons, groups or institutions in Germany.
2. Confiscated and plundered gold includes assets confiscated by the Third Reich from the Jewish population, beginning with the 1938 Anschluss, as well as theft from residents and citizens of annexed and occupied areas resulting from state or private plundering. The plundered gold was either transferred to the reserves of the Reichsbank, used on the black markets, or hoarded.
3. Victim gold is a term used to denote the gold assets the regime confiscated from the victims of concentration and extermination camps, primarily by the SS, headed by the commercial administrative headquarters (WVHA), and includes property from various camps and ghettos in Eastern Europe.
4. Gold from currency reserves of the central banks of occupied countries.
5. Gold from holdings that came into the possession of the Reichsbank before 1933, or were acquired through regular transactions before the outbreak of war.

Chapter 1

THE FINANCING OF WARFARE

'Throughout history, the ability to mobilize huge amounts of capital has been the true sinew of power and the most important ingredient in waging successful war.'[1]

From the sourcing of raw materials for weapons, the manufacture of the same and the paying and maintaining of combat personnel and equipment, fighting wars has always been a costly business. At the dawn of the Roman Empire, Cicero (106-43 BCE) pointed out that the crucial sinew of war is, and always has been, 'endless streams of money'.[2] Traditionally, wars would last only as long as a protagonist's financial resources, either its own or that plundered from the vanquished, held out. Given sufficient funds there were always well-armed mercenaries for hire, but once the coffers were empty armies would disappear almost overnight.

Athens is an example of how superior wealth allowed logistically inferior states to overcome the odds in war. When the Athenians uncovered rich seams of silver in the Laurion mines some 25 miles south of Athens in 490 BCE, much of the proceeds were allocated to building the ships with which Themistocles destroyed the Persian fleet under Xerxes at the battle of Salamis in 480 BCE. This proved to be one of the most significant battles in the whole of history. The Greek victory stemmed the tide of conquest by Asiatic peoples and laid the foundation for the flowering of a civilisation upon which all future European culture was built. The wealth that Greece amassed over the ensuing years would later finance the wars of conquest waged by the Macedonian king Philip II and his son, Alexander the Great. Alexander's campaigns, which reached as far as India, would, at their peak, cost half a ton of silver a day, but the loot he acquired from conquest more than compensated for this and allowed him to create one of the largest empires the world has ever seen.

Rome was another example of how wealth acquired through conquest financed yet more conquest and built an empire. After the fall of Carthage in 146 BCE and the ensuing plunder of its riches, the Romans conquered and looted Sidon and Greece before turning to Spain, where they gained control of the silver mines near Rio Tinto in the Huelva province that had already been worked on a small scale for 2,000 years. They immediately set about expanding mining operations until they had over fifty excavations worked by thousands of slave labourers. This wealth fuelled further military campaigns that saw Roman armies plunder the wealth of conquered peoples all across the Mediterranean; wealth that had been accumulated by the vanquished over many generations. It was a costly business, though. In the early days of empire, up to half of all expenditure of the Roman state went on its military, but later, when opportunities for looting were becoming a rarity, the failure of the state to tax the enormous wealth of its leading citizens became a significant factor in the decline of its military power. The Roman elites, whose personal wealth had grown out of the trading and exploitative opportunities that came with empire, stubbornly refused to recognise their debt to the Roman armies, whose foreign conquests had created the environment within which they had prospered. While the population of Rome grew rich, less and less of that wealth was spent on the military, and such wealth as was accumulated by the military, such as Pompey, whose armies of occupation controlled the Spanish silver mines, would eventually be used up financing their own personal political ambitions and result in civil war. Ultimately, towards the end of its empire, it would be the failure to adequately protect the wealth-producing areas of North Africa from attack and conquest by the Vandals that ripped into Rome's economy and began to erode its ability to defend itself. Its self-confidence ebbed as its enemies grew bolder. Trading networks suffered and provinces saw opportunities to break away from Roman domination. As a result, Rome's armies in Northern Europe became under-resourced and demoralised and eventually fell to the Huns and Goths, whose forces were supported by a much less sophisticated economic model. All of Rome's technologically superior military machine fell apart when the state was no longer able to finance it.

The fall of Rome led to a dark age, when the empire fragmented into localised regimes that lacked the administrative skills and resources to build sophisticated military machines. It was only when the Vikings swept in from Scandinavia during the ninth century and succeeded in occupying much of Britain and Northern Europe that provinces, once again, acquired common values and embryonic governments. Ironically, it was this invasion of the Norsemen that coerced Britain particularly into a more integrated state with a unified purpose, as it developed a system of taxation that would allow the kings to meet the huge demands of Danegeld, the annual payment the Norsemen demanded as tribute in return for peaceful occupation. This developed into Heregeld (army tax), which Anglo-Saxon kings raised to support a standing army.

Britain was not the only state to grow rich and militarily powerful through taxation. The Norman king William the Conqueror developed his own Danegeld-inspired system of taxation to accumulate surplus funds to finance a campaign of conquest, which eventually included Britain in 1066. Meanwhile, William's descendants, ruling from London, would go on to exert an influence well beyond the country's shores. With a state economy founded on silver currency, however, debasement of its coinage slowly drained its ability to pay for mercenary armies until drastic measures involving the brutal removal of fraudulent mint-masters once again gave Britain a stable currency that became the standard coinage throughout Europe. The taxation system inherited from Alfred the Great that had underpinned the Danegeld payments had become so efficient by the thirteenth century that per capita state revenues in Britain were, on average, more than double those of its European mainland rivals at the time, which gave it a significant advantage when financing its military. This paled into insignificance, however, when compared with the per capita state revenues of ancient Persia, ancient Egypt and even Rome at the height of its powers.[3]

The economic impact of the First Crusade at the end of the eleventh century had been to transfer wealth from the European states, who mortgaged themselves to finance it, to the countries that supplied the mercenaries and the Middle East countries where much of the coinage was spent. Feudal barons literally impoverished themselves to take part in the Crusade and pay for the upkeep of their strongholds in the east. Taxation of nations to pay for the Crusade, however, was resented by the people whose wealth was inexorably moving east and those that had been left to administer the countries began to resent seeing the nation's wealth drain away. They began to delay and eventually prevent the transfer of funds to the east. The Crusader empire quickly crumbled through lack of finance. The withheld funds that had been so efficiently collected to finance the Crusade were used instead to create a much more centralised state power structure, with more opportunities for ruling monarchs to finance their military adventures. The cost of this was that the kings now had to persuade the feudal lords to cooperate in the raising of taxes and this they would only do in return for a slow erosion of regal prerogative.

Interestingly, the transfer of funds to pay mercenaries and maintain the strongholds in the east during the crusades had required new and innovative economic structures. Rather than carry huge amounts of coin across the continent, a precarious venture at any time, the Crusaders deposited silver in a western castle run by the Knights Templars and in return received a note of credit which they could present to another Templar castle closer to the action and, in return, receive silver coin there, minus a substantial fee, of course. These were the first operations of what would become the international banking system. The Italians were the first to take advantage and it was there the powerful Italian merchant banking families like the Franzesi Brothers, who became bankers to Philip IV of France in 1290, and the Riccardi of Lucca emerged. These bankers became rich by lending to states that wanted to wage military campaigns and had to be careful about which side to back in a dispute. States that borrowed heavily and failed to benefit financially through their wars became indebted to the bankers unable to repay the loans. In such cases, the bankers had to be very careful and not demand too much too soon, because rulers were not beyond simply refusing to acknowledge the debt or even taking bankers hostage and bargaining their lives against cancellation of the debt. There was always the risk that the bankers themselves would become the target of military action. Some bankers such as the Bardi and Peruzzi families overextended themselves with loans to Edward III, who subsequently defaulted, leading to the collapse of their banking enterprises and plunging Europe into a financial crisis. The French lands that had been under the English crown since the Norman conquest were reclaimed by indigenous rulers as British kings became increasingly unable to pay for the mercenary armies to defend them, and Italian bankers in general became wary of lending to states for the purpose of waging war.

A new age of warfare emerged with the capture of the gold and silver wealth of the Americas by the Spanish in the sixteenth century, which allowed them to finance a major military conquest in pursuit of a new empire. However, once again it was by overextending its military adventures that the country, despite its control of New World riches, began to default on its loans and slipped into decline as a world power, taking down the once fabulously wealthy Fugger banking family with it in 1657. The Ming Empire in China had linked its own economy to New World plunder and also faltered alongside the Spanish. Thereafter, rather than confront the Spanish in direct combat, the British chose to exert pressure on Spain's main creditors (by then a number of Genoese banking houses), to refuse any more loans to Spain. In an early example of economic warfare, Sir Francis Walsingham is reputed to have cornered large numbers of bills drawn on these banks in order to squeeze their capital reserves which, in turn, reduced their ability to lend to Spain and delayed the build-up of resources to equip the Spanish fleet. It became not so much a question of how wealthy a nation was per se, but how much it could raise in loans; in other words, its credit rating determined a country's capacity to wage war.

In another revolutionary innovation, in 1694 the British king William III increased his ability to raise capital to finance his war against Louis XIV of France by extending the concept of loans to include long-term debt. This was achieved by establishing the Bank of England to administer all the nation's finances. The government was then able to borrow money from the bank and, rather than be required to repay the loan within a fixed, short time period, the bank would demand only payment of interest on the loan while retaining the value of the loan as an asset on their books.

The War of the Spanish Succession (1702-1713) saw almost all European nations end up in penury, but it was the British who would come out of it best by slowly extending the loan period of its debts. All loans at this time were based upon gold and silver, and when John Law tried to create a system based on printed money, it collapsed spectacularly in 1720 when confidence in the new currency disappeared almost overnight and plunged France into a debt crisis that would last for a generation. Britain avoided catastrophe by creating the South Sea Company in 1711, which took on much of its war debts. When the South Sea Bubble burst at the same time as France's disastrous Mississippi Company went bankrupt, instead of defaulting, Britain agreed to pay perpetual annuities to debtors, which at least gave them something rather than nothing, in return for the debtors never asking for repayment of the original loan. This inevitably saved Britain's credit rating, while that of France was greatly diminished, but resulted in Britain accumulating a 'national debt', shares in which became tradeable between private investors. This allowed Britain to finance debts that grew well beyond what it could otherwise service based on its size and population.

When Britain migrated from an agrarian society into an industrial one, the taxable base grew enormously and inevitably increased Britain's ability to service its debts and so increase its capacity to raise money through further loans and crucially use these loans to create an armament industry on the back of the Industrial Revolution. The system allowed the country to leave much of its wealth circulating in the economy rather than accumulating in vaults and this again created an environment in which the economy flourished.

When the First World War broke out in 1914, Germany had some £70 million in gold stored in the 'Julius Tower', a fortress in Spandau which had been amassed as a result of reparations paid by France after the Franco-Prussian War. The German states had united and adopted the mark as their common currency, basing it on the gold standard. Other countries followed suit, which left silver rather out on a limb and countries such as India, China and Japan, who kept silver as the basis for their coinage, suffered a wave of inflation as a glut of silver hit world markets and depressed its value. The French debt was met through loans and the French continued to rely on loans over taxation to finance its contribution to the First World War, which partly explains the French insistence on German reparations afterwards.

This German gold reserve in 1914 gave them the confidence to risk future wars and so exert its influence over its neighbours who had nothing like those sorts of gold reserves. Britain, however, was not intimidated, believing in the end that its ability to raise loans would more than equal Germany's financial clout, and since loans could be extended, they would still be financing a war long after Germany's gold had been used up. As it happened, £70 million would be enough to cover no more than a single month of German government expenditure at the height of the conflict.

On the Allied side, it was only access to huge U.S. financial resources that prevented the collapse of the British economy. Private loans raised in the U.S. accounted for almost half of Britain's wartime loans and even that was insufficient when, in 1917, the U.S. government was obliged to step in and lend money to Britain. While finance was always a problem for both sides in the war, industrial capacity to sustain conflict was never a limiting factor as long as it could be supported by financial loans. Britain had raised taxes by a factor of four and had plundered those revenues designed to establish a social welfare system, but could still not meet the cost of the war. Nevertheless, it was able to sustain a long conflict even though it was falling ever deeper into debt. By the end of 1918 it had increased its national debt by a factor of ten and was forced to curtail its sale of perpetual annuities in favour of time-limited bond sales. Furthermore, the country had resorted to simply printing money to pay for the war, almost creating conditions for the sort of ruinous inflation that was to overcome Germany a few years later.

Britain's fiscal system had shown itself to be sufficiently robust to fund a global war against another industrial power, but in doing so, the country had mortgaged itself and lost its dominant position of global financial leadership to the U.S. The war ended when most warring nations had reached the end of their financial rope. While their industries could still expand production of war matériel, there was no money or credit available to pay for such an expansion.

As Hitler rose to power, in January 1933 the economic situation in Germany was dire. Stocks of raw materials had been depleted, factories and warehouses lay empty, and about 6.5 million people were unemployed and on the verge of malnutrition, while the country itself was crushed by debt and its foreign exchange reserves approached zero. During the latter half of the 1930s, Germany tried to create an autarky, or self-sufficiency, of sorts, although they had little chance of achieving this in its totality. Since they relied heavily on imported food, which would have required increased agricultural production, for instance, this would have impacted negatively on their industrial capacity. What they hoped for and planned for was to achieve military autarky by employing their industrial base in support of war production as protection against economic blockade by enemies. This involved the complete reorganisation of the economic and political life of the country on a scale that could never be accomplished in a peacetime democracy.

Putting the domestic economy on a war footing and maintaining economic stability required low inflation to control prices and a strong currency. One requirement of the state strategy to control the exchange rate of the Reichsmark was a ban on the export of capital, especially gold and other precious metals. Thereafter, President of the Reichsbank Hjalmar Schacht's expert management of the German economy and Reichsmark exchange rates achieved the desired results. Trade thrived, but alongside this was the increasing tendency for Germany, in a deliberate policy, to delay payments to countries they were trading with. This resulted in a build-up of involuntary credit other countries extended to Germany and in effect resulted in interest-free loans from countries that now developed economic dependency on Germany and became locked into continuing their trading relationship on ever increasing onerous terms or risk total German default on their debts to them.[4] Such an economic model would not withstand a prolonged exposure to war. When other European nations contemplated Germany waging another war, they assumed that its economy would be able to withstand only a short war or the country's economy would collapse through failure to finance imports. Germany had, to some extent, overcome this limitation by its annexation of Austria and Czechoslovakia, which had allowed it to incorporate the gold reserves and resources of those countries, especially the Czech armament industries, into the German economy. Hitler may also have gambled on taking over Poland and Ukraine without precipitating a major war, but in the end had to deal with the reality of finding enough money to pay for a long war. This meant that trade with neutral countries like Sweden, Spain and Portugal, or the U.S. for that matter before Pearl Harbor, was essential to maintaining the output of its armament industries. None of these countries, however, was likely to accept Reichsmarks in payment for goods. The only acceptable currency available to them was gold and Swiss francs.

Schacht had transformed the German economy with an ingenious new economic device involving the issuing of bills of exchange drawn against newly produced goods, which maintained a balance between the amount of goods and the amount of cash in the economy. In this way, Germany was able to exit a long and deep depression, and to attain non-inflationary full employment in a short span without resorting to price controls or rationing. Through careful handling of this thriving economy, Schacht was able to assiduously build up a hidden gold reserve of some 500 million Reichsmarks in the Goldankauf, Treuhandgesellschaft and Asservat Devisen Reserve accounts, similar to the way in which the country had done before 1914. Schacht had accumulated this secret hoard without making it known to many of the top Nazis, whom he understandably suspected would plunder it for their own uses, and he would later claim that the motivation for building this reserve had nothing to do with preparing for an aggressive war. He fell foul of the Nazi hierarchy, however, and was replaced in 1939 by Walther Funk, who quickly brought the existence of this treasure to the attention of Hitler and Göring. Funk, however, was no banker, and it was his deputy, Emil Puhl, who was the real power behind the throne and would become responsible for using this reserve and the looted gold to finance the war effort. Under his control, with customary German attention to detail, books were maintained recording all gold receipts, re-smelting, and subsequent transactions. These records would prove invaluable when the reckoning came in 1945.

By the end of the Second World War, argues James Lacey of the U.S. Army War College, even the U.S., as the only power still possessed of the financial resources to continue the conflict at the same intensity, was showing signs of financial strain. As a result of the war, it had grown its national debt from 40% of Gross Domestic Product (GDP) to

120%, but it was still at 107% by the middle of 2022 due to the financing of domestic programmes, and Britain's was 81%. Whilst the U.S. has a massive economy in 2023 and remains the world's reserve currency, it has the capacity to manage its current debt load, but the extent to which either it, or Britain, could manage its debt load in the event of a future war is problematic. China, by comparison, had a debt to GDP ratio of around 50% in 2022, and Russia 12%. There is no clear opinion of how far the ratio can be stretched, but there will certainly be a breaking point if it continues to rise at this rate. In some future national emergency, it is quite likely that the U.S. may find itself in a position where it cannot raise the funds required to defend the nation; a state of affairs that has been all too common over the long sweep of history. Today's strategists and policymakers must take this financial limit into account.

Chapter 2

NAZI PLUNDER OF EUROPEAN MONETARY GOLD

'The Reichsbank possesses no more gold.'
Reichsbank President Hjalmar Schacht to
Adolf Hitler, 7 January 1939

In the summer of 1936, the German economy was in crisis, forcing the government into drastic action. In a draconian measure, Hermann Göring, in his capacity as Reich Plenipotentiary of the Four Year Plan and de facto controller of the German economy, ordered that every ounce of gold in the country and all Germany's remaining foreign assets were to be put at the disposal of a special investigative service for foreign currency assets, headed by Reinhard Heydrich of the SS.[1] At the beginning of March 1938, Germany's official gold reserves were almost depleted, but Schacht had squirreled a significant amount away in secret accounts that were consequently not available to prop up the domestic economy. By this time Göring was desperate for foreign currency to purchase raw materials from outside the country for the rearmament programme, with all thought of autarky now also blown away by the need to meet demand for domestic consumer goods that would ensure the German people retained confidence in the government. With Hitler eying the political prize of gobbling up the Austrian state, its gold reserves in the vaults of Viennese banks were by no means an irrelevance.

Austria

On 12 March 1938, German forces marched into Vienna and enacted the Anschluss. Austria thus became part of the Third Reich and gave Göring and Schacht the opportunity they needed to take possession of all 78,267 kg of Austrian monetary gold and foreign currency reserves. Monetary gold was that owned by the state and held as a national reserve to validate its currency and was an integral part of monetary systems based on a gold or a gold-foreign exchange standard. An order was signed by Schacht, German Finance Minister Johann Schwerin and Interior Minister Wilhelm Frick that liquidated the Austrian National Bank (Öesterreichische Nationalbank, OeNB) which then became part of the Deutsche Reichsbank, whose officials assumed all power at the Vienna Reichsbank head office and at all other Reichsbank offices located throughout the annexed Austrian territory. Very soon, all officials, employees and workers of the bank who did not conform to the demands of the new regime were dismissed, sent into retirement, or arrested. The monetary gold had been boxed up prior to the Anschluss in readiness for evacuation to Brno in Czechoslovakia and then London, but had not been evacuated in time and was taken instead directly to Berlin and deposited in the Reichsbank. A further 22,341 kg of Austrian gold held in the Bank of England was transferred to the Reichsbank account through the Bank for International Settlements (BIS) in Basel on 1 April. The price of gold on the international market soared.

Monetary gold alone, however, was never going to satisfy the Nazis. There was significant residual wealth within the population of Vienna from the days of the Austro-Hungarian Empire to whet their appetite for more plunder. A law was quickly enacted on 23 March 1938 which required all Austrian citizens to declare their gold and foreign currency and sell it to the state bank. Of course, prices offered were low, but there was plenty of evidence of the sort of consequences that would flow if people refused to comply.[2] The Jews were an obvious and convenient target and immediately after the German occupation, a wave of anti-Semitic terror swept the country that the U.S. foreign correspondent, William Shirer, called 'much more ruthless and sadistic than anything [he had] seen in Germany'.[3] The Gestapo compiled a complete inventory of assets and valuables belonging to wealthy Jews, all of which would be sold to the Berlin Pawn Institute (Berliner Zentrale Pfandleihe). Altogether, in this way they stole 14.3 tons of private gold, largely from the Jewish communities.

Immediately after the occupation of the Austrian state, the Austrian monetary system was also incorporated into the Third Reich.

At the time there was little international criticism of these financial arrangements since the countries were deemed to be so close already, despite the means employed by Hitler to achieve his Anschluss. Even the U.S. seemed to condone it when a court ruled that the takeover of Austria had taken place 'in a manner acceptable to our notions of international law...and had not been disavowed by the [U.S.] Department of State'.[4] On 17 March 1938, the Reichsmark was introduced in Austria by decree. The exchange rate was set at 1.5 Austrian schillings to the Reichsmark. Plunder of religious institutions followed as rare coins were taken from thirteen Catholic monasteries in Austria, ostensibly as part of a collection to be established in the proposed Linz Museum, although this was never completed.

Thanks to the looting of Austrian gold, Germany in 1938 was able to run a trade deficit of almost 450 million Reichsmarks, briefly freeing the Nazi economy from the balance of payments constraint. The Reichsbank board member Emil Puhl wrote on 3 October of the same year, 'Without the [Austrian gold and foreign exchange] it would not have been possible to obtain enough foreign raw materials [and build up stocks] for warfare'. Such was the voracious appetite for raw materials of the German war economy, however, that by the start of 1939, despite the injection of OeNB gold reserves, the country was again on the verge of economic collapse with a balance of payments deficit of several billion marks. Schacht called the situation 'alarming in the extreme'.[5] He became more open in his criticism of Hitler's economic policy, apparently believing that his reputation and position made him indispensable to the German economy and therefore untouchable, even telling Hans Bernd Gisevius that he could slow the breakneck speed of armament production because he had 'got Hitler by the throat'.[6] Schacht even tried to open up a line of communication for mediation with the British government through his friendship with Bank of England governor Montagu Norman, who was godfather to one of Schacht's children, but Prime Minister Neville Chamberlain would have nothing to do with him.

Schacht's reading of the political landscape did not match his financial acumen, however. The pressure being exerted by Göring for ever more investment in war industries as opposed to domestic manufacturing and export goods was becoming intense and, at that time, Göring's power and influence were considerable and growing by the day. Imports were far out stripping exports. It was not only Göring's economic ignorance that bothered Schacht, though. The anti-Semitic violence in Austria that followed the Anschluss caused him grave concern. 'We have no room in the Reichsbank for people who do not respect the life, property and the convictions of others', he said, condemning the Nazis' 'wanton and outrageous undertakings [that] make every decent German blush'.[7] His position was rapidly becoming untenable not only for his open opposition to Hitler, but also for the state of the German economy, which outwardly was strong with full employment but which, in reality, was seriously over-extended and facing the repayment of 12 billion Reichsmarks' worth of loans that had been raised in 1935 to finance German rearmament. Attempts to issue bonds in the private equity market to meet these payments in November 1938 failed by a large margin to raise the necessary funds. When Finance Minister Lutz von Krosigk asked Schacht for 200 million Reichsmarks to pay government salaries, Schacht refused him in the hope of bringing the seriousness of the situation to the attention of the country's leaders, but their attention was elsewhere and their solutions to the problem were quite different to those proposed by Schacht.

Exasperated, on 7 January 1939, on behalf of the board of the Reichsbank, Schacht wrote a memo to Hitler in which he said:

> The Reichsbank possesses no more gold or foreign exchange reserves… The reserves formed by the annexation of Austria have been used up… our last remaining foreign credit for the importation of goods [has been used up]…In the last ten months [banknotes in circulation] have risen faster than in the whole of the preceding five years [and] cannot maintain value…No increase in the production of goods can be achieved by increasing the amount of paper money.[8]

Schacht's message was spelled out clearly: Germany was spending too much money on armaments and had too little foreign currency to pay the bills. The war industries were booming and brought full employment, but they also increased demand for consumer goods, thus raising the spectre of inflation and pressure on the Reichsmark that would further increase the cost of imports.[9] It was Schacht's misfortune to have to deal with Hitler who, like Göring, was essentially an economic illiterate who believed, without justification, that all the country's financial difficulties were transient and within ten years Germany would 'eliminate the burdens of war without disrupting internal purchasing power'.[10] Predictably, Schacht's memo left Hitler incandescent with rage. On 20 January he summoned Schacht to the Reich Chancellery and, without ceremony, personally handed him a written notice of dismissal. It read, 'In the complete realisation of the additional tasks demanded of economic life for the re-establishment of Greater Germany there is need for uniform leadership in economic life'.

Clearly Hitler saw Schacht as the one who was out of step and five of the seven directors who had signed the memo with Schacht were forced out also. The new Reichsbank boss, Walther Funk, who had already replaced Schacht as Minister of Economics in 1937, was a man much given to alcoholic excesses and who would soon show himself to be 'less and less equal to his post'.[11] However, the man's banking credentials were only of secondary importance to the Nazis. His brief included a call to 'bring to a state of completion corresponding with Nazi principles the reform [of the bank which will become] unconditionally subordinate to the sovereignty of the state'.[12] This presented no problems to one whose obsequious pandering to the Nazi hierarchy had seen a meteoric rise and elevated him, like many other Nazi lickspittles, to offices way beyond any justified by their meagre talents.

It was no surprise that it had been the Luftwaffe chief Hermann Göring, who had long battled with Schacht for control of the economy, who championed Funk's cause in anticipation of him channelling ever more Reichsmarks into the Four Year Plan for German re-armament. While Funk applied himself to furthering his personal agenda, it was his deputy, Emil Puhl, an ambitious, industrious and level-headed individual who was left to carry out the major functions of the office in which he was ably assisted by the assiduous Albert Thoms, who would go on to become the 'irreplaceable' recorder of all Nazi gold transactions during the war.[13] It suited Puhl's purpose to be outside Hitler's privileged circle, which meant that he did not have to contend with constant badgering and criticism and was left to get on with the job, while Funk said whatever needed to be said to mollify the Führer. Puhl, however, was on excellent terms with Himmler and Heydrich of the SS and it was Puhl who would go on to develop close links between the Reichsbank and the Swiss bankers.

Czechoslovakia

With the German economy once again in crisis so soon after looting the Austrian treasure, Hitler looked to Czechoslovakia for a way out. Czech gold reserves had benefitted throughout the early 1930s thanks initially to inherited wealth from the Austro-Hungarian Empire, but also because of a buoyant arms trade. In 1935, Czechoslovakia had been the largest arms manufacturer and exporter in the world. The production of tanks, light arms and other weaponry at the massive Škoda works in Plzeň and the Brno munitions factory dwarfed British production. Much of the gold reserves, however, had been built up through contributions from the Czechoslovak population. Under a system devised by the

First Republic's Finance Minister, Dr Alois Rašín, these reserves had been accumulated through national collections between 1919 and 1924. Whatever the limitations and failures of Czechoslovakia's interwar democracy, the state was a financial success. Immediately after the First World War, there had been relatively adequate supplies of essential foodstuffs and the country had benefited from the absence of war devastation. A combination of industrial inheritances from the Austro-Hungarian Empire, stable securities and a buoyant arms trade meant that the Czechs had weathered the economic crisis of the early 1930s better than most. In 1919, the state had no reserves to speak of, but by 1926 the Czechoslovak National Bank held some 40 tons of monetary gold, and on the eve of the state's demise in September 1938, Czechoslovak accounts held 94 tons, although only around 7 per cent of that was in domestic vaults. Throughout the 1930s, the Czech government had been secretly transferring gold abroad to the Bank of England through the BIS as insurance against the growing threat from Nazi Germany.

The looting of Czechoslovakia's gold reserves began as a consequence of the Munich Agreement of September 1938, after which Czechoslovakia was required to provide Germany with 14.5 tons of monetary gold in payment for the Czech currency being converted into German marks in the Sudeten areas during the first two months of 1939. There was, however, a second financial penalty imposed on the country after 15 March 1939, when the short-lived Czecho-Slovak Republic was extinguished as the Nazi takeover of the rump of Czechoslovakia saw Hitler enter Vienna in triumph at the head of his armed forces. The Česká národní banka (Czechoslovakian National Bank, ČNB) was not liquidated but reorganised into the Národní banka pro Čechy a Moravu (National Bank for Bohemia and Moravia). Along with the German soldiers came Dr Friedrich Müller, special commissioner of the Reichsbank, who headed directly for the National Bank for Bohemia and Moravia in Prague and demanded, at gunpoint, that the directors Josef Malik and Frantisek Peroutka sign a formal request for the transfer of 23 tons of gold held at the Bank of England from the Czech BIS account (BIS account No. 2) to a new BIS account (No. 17). Although it was never explicitly documented, it was clearly understood that account No. 17 was kept on behalf of the Berlin Reichsbank. There would be no physical movement of gold, only a book entry showing the gold was under new ownership.

In a letter dated 15 March, the day the Nazis marched into Vienna, the British Chancellor of the Exchequer, Sir John Simon, had sanctioned the freezing of all Czech assets. The government would indemnify the bank and pass the necessary legislation as soon as possible. Two days later the freeze was extended to all Czech assets held by all British financial institutions. The British government was taking steps to have some bargaining counters with which to protect British assets in Czechoslovakia now under threat from the Nazis. Malik and Peroutka tried to protect the country's gold and played for time. They managed to get word out to the Bank of England and BIS headquarters in Basel that any instructions sent under their names concerning transactions in Czech monetary gold would be made under duress and should be ignored. Montagu Norman at the Bank of England initially refused to sanction the transfer ownership of the 23 tons of gold in his vaults between the BIS accounts, but after due consideration apparently arrived at the conclusion that he 'saw no way that the transfer could be prevented'.[14] Consequently, some £5.6 million belonging to the Czechoslovak National Bank and held in the Bank of England in the name of the BIS was transferred to the ownership of the German Reichsbank on 19 May 1939. Within ten days the balance of the account, a further £1.2 million, was transferred to other accounts and used in settlement of German trade deals. The British government continued, quite disingenuously, to insist that it had no knowledge of in whose name BIS-numbered accounts were being held in London. In his contribution to the London Conference of 1997, Eduard Kubu would call the gold 'the property of the victims of an act of violence' and accused the Bank of England, with the connivance of the British government, of irresponsibly surrendering to the Nazis.[15]

Immediately afterwards, the British government was forced to defend itself against a charge of economic appeasement, which it was said by its critics to have adopted as a continuation of political appeasement by other means in a 'last ditch effort to keep channels of communication open with Nazi Germany'.[16] It did so by claiming that the Bank of England had acted without government knowledge. The Bank of England, especially Governor Montagu Norman, and Otto Niemeyer, the director in charge of its overseas and foreign department and current chair of the BIS, then came under attack for agreeing to the transaction without referring the matter to the government. Yet Norman's own opinion was that he had not thought it his duty to make statements about BIS transactions to the British government. His opinion, which he publicly expressed, was that it was 'more important to keep [the BIS] as a non-political body than it was to keep [the gold] out of Hitler's hands'.[17] Simon claimed, in what was described as an 'excessively legalistic, cynical and insincere' manner, that he had no knowledge about ownership of BIS accounts and had no right to ask.[18]

On 21 March, the French government, unaware that the transaction had taken place two days earlier, protested and insisted that it be blocked. The Bank of England's executive director, Cameron Cobbold, did not think it was any of their business what the BIS did and chose not to enlighten them and, indeed, seems to have taken the same view towards the British government when he said that it was 'a matter exclusively for the Board of the BIS and that he could not see how HMG was concerned'.[19] It was not until 4 April that he told the Treasury, 'the bird had already flown'. The British Foreign Office took the view that whilst immunities conferred on BIS assets by protocols to which Britain was a signatory prevented the government from placing an embargo on the gold, the break-up of Czechoslovakia and the Nazi's presence in Vienna cast serious doubts over the validity of any orders coming from the NBC, and that the BIS should refrain from handing this gold over to the Reichsbank until the situation was clarified. The Foreign Secretary, Lord Halifax, went as far as to express his wish that the gold be prevented from falling into German hands, although he surely must have known that it had already done so. The British Treasury agreed that no transaction should take place until the status of the Czech state had been clarified, but again, all this was happening days after the deal had been done and the gold had gone.

On 5 May 1939, an account was created in the Berlin Reichsbank in the name of the National Bank of Bohemia and Moravia, with a deposit equivalent to the value of gold transferred from the Bank of England through the BIS. The BIS claimed that it was simply following instructions given to it by the legitimate signatories of the National Bank of Bohemia and Moravia, which had been created out of the now defunct Czechoslovakian National Bank and, for all outward appearances, was an autonomous entity. It should be noted that throughout this time, the gold remained in the vaults of the Bank of England in London and only its ownership had been changed. The British action was roundly criticised in the House of Commons, where Brendan Brecken called it 'a very squalid form of financial appeasement' and Churchill condemned it saying the transaction 'stultified altogether the efforts our people are making in every class and in every party to secure National Defence'.[20] All remaining Czech gold deposits in Prague were removed, along with 1,009 kg from the safes of the Škoda works and the Brno munitions factory. In contrast to its complicity over the Czech gold transfers, it is worth noting that later in July 1940, when the central banks of Lithuania, Estonia and Latvia ordered the delivery of gold in their BIS accounts to be transferred to the Russian State Bank, the BIS refused to recognise the instructions because the orders were influenced by the will of the Soviet Russian government.[21] A poor defence in the light of what had gone before.

On 26 May, Sir John Simon wrote to Montagu Norman asking whether the Bank of England still held the Czech gold, as the information might help him to answer questions in the House of Commons. Norman replied four days later without answering the question, but pointed out that the Bank held gold from time to time for the BIS and had no knowledge whether it was the property of the BIS or that of their customers. Hence, they could not say whether the gold was held for the National Bank of Czechoslovakia, which had been dissolved in March. On 14 June, the Bank of Bohemia and Moravia sent to Berlin its remaining 6.4 tons of gold, mostly containing coins of historic value, after its director, who had been falsely accused and arrested by the Gestapo, committed suicide.

It is worth looking at the wider environment in which the Bank of England and the British government operated at this time and both institutions' relationship with Germany. Cain and Hopkin, in their analysis of British imperialism, contend that Britain and its empire had been controlled since 1688 by an order 'fusing the interests, values, families and power structures of the old landed elite and a newer financial and service bourgeoisie'.[22] This governing elite strove above all to restore the financial power of the City of London in the face of the advances made by New York during the First World War, and this required the creation of strategic partnerships with the largest economies outside the U.S., most crucially Germany. Despite the growth of fascism in Germany, the British government and the leading financial powers in the City of London saw confrontation as self-defeating. The sheer cost of rearmament would destabilise Britain's economy, so it chose instead to develop financial partnerships with Germany, which it hoped might strengthen the position of moderate Nazis and the Economics Minister, Hjalmar Schacht. There grew up a complex of financial arrangements between British financial institutions and Germany, which enjoyed the active support of the British government throughout the pre-war life of the Nazi regime.

It now became a question not of how much the government knew, but of the nature of its relationship with the Bank of England and how much power it had to intervene in the bank's affairs in relation to BIS transactions. In cannot be assumed that the Bank of England was acting entirely independently of British government policy when it continued to follow BIS instructions to sell gold after the Czech affair on behalf of the Nazis. There was a further transaction on 1 June when there were sales of gold (£440,000) and gold shipments to New York (£420,000) from the No. 19 account of the BIS, which represented gold shipped to London by the Reichsbank. This time, for appearances' sake, before acting, the Bank of England referred the matter to the Chancellor, who said that he would like the opinion of the law officers of the Crown but, after frustration over delays, went ahead with the transfers anyway. The law officers subsequently upheld their action.

Throughout this period, the Bank of England had presented, as self-evidently true, the idea that it had no legal right to frustrate an order of its customer, the BIS, but a number of legal opinions advanced during the controversy raised significant doubts about the legality of the BIS's action. Firstly, the instruction was given under duress (known as early as 17 March), and secondly, there was a question mark over whether the NBC had the legal right to make such an order without the endorsement of a constitutionally founded Czechoslovak government. There was no international recognition of the Czech government after the invasion of 15 March.

The spotlight falls on Montagu Norman who, as governor of the Bank of England and director of BIS, was acutely aware of the details of the transaction at all times, and had all the authority required to deny the instruction to transfer the gold. Norman had long been a supporter of Germany in international financial matters, primarily for its support in challenging U.S. financial ambitions, and was a close friend of Schacht. He had even repeatedly challenged Chamberlain's tough stance on Germany's threats to default on various components of its debts to British financiers' traders. It could be argued that to thwart the BIS over the Czech gold transaction might have seen 'the end of German transfers of interest to the BIS and might even mean the end of the BIS altogether'.[23] It was tacitly accepted that preservation of BIS neutrality was so important that it would retain its absolute right to direct the Bank of England to transfer its assets even in time of war, a view that the Treasury seemed to endorse, at least in 1939.

After the pillage of Czechoslovakian gold, European bankers started to look for ways of protecting their own gold. Already after the Anschluss, gold had flowed into the U.S. from Europe at an increased rate, but it was the Munich Agreement of 30 September 1938 that triggered a significant rise in activity. Increased national expenditure on armaments across Europe targeted U.S. manufacturers and it was the requirement for gold to pay for purchases that, in part, was responsible for the transfer of monetary gold into the vaults of the New York Federal Reserve in Washington. The other obvious reason was to put the gold reserves of those nations threatened by Germany beyond its reach in the event of invasion. By 30 September 1939, some thirty-nine countries had deposited at least some of their monetary gold in New York banks. U.S. Treasury Secretary Henry Morgenthau Jr. warned President Roosevelt that the sheer volume of gold entering the U.S. meant it now held about 60 per cent of the world's supply, which was threatening to destabilise the whole international monetary system.

Poland

On 1 September 1939, when Germany invaded Poland, the former had declared reserves of 28.6 tons of gold and another 82.7 tons in a secret fund. The Reichsbank also held 99 tons in its Austrian account and 43 tons in its Czech account. Poland had been the next victim of Hitler's vaulting ambition, but he found its coffers disappointingly empty. During the first few days of the German invasion, officials of the Polish National Bank in Warsaw crated up 13.5 tons of gold and sent it to Brest in buses. Another 15.1 tons in vaults at Siedlce followed. The remaining gold was crated and shipped out along with members of the Polish government on 5 September. Under the supervision of the 'bald-headed and owlish'[24] Colonel Adam Koc, the gold had been loaded into decrepit buses and trucks belonging to the Warsaw Bus Company. The idea of using buses was so as not to attract too much attention as they passed through the flood of refugees going south towards Lublin. Upon arrival, the gold convoy was ordered to continue to Lutsk (now in Ukraine), travelling by night and hiding in woods by day. Koc brought in Henryk Floyar-Rajchman, whose job it would be to get the gold to Romania, and Ignacy Matuszewski, who would be responsible for taking it from there to the French National Bank in Paris. The governor of the Polish Central Bank, Zygmunt Karpiński, was given full authority to 'dispose' of all stocks of gold deposited in foreign banks in the name of the Polish National Bank, and so left immediately for Paris.

Polish monetary gold was now spread out in a number of locations across the country and arrangements were made to collect it all and bring it to the Romanian border, with buses and trucks travelling by night to avoid attack by Luftwaffe aircraft. The Germans were not the only ones to worry about; Soviet agents had become aware of the existence of the gold convoy and were also trying to locate it.[25] On the Romanian border, Koc had been able to negotiate the use of a train on which the gold was loaded at Śniatyń on 14 September. This train took the gold to the Romanian port of Constanţa, on the Black Sea.

Meanwhile, the German ambassador in Bucharest was informed of the gold transport and had unsuccessfully tried to browbeat the

Romanian government into preventing the convoy from crossing the border into Romania by suggesting that failure to comply would be 'a heavy violation of [its] neutrality policy'.[26] Meanwhile, Floyar-Rajchman had returned to Dubno to retrieve 4 tons of gold that had been unloaded there by Polish military officials, ostensibly to finance the war effort. What was now seen as an inevitable German victory over Poland meant that this gold would fall into German hands if left where it was, so it too was taken across the border to Bucharest. However, when the trucks tried to enter the Polish embassy, they were halted by Romanian troops and the gold was confiscated. The gold remained in Romania for the rest of the war on the pretext of financing the welfare of Polish refugees who had fled into the country.

Britain, desperate to keep the Polish gold out of German hands, now offered assistance in the form of the creaky 4,000-ton tanker SS *Eocene*, skippered by Robert E. Brett. The ship docked at Constanța on 14 September, and, during the night, 1,200 cases of gold were manhandled off the newly arrived train and onto the ship, which also took on twenty-seven Polish passengers. Meanwhile, the Romanian crew had disappeared, fearing the ship would be attacked and sunk, meaning Brett had to pay huge bonuses to the replacement crew. The next day, the ship set sail for Istanbul and dropped anchor in the Bosphorus at Kabataş where it was circled and photographed by a German yacht. The Turkish authorities were not prepared to invite German reprisals by allowing the *Eocene* to progress out into the Mediterranean and refused permission for the British to transfer the gold to a British destroyer. Neither were they willing to submit to a German proposal to have the gold unloaded and stored in a local Turkish bank. A compromise was reached in which the *Eocene* was allowed to pull up at the Haydarpaşa terminal in Istanbul and offload the gold onto a train, which would then be allowed to leave for Beirut. For this concession, Turkey demanded a payment of $30,000.

When the train reached the Syrian border, French military officials took control and brought it into Beirut harbour, where the bulk of it was loaded onto the French cruiser *Emile Bertin*, reputed to be the fastest warship in the world.[27] The rest was loaded onto the destroyers *Vaubin* and *Epervier* and taken to Toulon, and then by train to Nevers, where it was deposited in the Bank of France. There it stayed until June 1940, by which time German forces had invaded France and the Low Countries and were threatening to take Paris. On 7 June the Polish gold was taken by train to the port of Lorient, in Brittany, in preparation for its evacuation to Canada. Its fate now became entwined with that of the Belgian and French gold that was also being readied for evacuation.

Denmark

In December 1939, Denmark, along with other Nordic countries, had discussed strategy to protect their gold reserves. Denmark was quickest to react by sending one third of its total reserves to New York at the turn of the year and followed up with further shipments in early 1940. On 13 February it sent 2,000 bags on the SS *Randsford* and a week later a similar quantity on the SS *Trafalgar*. All its gold coins were melted down in the U.S. and made into gold bars. A final shipment emptied the Bank of Denmark vaults in early March. Henrik Kauffmann, the Danish ambassador in the U.S., was given full authority over the gold.

Norway

Norway, too, had shipped out three-quarters of its gold and had it stored in the vaults of the New York Federal Reserve. More than 170 tons had been shipped by the end of January 1940. On the morning of 9 April 1940, when the German invasion of Norway began, the Norwegian king, Haakon VII, and members of the Norwegian cabinet fled Oslo and travelled north to Elverum. At the same time, the Minister of Finances, Oscar Torp, had had the country's entire gold reserve, 120,000 pounds in 1,538 cases, loaded onto twenty-six trucks and transported out of Oslo to a well-guarded concrete cellar in the Norges Bank in Lillehammer, a little under 100 miles north of the capital.

Fredrik Haslund, one of the drivers who had taken members of the Norwegian government to Elverum, had been trained as an engineer in Germany. On 17 April, he was tasked with leading a team to collect the gold from Lillehammer. Under close armed guard, the cases of gold were taken in trucks to the nearby railway station and loaded onto a train, which travelled by night and found what forest cover it could to hide under by day. Its destination was Åndalsnes, a town on the Romsdalsfjorden at the mouth of the river Rauma. Unfortunately, the town was being targeted by Luftwaffe bombers trying to prevent a landing of British troops. Haslund stopped the train a little way short of the town. During the night he was able to move into the port, but had time only to unload 200 cases onto the British cruiser SS *Galatea* before retreating for cover at daybreak. He described the conditions as follows: 'The snow-covered peaks gleamed like gems in the clear air of this spring night. All about us was the profound night silence of the mountains. But the tiny centre formed by the ship seethed with activity.'[28]

German troops were closing in and Haslund decided that it was too dangerous to remain in the vicinity. He rounded up twenty-five trucks from the town and offloaded the gold onto them from the train. The trucks were then transported across the Romsdalsfjorden, two at a time, during the following night. They set off towards Åfarnes in small groups with several hours between as a security measure. On the way they were subjected to occasional strafing by Luftwaffe aircraft but managed to continue unscathed. It took another three ferry crossings from Åfarnes before they reached Molde, where they were forced to halt for five days as the town was being bombed incessantly by the Luftwaffe. Members of the Norwegian Royal Family and government were also at Molde preparing to evacuate on the British cruiser HMS *Glasgow*, which had two destroyers for company. Two smaller boats started ferrying the gold onto the British ship, but before they could complete the task, the *Glasgow* was forced to weigh anchor and leave. Haslund now loaded the gold onto two fishing boats supplied by the Norwegian resistance and continued to the far north. He had no idea how far northwards the German troops had progressed and decided to go as far as he could to Tromsø, where he found the British cruiser HMS *Enterprise*. The 550 cases of gold were safely loaded on board, at last, and were shipped to Britain. Weeks later, on 15 June, the gold was loaded onto the Norwegian cargo ship MS *Bomma* and transported to Baltimore, where it arrived on 28 June. From there it was deposited in the Federal Reserve Bank of New York.

The Netherlands

As early as September 1938, 362 tons of Dutch monetary gold was shipped out to New York, London and Pretoria. The remaining gold was stored in crates at the Amsterdam branch of the Dutch National Bank and at the Bijk branch on the Boompjies in Rotterdam. When the German attack came on 10 May 1940, the 78 tons of gold which had been held in Amsterdam was loaded onto a dozen lorries and taken to the port of IJmuiden, where it was loaded onto the SS *Iris* and SS *Titus*. The *Iris* was escorted by the British cruiser HMS *Arethusa* and the destroyer HMS *Boreas* to Tilbury Docks in London, where it docked on the morning of 11 May. The *Titus* came right behind, escorted by the destroyer HMS *Keith*. From Tilbury, the gold was taken to the vaults of the Bank of England.

Rotterdam had come under immediate Luftwaffe attack following the invasion and its southern and eastern outskirts had already been taken by German forces. They were only 200 metres from the Rotterdam branch of the Dutch National Bank, which they targeted with sniper fire. The bank vaults still held 114 tons of gold but only 11 tons of that could be removed in time. Four trucks took it in 170 crates to be loaded onto Pilot Steamer No. 19, originally designed and built to operate in Dutch coastal waters but commandeered by the Royal Dutch Navy to act as a coastal surveillance vessel. As it left the harbour in the early morning of 11 May, moving down the Nieuwe Waterweg Channel it passed over a magnetic mine dropped by Luftwaffe aircraft and was blown apart. Only two crewmen survived. On 31 May, W.A., the Van den Taks Bergingsbedrijf salvage firm, was ordered to clear the wreckage. They recovered 776 gold bars, which were claimed by Germany as war booty and sent to Berlin in April 1941 to be deposited in the Reichsbank's Dutch account. A request from Britain for the Netherlands to lend them the gold that had been sent to Britain to finance its war effort was refused. A similar request to Norway was also rejected.[29]

By the middle of 1940, Britain was facing bankruptcy, with all its gold reserves virtually wiped out. It was only by negotiating a lend-lease agreement with the U.S. that it was able to continue its war effort, but the terms demanded that Britain exhaust all its resources first. When Britain appealed for loans of part of the £400 million in gold deposits in London belonging to other European countries, Belgium was one of the few to respond positively by making £59 million of gold available. At the same time, the Czechs had offered £7.5 million in loans. The Belgians, however, wanted a deal which would give them preferential trade terms after the war, but the British Foreign Office, who had no great affection for the Belgians, would make no promises and negotiations became protracted. An agreement was reached eventually; a vital step in keeping the British economy afloat until the U.S. lend-lease could come into play.

Once the Germans were firmly in control of the Netherlands, they started shipping out the remaining Dutch monetary gold to Berlin on the pretext that it was the Dutch contribution towards the war against communism in the east. Unfortunately for the Dutch, they still had large quantities of gold in their vaults when the Germans invaded. By 1945, the Germans would take more than 192 tons, assisted by the pro-Nazi Dutch bank presidents Trip and Post van Tonningen. Occupation laws now forbade ownership of gold and all citizens were required to sell or deposit their gold in the Netherlands Bank. All safety deposit boxes in the country were opened, yielding some 10 tons of gold. The whole haul of non-monetary gold amounted to 35,476 kg, all of which was sent to Berlin between 1940 and 1943. As the war progressed, the Germans systematically plundered the Dutch gold in their Berlin vaults by claiming it as part of the Netherlands' contribution to the war against Bolshevism in the Soviet Union.

Belgium

The Grand Duchy of Luxembourg had accumulated 357 bars of gold (4.3 tons) during the 1930s and in 1938 had transferred it to the National Bank of Belgium, which was given instructions to protect it in the same manner they were protecting their own bullion. During the late 1930s, Belgium also saw a huge influx of gold deposits coming in from wealthy French citizens worried about the security of their assets, which they saw as being threatened by left-wing governments in Paris. Following the Anschluss, Belgian bankers started drawing up plans to safeguard the gold in Belgian banks which had amassed considerable gold reserves, amounting to some 600 tons, and thus making Belgian reserves the fourth largest in the world. During 1938 and 1939 they had prudently followed a policy of transferring this gold abroad to the Federal Reserve Bank of New York (117.5 tons), the Bank of England (308.6 tons) and the Bank of France (178 tons) as a hedge against political instability in Europe. The gold was deposited in the Bordeaux and Libourne branches of the Bank of France under terms which meant that the Belgians had no further access to it and were not even allowed to know the combination of the vaults in which it was kept.

After the fall of Poland in September 1939, a further 198 tons of Belgian gold in 4,944 cases was deposited in the Bank of France, along with gold assets of the Luxembourg Savings Bank which Belgium had been holding, in preparation for transfer to the U.S. By the time of the German invasion of Belgium in May 1940, 40 tons were still held in the port of Ostend awaiting evacuation. Within days Belgium was facing capitulation and it seemed as if the gold would be stranded and swept up in the German advance, but on 19 May a Belgian coastguard vessel, commanded by Lieutenant Van Vaerenbergh and bearing the number A4, sailed into Ostend from Dunkirk in the late afternoon. Ostend had been mined by the Luftwaffe but the A4 had been demagnetised. Hubert Ansiaux, the governor of the National Bank of Belgium, was able to convince the local Belgian naval commander to make the ship available to him. The gold was loaded and the A4 steamed up the coast to Nieuwpoort and crossed to the Thames Estuary, where the British Admiralty instructed it to sail on to Folkestone. From Folkestone, the A4 was directed to Dartmouth and from there to Plymouth, where it tied up on 26 May. From Plymouth the gold was taken by road and deposited in the vaults of the Bank of England. Immediately upon his arrival in London, Ansiaux contacted the British government and the Bank of England to devise a plan to recover the Belgian gold held in France. The massive influx of Belgian refugees into France during the last days of May had created significant problems of currency exchange, which required the Belgians to transfer to France 65 tons of Belgian gold held in the Bank of France.[30] On 21 May, the occupying German authorities in Belgium issued a decree that anyone in possession of safety deposit boxes was to present themselves at their bank and open the boxes to have the contents listed. All gold and foreign currency would then be placed in safe custody of the bank. On 17 June another order would go out forbidding ownership of private gold and demanding that it be offered for sale to the Reichsbank in Berlin.

When the Belgian king, Leopold III, personally surrendered to German forces on 28 May, he was incarcerated in Laeken Castle, 3 miles north of Brussels. The Belgian government in exile, however, opposed the surrender as an illegal act since it had not been authorised by the Belgian prime minister. Leopold made a personal plea to Hitler for the Belgian gold held by France to be returned to Brussels, but this was treated with contempt by Hitler, who did not even bother to reply. Ansiaux, now in London, wanted British help to have the Belgian gold extracted from French control and shipped to the U.S., but no Royal Navy vessels could be spared from the Dunkirk evacuation to escort the gold across the Atlantic. Meanwhile, the Belgian gold held by the Bank of France had been entrusted to the French Admiralty; the only organisation able to facilitate its transportation beyond reach of the German invaders. The gold was transferred from Bordeaux and Libourne by train to Lorient in Brittany on 7 June, along with the Polish gold held at Nevers, with a view to shipping it to the U.S., and on 17 June, at Lorient, 4,944 cases of Belgian gold and 1,208 cases of Polish gold was loaded onto the French light cruiser *Victor Schoelcher*, but by this time German forces were closing in on the port and Luftwaffe aircraft were dropping mines into the harbour. The Poles had been assured that this ship would cross the Atlantic to Halifax in Nova Scotia and that a Polish bank official, Stephan Michalski, was on board to accompany it. The ship left port at midnight and, in what Michalski called a 'courageous effort',[31] sailed close to the rocky coast to avoid mines before passing the harbour mouth at the Port Louis Citadel and making for open water.

The skipper of the *Victor Schoelcher*, Captain Moevus, still did not know his destination but was told to rendezvous with a flotilla heading west from the port of Brest. Moevus asked for his destination 'in the event of separation' and was told Casablanca. There has been much debate over the decision to send the *Victor Schoelcher* to West Africa instead of the Americas. It may have been because discussions that took place in the French government on 14-15 June centred around a possible move to North Africa in order to continue the struggle from there. Or it may have been to do with the armistice signed the next day by Marshal Pétain, whereby the French government hoped for some form of autonomy.[32]

Whatever the reasons, on the following day there was a new twist in the tale. Moevus was ordered to leave the convoy and go to Royan, on the Gironde Estuary. Reports came in all day about ships hitting mines or being struck by torpedoes all across the estuary. Michalski was furious and demanded clarification of the order. A flurry of signals passed between the ship and the French Admiralty to find out where the order had come from. Eventually, the French Admiralty concluded that it had not emanated from any of their officials and Moevus was instructed to continue to Casablanca, where the *Victor Schoelcher* arrived on 23 June. Michalski was now told to transfer the Polish gold to a Polish ship anchored in Dakar for transportation to the U.S. The Polish government in exile feared that the gold would end up in Martinique, still under Vichy control, and appealed to Britain to rescue it. Churchill ordered the Royal Navy to intercept any vessel leaving Dakar and began planning Operation Menace.

Ansiaux had flown to Bordeaux on 18 June, accompanied by a high-ranking British naval officer, Commander Richard Onslow, with authorisation to requisition the British cruiser HMS *Arethusa* moored at Le Verdon and transfer the Belgian gold to Britain. He went to the branch of the Bank of France and met a representative responsible for the Belgian gold. This man told him that the gold was no longer being held in the strongrooms at Bordeaux and Libourne but had been sent to another port, the name of which he would not divulge. Ansiaux was advised to go to the French Ministry of Finance, where he submitted both an explicit request for the custody of the Belgian gold to be lifted and authorisation for it to be shipped, perhaps via Great Britain, to the United States by the British Navy. It may be that the signal Moevus had received had been sent by the British, who believed that the Belgian gold was still in Bordeaux.

The French refused to discuss the matter until Ansiaux agreed to authorise an 'immediate' payment in gold to the Bank of France in relation to the currency exchanges brought on by the massive influx of Belgian refugees. The Belgians eventually agreed to transfer ownership of part of the gold to France, but it was too late to salvage the rest as by this time it had been loaded onto the *Victor Schoelcher* in Lorient and was now somewhere in the Bay of Biscay, or, for all Ansiaux knew, heading across the Atlantic. The gold was now subject to French naval authority and the French refused to disclose the name of the ship or its destination, citing military secrecy.

Meanwhile, appeals to French government ministers in Bordeaux failed to get any response.

When the Belgian gold, along with that of Poland, arrived in Casablanca, Pierre Fournier, the governor of the Bank of France, tried to intervene and have the Belgian gold separated from that of other countries at the port. He was told that it had all been mixed, but that was misleading and would later prove to have been incorrect as the Belgian gold had remained sealed in its boxes and so was easily identifiable. By 5 July all the gold had been taken a further 1,800 miles further south to Dakar, which was under the de facto control of the French Vichy government. Ansiaux now went to Vichy on 29 July and tried to negotiate with Fournier to have the Belgian gold sent to the U.S. Fournier appeared sympathetic to Ansiaux's request, but regrettably advised that he was constrained by political considerations and would require specific authorisation from the French government to comply. The following day, the French minister of finance acceded to German demands to have all foreign gold assets in French overseas territories frozen.

The fate of the Belgian gold now became inexorably tied up with that of the Polish gold. Both had been evacuated from Brittany and both were now in Dakar. On 20 August 1940, during the negotiations of the Franco-German Armistice Commission at Wiesbaden, Johannes Hemmen, the blunt and aggressive economics expert and German plenipotentiary minister in France, angrily demanded that France itemise all foreign gold in its custody and take steps to have the Belgian gold repatriated to Brussels without delay. At the same time, he made strenuous efforts to persuade Yves Breart de Boisanger, the head of the French delegation to the Armistice Commission and governor of the Bank of France, to return the Polish gold to the Polish National Bank. He was less than pleased to discover that all the gold in French hands had gone to West Africa, an area very much in the Italian sphere of influence, and it had been made clear that, from a diplomatic perspective, he was to 'avoid anything which might lead to conflicts of authority with the Italians concerning Africa'.[33]

Hemmen was constrained by political considerations to stop short of demanding that de Boisanger comply, which would have been his preferred approach. Instead, he was forced into moderation by Germany's need for the full cooperation of the Vichy government to smooth the occupation process and the determination shown by the German authorities at this stage of the war to exhibit some sort of legality to their actions. A stalemate ensued. The French objected to the transfer of the Polish gold on the grounds that the directors of the Bank of Poland were no longer in Warsaw, and therefore the bank was no longer a viable, functioning entity, and the Germans, for diplomatic reasons, were unwilling to go into Dakar and simply take it. Furthermore, the French argued that the Polish gold should be transferred to French ownership in compensation for the massive loans France had made to Poland during the inter-war years. Hemmen dismissed this out of hand and argued that the Polish state no longer existed and there was therefore no Polish administration capable of authorising such a transaction. He was, however, eager to give the looting of the gold a semblance of legality and agreed to hold talks to discuss the fate of the Belgian gold. It was a feature of dealings with the Vichy government at this time that the Germans were willing to go to some lengths to ensure smooth cooperation and avoid serious disruption.

Despite his frustration, Hemmen also had to contend with other diplomatic considerations. He was wary of doing anything that might prejudice the delicate relationship between Hitler and Mussolini, but he was clear that if the gold fell into British hands, de Boisanger would be held personally accountable. West African ports were vulnerable to attack by British warships and a raiding party might easily go ashore and take the gold. As a compromise, Hemmen and de Boisanger agreed to have the gold moved away from the coast to the small military camp of Thiès, and then to Le Fort de Médine at Kayes, some 300 miles further inland on the Senegal-French Sudan border. Their fears were not unfounded.

On 23 September, Britain launched Operation Menace, an attack against Dakar, with the objective of capturing the gold. In the raiding party was Charles de Gaulle, the nominal leader of the Free French. The task force comprised an aircraft carrier, HMS *Ark Royal*, two battleships, HMS *Resolution* and HMS *Barham*, five cruisers, ten destroyers and a fleet of transports carrying 8,000 troops of the 101st Brigade of the Royal Marines and the 13th demi-brigade of the French Foreign Legion. Their orders were to negotiate with the French governor for a peaceful occupation, but if this was unsuccessful, to take the city by force. De Gaulle broadcast a series of messages to the port's defenders calling upon them to abandon Vichy and turn the town over to him, but all to no avail. On 23 September a raid was launched but bad weather prevented a landing and so the port was subjected to bombardment by the British fleet. The Vichy naval force in the harbour refused to give ground. Faced with this resistance, the British commander, Admiral John Cunningham, consulted Churchill and was told, 'Having begun, we must go on to the end. Stop at nothing!' Just before midnight, the Allies broadcast a demand for surrender to the Vichy Governor-General, Pierre Boisson. Four hours later, this was rejected.

A landing by the Free French, even backed by the British, no longer looked practical. The only way of continuing was to intensify the bombardment, risking the lives of civilians in Dakar, but such a course would be counterproductive to the Free French cause. De Gaulle met with Cunningham and called for a change of plans, but Cunningham had his orders. He was to stop at nothing. A third day of fighting started with a renewed bombardment, but it was futile. British ships were suffering from mounting damage, with the battleship *Resolution* holed and flooded by Vichy torpedoes. Eventually, Cunningham accepted that his cause was lost and so retreated out to sea and returned home, just at the point where Boisson had been on the verge of surrender. Operation Menace had been an embarrassing failure for the British.

The Polish government in exile now exerted diplomatic and then legal pressure to try to force the Vichy government to transfer the Polish gold in West Africa to British and American banks. On 3 September 1941, the New York law firm of Sullivan and Cromwell filed a lawsuit against the Bank of France and as a result, the court promptly seized a part of the French gold deposited in the Federal Reserve Bank in New York. At the same time, the Polish government in exile agreed a confidential memorandum with representatives of the Free French government in London, signed on 27 October 1941, providing for the return of the gold to the Bank of Poland. It was agreed to transfer the gold from Kayes to the Bank of England, the Bank of Canada in Ottawa and the Federal Reserve Bank in New York.

The Germans expedited plans to obtain the gold before it could be shipped across the Atlantic. On 6 September 1941, Hans von Becker, head of the Bankaufsichtamt, the body set up by the Germans to supervise banking operations in Belgium, demanded that all the Belgian gold in West Africa be brought back to Brussels, but the Belgians claimed that it had been entrusted to the care of the Bank of France and it was they who controlled its movement now. Albert-Édouard Janssen, the governor of the Bank of Belgium, agreed to its repatriation on the condition Belgian retained free disposition of it to pay for the import of food and fuel into the country, despite Ansiaux still trying to have it taken to the U.S. The Bank of France sided with Janssen.

In October, the Vichy government, under pressure from Hemmen, ordered the Bank of France to repatriate, under its own responsibility, the Belgian gold to Brussels. Heated debate ensued between von Becker, the Bank of Belgium and the Bank of France about responsibility for the transfer and the ultimate control over the gold. As ever at this stage in the war, the Germans were anxious to preserve a semblance of legality to their actions and in this regard, on 29 October, the Wiesbaden Convention was signed which, in effect, gave the Germans everything they demanded. The first gold shipment of 2,400 kg left Kayes by air for Marseilles, at French expense, on 4 November and a second similar one followed two weeks later. It was clear that air transport was not a practical solution, so the next consignment of 1,199 crates, with a combined weight of approximately 60 tons, was transported by train from the military base at Kayes back to Dakar. From there, it was shipped back to Casablanca, freighted by train to Oujda in Morocco, on to Oran and then on to Algiers. Transporting the remaining 3,652 crates proved to be rather more difficult. Patrolling British and American ships had made the sea route unsafe, so the crates left Kayes by train in April 1941, bound for Bamako, a small colonial garrison on the banks of the River Niger. From there the gold went downstream to Koulikoro, then to Bourem in what was then the French Sudan. This part of the journey took three weeks and once in Bourem, the crates were loaded onto trucks of the Compagnie Transsaharienne, which took them across a thousand miles of barren wastes of the Sahara Desert to Colomb-Béchar in Algeria. From here the crates were transferred by rail to Algiers and airlifted to Marseilles, where they joined other crates that had been flown directly from Dakar.

The whole operation was beset by complications and logistical dilemmas. River transportation in the early stages was hazardous due to frequent flash-flooding and torrential rainstorms. Transportation overland across the North African deserts was by trucks which frequently broke down with few or no spare parts to mend them. It was not uncommon to use camels when trucks irretrievably broke down. Schedules were constantly revised but progress was slow, with rarely more than 10 tons arriving in Marseilles in any one week. Eventually, it all ended up in Berlin by 26 May 1942, where it was deposited in a National Bank of Belgium account in the Reichsbank. Gold which had been sent by Luxembourg to be held in Marseilles was also scooped up at this time and paid for in Reichsmarks, which seemed to make it a legitimate transaction, although Belgium refused monetary compensation for its gold. The 500 million Reichsmarks that the Reichsbank had credited to the Belgian National Bank for the purchase of the gold was returned. In February 1941, the Belgian National Bank brought an action against the Bank of France in the Supreme Court in New York for the return of the Belgian gold. The court ruled that

$260 million worth of French gold stored in New York should be frozen, pending resolution of the claim.

All the gold was melted down, formed into new bars, and a new seal was added to it to make it look like pre-Second World War gold bars. While much of it was assigned to finance Hermann Göring's Four Year Plan, a portion was siphoned off to establish a special fund under the control of Joachim von Ribbentrop at the German Foreign Office. This would later spark a furious row between Göring and Ribbentrop. Göring was adamant that this 'confiscated' gold represented Germany's 'last reserve' and should be 'utilised in the most sparing manner'. A seriously aggrieved Ribbentrop felt sufficiently confident of his own authority to parry with a protest at Göring's 'arbitrary stance on the issue' and reminded the Reichsmarschall that it had been his man, Hemmen, and the Foreign Office's 'initiative...quick and energetic intervention' that had facilitated the return of the Belgian gold in the first place.[34] Ribbentrop had clearly overstepped the mark with this injudicious riposte and he was quickly reminded of his diminishing influence over German foreign policy and reduced status in the German hierarchy. The Belgians were given a receipt for 198 tons of gold to be paid for in Reichsmarks, which could only be spent in Germany on German goods. The Belgians rejected the offer but in October 1943, the Belgian gold was sequestered, in return for Reich treasury bonds, then melted down and reformed into new bars with new stamps and new date. After the war, Emil Puhl gave evidence to show that looted Belgian gold was used to make payments to Romania (80-100 million Reichsmarks), Hungary (20 million Reichsmarks), Bulgaria (20 million Reichsmarks), Slovakia (20 million Reichsmarks), Albania (20 million Reichsmarks) and Greece (30 million Reichsmarks).

In 1942, Hemmen was still arguing with de Boisanger over custody of the Polish gold still in West Africa. He claimed that denying German access to Polish gold while allowing Germany's enemies to draw on Polish deposits abroad was a violation of the Armistice agreement. The Bank of France argued that while it held the Polish gold in its vaults it had no jurisdiction over it, as that was down to the Vichy government. By the time an agreement was reached to transfer the 65 tons of Polish gold to Claremont-Ferrand, however, the whole of North Africa was being threatened by Allied landings, which would cut off all links between Vichy France and Dakar. At the end of January 1944, two envoys of Bank Polski SA, Director Wiktor Styburski and General Treasurer Stanisław Orczykowski, arrived in Kayes and arranged for the gold to be transported to Dakar, where it came under the protection of the Free French military authorities. The first batch arrived in New

York from Dakar on 4 April 1944 on board the USS *Breeman* and USS *Bronstein* and was deposited in the U.S. Federal Reserve Bank in Manhattan.[35] The gold for London was sent in small batches through more dangerous waters between 5 May and 25 August 1944 and the gold for Canada arrived in Ottawa in September and October 1944.

France
In 1939, the Bank of France held 2,500 tons of gold, most of which was in La Souterraine, deep beneath the Hôtel de Toulouse, the headquarters of the central bank, in the 1st arrondissement of Paris, with a minor amount held in other branch locations. After the Chamberlain–Hitler Munich Conference in 1938, France decided to send 600 tons of gold to the United States for storage in case they needed to purchase arms quickly. After the fall of Poland, French Minister of Finance Lucien Lamoureux began moving the gold from La Souterraine to the Bank of France branch bank vaults near the western port of Brest, in Brittany, the south-western port of Le Verdon, on the Atlantic just north of Bordeaux, and the Mediterranean port of Marseille in the south. At the same time, the French navy transported 400 tons of gold in four convoys to the United States using their smaller, fast cruisers to do the job instead of their larger, more formidable, but slower, naval ships.

The aircraft carrier *Bearn* left the port of Toulon near Marseille with 195 tons of gold and sailed to the Azores. Two fast cruisers, one of which was the *Emile Bertin*, carrying a further 210 tons of gold, had sailed from Brest and met up with the carrier in the Azores and all three ships sailed together to Halifax. The gold at Le Verdon, consisting of 3,080 heavy sacks and 758 cases, was loaded onto a small mail-carrying vessel and taken to Casablanca, where it was offloaded and put into vaults of the Moroccan State Bank. The intention was to await the arrival of the USS *Vincennes*, which would then take it across the Atlantic to Canada. The U.S. ship arrived on 10 June but to avoid violating U.S. neutrality, the gold had to be reloaded onto a French vessel and transferred to the *Vincennes* at sea, and ownership of the bullion had to be transferred to the U.S. for the duration of the trip. The $242 million in gold was then deposited at the Federal Reserve and exchanged for U.S. dollars.

On 11 June 1940, the *Emile Bertin* crossed the Atlantic again from Brest with 255 tons of gold, but was this time pursued by three British warships intent on capturing its golden cargo. The *Emile Bertin* was quickly ordered by the Bank of France to go to Martinique in the Caribbean, instead of Halifax. It arrived at Fort-de-France on 24 June.[36] The French had already shipped $245 million worth of gold to Fort-de-France in the Spring of 1940.

The 16,201 cases of gold bars and coins stored at Fort de Portzic, just outside Brest, was hastily loaded onto six private passenger vessels as German forces took Rennes. There were now no French forces between them and the gold at Brest. It took two days, working day and night, to load the gold and the ships using prisoners from the Pontaniou prison, who were promised pardons in return. Loading was finished on 18 June and the ships put to sea and joined up with the *Victor Schoelcher*, which was carrying the Belgian and Polish gold going south to Casablanca.

Still more gold was gathered from a variety of locations and loaded onto a French light cruiser, the *Primauguet*, at Le Verdon on 19 June and taken to Casablanca, but the harbour there was so congested that the ship could not dock. Furthermore, the signing of the armistice between France and Germany meant that the French ships might now be attacked by British warships, so the French Admiralty ordered the *Primauguet* to move further south to Dakar. At this point there were 735.7 tons of French gold in Dakar, 476.5 tons in New York, 345.5 tons in the Canadian National Bank in Ottawa, 258.1 tons at the Bank of England, 254.2 tons in Martinique and 10.4 tons still in Casablanca. Fear of an attack by the British now saw the gold at Dakar transferred, along with the Polish and Belgian gold under French control, to Thiès, 40 miles inland.

Greece
On 31 October 1940, the National Bank of Greece had packed gold coins in twenty-seven numbered bags and placed them in three large boxes. Along with seven boxes of silver coins, these were then sealed with the letters ETE. On 12 April 1941 these ten boxes were shipped to Crete and placed in the vaults of the bank in Heraklion. At the same time, 25 tons of Greek monetary gold was shipped out through Egypt to be held in the vaults of the Bank of England. Two months later, Crete was occupied by Germany and the ten cases were seized. When the whole of Greece came under German occupation, all citizens were ordered to exchange personal gold for drachmas and 6.5 tons was taken from Jews, who were deported to concentration camps.

Albania
Up until 8 September 1943, Albania had been under Italian control but when the Kingdom of Italy and the Western Allies signed the Armistice of Cassibile, which formalised the capitulation of Italy, the country was invaded by German forces. However, the Germans did not incorporate Albania into the Reich but declared it to be independent and neutral.

Despite this assertion, however, on 12 September, the German Ministry of Foreign Affairs requested that all Albanian gold held in the vaults of the Bank of Rome be transferred to the Reichsbank in Berlin. The 2.5 tons of Albanian gold were removed by SS troops under the command of SS Lieutenant Colonel Herbert Kappler and flown to Berlin on 16 September 1943. Later, in October 1944, the Germans removed 280,000 gold francs from the Albanian National Bank vaults in Tirana and this, the gold from Rome, and more than 5 million gold francs' worth of gold plundered from the Albanian people, was stored in fifty-five cases and sealed with steel strips and numbered AN1 – AN55.

Italy

In September 1943, Marshal Pietro Badoglio, who had taken over as leader of the Italian government after Benito Mussolini was deposed and imprisoned, surrendered southern Italy to the Allies and signed an armistice agreement. It was hoped that this would prompt the Germans to withdraw their forces from the country, but Hitler ordered that a line should be held as far down the peninsula as possible to keep strategically important airfields in northern Italy out of Allied control. On 10 September the German ambassador and plenipotentiary, Rudolf Rahn, was given responsibility for the defence of Rome. Immediately prior to this, Italian officials had tried to make plans to keep their gold reserves out of German hands by removing them to Piedmont, from where they could be easily sent over the border into Switzerland at some future date. This was clearly impossible without the Germans becoming aware of it and alternative plans to send the gold to Sardinia proved equally impractical.

No less than four German organisations, Himmler's SS, Hermann Göring's Economic Ministry, Joachim von Ribbentrop's Foreign Ministry and Funk's Reichsbank, now competed to obtain control of the Italian monetary gold. Göring demanded that the gold be transferred immediately to Berlin, where his authority would have given him a decisive control over it, but Rahn, a close ally of von Ribbentrop, argued against this saying that it had to remain under the control of the Banca d'Italia to avert the economic and financial collapse of the part of Italy that remained in German hands. However, he was unable to prevent the transfer of a little over 2 tons of gold that the Italians had looted from Albania. Whatever was going to happen to the rest, however, with Allied forces closing in on the city from the south, it was clear the Germans would not allow the gold to remain in Rome.

Italian bank officials now hatched a bizarre plot to keep the gold out of German hands; a false wall would be built in the vaults, behind which the gold would be hidden. False documents would then show that the gold had earlier been shipped to Potenza, which was now under Allied aerial attack. Before the wall was completed, however, the Germans demanded an inventory of the gold. Italian bank officials feared that if they resisted, the Germans would simply march into the vaults and take the gold as plunder. By cooperating with them, this would at least allow them to retain some control over it. The half-finished wall was quickly pulled down and all trace of it removed.

Rahn had been moved out to head up the Italian Socialist Republic in the north of the country, which had been set up by Mussolini after his escape from captivity. Rahn was replaced by Eitel Friedrich Moellhausen, who now wanted the gold moved out of Rome by air. However, he was quickly assured that this was impossible and so, instead, he instructed Giacomo Strinasacchi and Alessandro Cembran of the Banca d'Italia to move all the bank's gold deposits from the Palazzo Koch Palace on Via Nationale, north to Milan. On 22 September a total of 175 barrels and 20 bags was shipped and a further 451 barrels and 523 bags followed on 28 September. The Italians considered the movement of gold to Milan should not be seen as a delivery of the gold stock to the Germans, or even a forfeiture as spoils of war; it was simply a transfer of the gold from one bank building to another in compliance with the German request. The gold, they said, remained the property of the Banca d'Italia and continued to remain under its jurisdiction and administration. It was clear, however, that the transfer of gold to Milan meant that the bank had lost full control of their own gold reserves and that every future decision would have to be made with the agreement of the German authorities.

Göring now made another attempt to obtain control of the gold. On 18 October he ordered it to be transferred again, this time to Fortezza, a town in South Tyrol located in the Isarco Valley, where it could be stored in a military fort of Habsburg origin. It had the advantage of being on the road to Brenner, an ideal avenue of retreat for the Germanic forces should that become necessary, and was also located in the territory of Alpenvorland, a form of German protectorate that included the fiercely pro-Nazi regions of northern and southern Tyrol. Rahn, thinking that he was acting for Ribbentrop, tried to prevent the transfer, but Ribbentrop was losing ground both in terms of his influence and mental balance, and felt unable to oppose Göring's plan. At the same time, the bank sent small quantities of gold to a number of branch offices all over central and northern Italy and to colonial outposts such as Rhodes and Addis Ababa. Much of this gold remains unaccounted for.

The 626 barrels of gold, each weighing 180 kg, and 543 bags, weighing 70 kg, were loaded into twelve rail cars on 16 December in Milan. The cars were wired shut and sealed with lead stamps of the Banca d'Italia. Under heavy guard they were then taken, often under aerial attack, to Fortezza, where the gold was unloaded by Russian prisoners. It was stored deep in underground tunnels under the protection of the German military authorities and was now under de facto total German control. The tunnels were fortified with reinforced concrete and a triple-lock steel door. There were always twenty-six SS guards and two bank officials in the vaults at any one time.

Göring bullied Mussolini, now a much-diminished figure physically and politically, to hand over the gold for 'the common good of the war',[37] and on 5 February 1944, an agreement was arrived at in Fasano, a town on Lake Garda, between Rahn and delegates of the Italian government, Serafino Mazzolini, deputy-secretary for Foreign Affairs, and Pellegrini Giampietro. Banca d'Italia officials were not even told that a meeting had taken place. The underlying principle of the agreement was that 'the entire amount of gold owned by the bank of Italy [will be] available to the Ambassador and Plenipotentiary of Greater Germany in Italy', and put at the disposition of the German government, and Italy should contribute its gold to pay for the German troops that had been forced to replace the Italian troops on the southern front and who were now defending Italy.[38] Two other bodies eager to get their share of the loot were the Swiss National Bank (SNB) and the Bank for International Settlement (BIS), in Basel. They claimed that they had loaned the Italian government large sums of money to finance its rearmament in 1939 and now wanted reimbursement in gold. Mazzolini argued that it was important to retain financial credibility abroad, which required Italy to meet these requests in full. Despite Mussolini's position, which had been that he had 'always wanted our country's credit abroad to be kept absolutely intact', the governors of the bank initially refused to comply with the Swiss requests. Indicative of the lack of control the bank now had over the gold, on 19 April it was agreed to transfer 12,604 kg of gold to the BIS and 10,784 kg to the SNB. Mazzolini defended the transfers by arguing that they were necessary to safeguard Italy's good name and relationship with the two institutions after the war. Nor were the Germans eager to fall foul of the Swiss banks at this stage and their decision here is indicative of the extent to which Germany was willing to compromise with them in order to preserve their working relationship.

Mussolini authorised the transfer of 1,863 gold bars and 238 bags of coins to be delivered directly to the Reichsbank in Berlin, but when this first shipment arrived at the railway station on 3 March 1944 after a tortuous three-day journey from Fortezza, 135 bags of gold coins were grabbed by Ribbentrop's men, much to the disquiet of the Reichsbank. This was far from the entire Italian stock, however, much of which had been retained at Fortezza so that Italy could maintain a gold reserve to uphold the country's financial credibility and avoid a total collapse of its currency. Giampietro, however, conceded that Italy's military position was untenable and was clear that there was no margin for mediation with the Germans, and so ordered the release of all the gold remaining at Fortezza to be handed over to them. Bank officials, however, still resisted and were able to delay the transfer of the gold despite strong pressure by the Germans to do so. This pressure was, in reality, waning, since the Allies had imposed restrictions on gold transactions that could be traced back to looted German gold, but one further shipment on 21 October 1944 of 1,620 gold bars and 8,560 coins was deposited in the vaults of the Reichsbank in Berlin. Of this second shipment, 1,607 gold bars were delivered to the Prussian Mint for re-smelting between 3 and 26 October. This was then deposited, along with 300 gold coins, in the 'German Foreign Ministry Deposit – Italian gold I' account. A portion of the gold was held on behalf of the Italian Embassy in Berlin and the remainder was placed in the 'German Foreign Ministry Deposit – Italian gold II' account.

In February 1945, the Germans decided to transfer the Reichsbank gold to the mines at Merkers, in Thüringen, central Germany. Records show that the Italian gold was transported in 2,439 large sacks and deposited in the mines by the end of March. The gold that had been handed over to Ribbentrop's Foreign Ministry in March, however, did not go to Merkers. It had been divided up into two parts, one of which, comprising a little over 2 tons, was taken to a place near the city of Plön in the Schleswig-Holstein region of northern Germany. Here it was buried in two different locations and remained there until discovered by Allied forces after the war, who identified it as being of Italian origin.

Of the remaining gold, forty-one sacks had been sent to a house in the forest near Ballenstedt. This and another forty-one bags that had been sent to a farm in Heiligenstedten, also in Schleswig-Holstein, were then transported to Fuschl Castle near Salzburg, in Austria, which had been requisitioned by one of Ribbentrop's officials, Bernd Gottfriedsen. The castle itself was not considered to be suitably secure and so all the treasure was taken to the farm of Alois Ziller, near Hintersee, and buried in a hole dug inside a large wooden shed.

In June 1945 this cache of gold was reported to the Allies, who recovered it and carried out a thorough investigation into its provenance. Despite many of the bags still having the original seals of the Banca d'Italia, the gold was handed over to the Austrian Central Bank on 19 February 1947 on the assumption that it was part of the gold that had been owned by them prior to 1938 and which had never left Austria. However, the Banca d'Italia was able to prove that it was Italian gold and so the allocation to the Central Bank of Austria was revoked and the gold awarded to the Tripartite Commission. In May 1945, the Allies returned the gold which had remained at Fortezza, 153 boxes and 55 bags, to the Banca d'Italia in Rome.

As well as monetary gold, the Germans also looted private wealth in Italy after 1943. SS Lieutenant Colonel Herbert Kappler, the Gestapo commander in Rome, was entrusted with maintaining order during the Nazi occupation. He established his headquarters not far from the Church of Saint John in Lateran on the Via Tasso and immediately got to work registering the city's Jews. On the morning of 26 September 1943, he summoned the president of Rome's Jewish community, Ugo Foà, and the president of the Jewish-Italian community, Dante Almansi, to his headquarters, where he delivered them an ultimatum: they were to deliver 50 kg of gold to his headquarters within 36 hours or he would deport 200 members of their Jewish community to Germany.

The population of Rome, Jews and non-Jews alike, took what gold they had to the city's synagogues. One eyewitness, Giacomo Debenedetti, recorded that:

> Cautiously, as if afraid of being refused, uncertain whether to offer gold to the rich Jews, some 'Aryans' presented themselves. They entered the hall adjacent to the synagogue full of embarrassment, not knowing if they should take off their hats or keep their heads covered, according to Jewish custom. Almost humbly, they asked if they could – well if it would be all right to … Unfortunately, they did not leave their names.[39]

By the time the deadline expired, the Romans had managed to gather 80 kg of gold. They delivered the required 50 kg to Kappler's headquarters and the rest was hidden.

Chapter 3

TRADING WITH THE THIRD REICH

'Too often, being neutral provided a pretext for avoiding moral considerations.'
U.S. Commerce Department Undersecretary, Stuart Eizenstat

The most widely accepted interpretation of neutrality is impartiality, and it was in this context that Hugo Grotius (1583-1645) in his treatise *De jure belli ac pacis* [On the Law of War and Peace] said non-combatant nations should 'show themselves impartial to either [belligerent] in permitting transit, in furnishing supplies to his troops and in not assisting those under siege', and 'From those who are at peace nothing should be taken except in case of extreme necessity and subject to the restoration of its value.'[1] For small states in a world at war, neutrality was complex and often simply a matter of survival.[2] Arguments put forward by neutral countries that traded with Nazi Germany during the war, and who sought justification for their strategy, included the fear they too would be overrun, but they have usually been seen as convenient excuses for self-enrichment.

Not all European nations were caught up in the Second World War as belligerents. Countries such as Belgium and the Netherlands had wanted to stay out of the conflict, but their geographical position made them strategically too important for the Germans to respect that desire and they were swallowed up in the drive against France. Other countries on the periphery, such as Sweden, Portugal, Spain and Turkey, who also declared neutrality, were more problematic for the Germans, who would have also liked to occupy them and strip them of resources to feed their war machine. There was obviously a limit beyond which Hitler was not prepared to stretch his forces in the role of occupying powers when he needed all available men for the ultimate goal of destroying the Soviet Union, so the solution for him was to secure trading relationships with these neutrals, thus giving Germany access to their products and services. The Allies were also hugely interested in competing for the same resources, for which there were limited viable substitutes.

In order to remain independent and survive, neutral countries had to make themselves economically useful to the belligerent by trading in goods and materials, labour provision, and capital, in the hope that these would prove to be sufficiently valuable for the belligerents to continue to respect their independence. Trading with both sides also reduced the risk of attack from either. For Sweden this meant providing Germany with iron ore and ball bearings, for Spain and Portugal supplying leather and wolfram, and for Turkey, chromate. Switzerland was a special case in that it not only supplied armaments but provided banking facilities essential for Germany to trade with other neutral countries. It should be remembered, however, that all neutral countries that traded with Germany during the war also traded with the Allies. For instance, Portugal provided the British with shipping services, while Sweden provided both the Allies and Axis powers with diplomatic, shipping, and insurance services. Even Switzerland supplied timing devices for bombs to both sides. Neutral countries managed their neutrality in different ways, according to the level of threat they perceived themselves to be under from Germany. Geographically, economically and politically, Spain, Sweden and Switzerland were the neutral countries most affected by the war. Unlike Portugal or Turkey, they were physically substantially surrounded by Axis forces and were prevented from trading with the rest of the world unless such trade was mutually agreed to by both Axis and Allied powers.

The neutrals resisted repeated Allied attempts to apply diplomatic and economic pressure on them to curtail trade with Germany by arguing that it would result in German reprisal, and even invasion, if trade with Axis powers was restricted. They also pointed out that if the Germans went down the road of occupation, then all Allied access to resources of the former neutral states would cease. Such reasoning could not easily be countered by the Allies in the early years of the war, when neutral vulnerability was all too apparent, but by late 1943, the Allies were much less willing to accept the neutrals' claim of the *force majeure* argument as a reason to justify their continued economic interaction with the Nazi regime. In 1943, as the course of the war clearly began to flow against Germany,

Allied leaders felt that the German military threat to neutral states began to recede. Most importantly, the charge of collusion shows that despite the lessening or ending of any real threat from Germany and, indeed, the making of considerable concessions to the Allies, such as the Portuguese granting Azores bases, Spain withdrawing its Blue Division from Russia and the rescue and aid to Jewish refugees, the neutrals continued for many months into mid or late 1944, or in the case of Switzerland until the closing days of the war in 1945, to continue to trade or ship critical materials to the German war industry.

Emil Puhl was well aware that although Germany had acquired significant quantities of gold to finance its war effort, neutral countries were, in the main, unwilling to accept payment for their exports in gold, especially after 1942 when the Allies began to apply pressure on them to stop trading with Germany. It is here that Switzerland played a major role by purchasing Germany's gold and paying for it in Swiss francs, which was one of the few currencies universally accepted. The Germans could then go ahead and make their purchases paying with the Swiss francs.

Sweden
Sweden had a traditional policy of neutrality dating from the Napoleonic wars. In the years immediately prior to the outbreak of the Second World War, Sweden withdrew from Europe and hoped that the Nordic region could remain outside any conflict. Sweden's subsequent strategy of neutrality was founded on three factors: its geographical position, which gave it only minor strategic importance within the overall German war plans; its declared willingness to defend itself; and its willingness to maintain pre-war levels of iron-ore exports. Sweden provided Germany's wartime industry with high-grade iron ore from Kiruna, in the north of the country, and ball bearings. It tried to balance Allied criticism of its trade with Germany through its traditional political and economic ties with the Western democracies, gaining some sympathy for their position surrounded by Axis powers or occupied countries, but there was some concern that it went too far in sustaining the German war machine.

Sweden was heavily dependent on imported coal and oil and required foreign currency to pay for them, meaning it had to maintain a high level of exports to avoid economic collapse. After the German occupation of Norway and Denmark in April 1940, however, the country became cut off from the West, depriving it of up to 70 per cent of its export market. It now became utterly dependent upon Germany and countries under German control to obtain coal and coke for industry, and artificial fertilizers for agriculture.

From the government's perspective, trade with the Axis powers was not so much a question of profit as one of survival. It is argued by many that if Sweden had stopped exports to Germany for political and moral reasons, and the Germans had invaded, it is possible that the latter would have exploited Sweden's industrial and economic resources with such ruthless efficiency as to extract a far greater contribution to their war effort than was the case.

On 12 April 1940, three days after the German invasion of neighbouring Denmark and Norway, Swedish Prime Minister Per Albin Hansson went on the radio to outline his country's policy:

> Sweden is firmly determined to continue to follow the line of strict neutrality. That implies that we must reserve for ourselves independence of judgment and independence of action in every direction. It is not consistent with strict neutrality to permit any belligerent to make use of Swedish territory for its activity. Fortunately, no demands in such a direction have been made of us. Should any such demands be made they must be refused.[3]

Despite this assertion, Sweden granted permission for what were designated as sealed 'Red Cross' trains, operating as regular commercial freight carriers, to transit its territories to take non-military goods, food, clothing, and fuel to the German Narvik garrison. The German 'medical personnel' on the trains, however, were critically needed military specialists, and the 'non-military' goods were, in fact, artillery and anti-aircraft guns, as well as ammunition. In return, the Swedes demanded, and received, from Germany substantial arms shipments for its own defensive build-up.

With its victory over France, Germany's position became much stronger, and Sweden lost much of its leverage to resist German demands. At a Swedish cabinet meeting on 18 June, a unanimous decision was taken to accede to German calls to allow their soldiers on leave from occupied Norway to travel to Germany on Swedish railways, but a spokesman still insisted that 'an acceptance of the German demand did not have to imply that we abandoned our policy of neutrality.'[4]

In late June 1941, Germany demanded transit of its forces from Norway across Sweden to Finland, and in return Sweden asked for, and received, aircraft engines, Daimler-Benz tanks, half-ton half-tracks from Demag, 21-cm Škoda cannons together with their ammunition and equipment, and a long list of optical and radio equipment. This agreement was taken by Germany to indicate that 'Sweden was finally beginning to see the realities of power in the new Europe'.[5] Germany was even able to influence Swedish internal politics by pressuring the Swedish government to suppress unfavourable comments about Germany. In this regard, the Swedish government failed to fully defend an important freedom of expression granted to a neutral country in international law. Further Swedish demands met an increasingly stubborn response in Berlin, however, when the Reich imposed an arms embargo and a withdrawal of German naval protection of Swedish shipping.

By 1943 it became apparent to the Swedes that Germany could no longer win the war, but there was still grave danger to any neutral country that tried to thwart it. An Allied-Swedish trade agreement of September 1943 did eventually bring about a progressive, substantial curtailment of Swedish commerce with Germany. Under this agreement, the U.S. and Britain agreed to allow an increase in exports to Sweden, including oil and rubber, in exchange for which Sweden agreed to cancel the transit of German military matériel and troops across Sweden, further reduce iron ore exports, end Swedish naval escorting of German ships in the Baltic, and reduce ball-bearing exports. This may not have been such a crucial blow to German industry because it could have continued military production by utilising its substantial high-grade iron-ore stockpiles and would have been able to take up any slack with ore from other occupied states.[6] All Swedish trade with Germany halted completely in November 1944.

An important issue that Sweden was forced to address much later, in 1998, was the extent to which its government knew about the Bank of Sweden's growing suspicions that gold, with which Germany paid for its imports, might be looted monetary gold. It seems that in 1943 the Swedish government turned down a proposal by the state bank to officially ask the German Reichsbank for assurances that upcoming deliveries would not contain looted monetary gold.

Turkey

To say that Turkey was neutral during the Second World war hides a complicated reality. Initially, the country assumed that the Allies would win the war and it was neither ideologically nor constitutionally committed to neutrality as part of a long-term strategy. Its change of heart came as an abrupt reaction to the unexpected fall of France. The Turkish government had become uneasy after the Italian invasion of Albania in April 1939, and entered into an Anglo-Turkish Agreement to 'conclude a definite long-term agreement of a reciprocal character in the interests of their national security', and 'in the event of an act of aggression leading to war in the Mediterranean area [both governments would be prepared] to co-operate effectively and to lend each other all aid and assistance in their power'.[7] A formal treaty was signed on 19 October 1939.

After June 1940, when Italy threw in its lot with Germany, however, Turkey found itself in the unenviable position of being obliged to go to war with Italy. It took the pragmatic view that such an action would invite invasion by the Wehrmacht and, instead, adopted a position of non-belligerency. The Allies initially made no protest, hoping that Turkey might eventually become an important ally later in the war. Instead of confrontation, Britain negotiated an agreement with Turkey to buy the following two years' supply of chromite at highly inflated prices on the condition that none whatsoever be sold to Germany.

In the spring of 1941, after the German occupation of the Balkans, the German government and the Turkish Republic, 'inspired by a desire to place relations between the two countries on a basis of mutual confidence and sincere friendship', concluded a German-Turkish Treaty of Friendship in June 1941. They agreed to 'bind themselves mutually to respect the integrity and inviolability of their territories'.[8] Thereafter, for most of the war, Turkey tried to balance its trade with Germany and the Allies. Germany strictly observed Turkey's territorial integrity, and Turkey carried on extensive commerce with Germany, particularly the export of critical chromite ore for the Nazi war effort. Chromium was one of the few raw materials essential for the German war industry and for which there were no adequate sources within German territory.

Dr Karl Clodius, the German foreign office minister, went to Ankara to negotiate an end to Britain's monopoly of Turkey's production and was able to persuade the Turks to agree that when the British deal expired it would ship 90,000 tons of chromite to Germany, providing Germany also buy, at grossly inflated prices, a large portion of the domestic farm commodities glutting the Turkish market. Before that, however, the Germans tried to organise a smuggling operation which almost caused the Turks to cancel the deal, but legitimate exports were begun in 1943, at which point Turkey was supplying almost 100 per cent of German war needs of the material. German Armaments Minister Albert Speer told Hitler in November 1943 that 'should supplies from Turkey be cut off, the stockpile of chromium is sufficient for only five to six months. The manufacture of planes, tanks, motor vehicles, tank shells, U-boats, almost the entire gamut of artillery would have to cease from one to three months after this deadline, since by then the reserves and distribution channels would be used up.'[9]

Roosevelt, Churchill, and Stalin all agreed it would be desirable to have Turkey in the war in 1943, but they lacked the means of enticing it. All Allied industry was working day and night to produce its own armament in preparation for Operation Overlord, the Allied invasion of northern Europe. Instead, Churchill tried diplomacy. Together with Foreign Secretary Anthony Eden, he met a Turkish delegation in Cairo on 23 November 1943, where the urgent requirement of Allied access to Turkish air bases was discussed. The Turks would not agree ostensibly because they feared German air strikes on Constantinople, Ankara, and Smyrna, but behind the scenes, the Deutsche Bank in Istanbul and the Deutsche Orient Bank were depositing a steady flow of bonds, cash, gold, bank deposits, and foreign exchange belonging to German firms and individuals. Six German insurance companies with branches in Turkey were linking Turkish insurance companies into their own operation with grants of German investment capital. Large flows of capital were entering the country and being invested in local real estate and other properties and business ventures. More than sixty German-controlled firms in Turkey, including I.G. Farben, Krupp, and Bayer, were engaged in building and public works contracting; building materials and tobacco merchandising; importing and exporting; chemicals and pharmaceuticals; shipping, forwarding, and transportation; machinery and electrical equipment. There was also the small matter of a 100 million Reichsmark order for German war matériel going to Turkey. While the Cairo meeting was taking place, Turkish and German businessmen and government leaders were deep in discussions about contracts and bond sales, all handled by Deutsche Bank.[10]

Turkey halted the export of chromite to Germany in April 1944 and suspended all commercial and diplomatic relations with Germany in August 1944. The United States began pressing Turkey to implement Safehaven controls (see Chapter 7) in 1944. On 4 November, the State Department sent diplomatic notes to Turkey, warning that it should neither acquire nor store any additional German gold. On 25 January 1945, they instructed the U.S. Embassy in Ankara to warn the Turks that they should preserve German assets for disposition in accordance with Allied policy. The Turks, however, did not respond, and as late as March had done nothing to control German assets in their territory.

U.S. experts estimated that Turkey, while not a major recipient of gold from Germany during the Second World War, received as much as $15 million in gold, much of it probably for its chromite exports. Some $3.4 million of this was Belgian monetary gold looted by

Germany. In addition, two German banks with branches in Istanbul (Deutsche Bank and the Dresdner Bank), took advantage of the high prices on the Turkish free gold market to sell looted gold provided by the Reichsbank in return for foreign currency, particularly Swiss francs. Some of this gold was traced to the Melmer account containing concentration camp gold. Other German gold acquired by Turkey during and after the war included coins and ingots from the account of German Foreign Minister Joachim von Ribbentrop at the Reichsbank, which had been stocked with gold looted from occupied Europe.

After the war, the British and U.S. ambassadors in Istanbul argued against treating Turkey as anything but an ally when it came to searching for looted gold. The United States subsequently dropped any plans to request Turkey to provide detailed information about its wartime gold supply. The Allies tried to get Turkey to negotiate over the $70 million of German assets in the country, but never did so with any vigour given Turkey's new strategic importance in the emerging Cold War with the Soviet Union, in the wake of threatening Soviet gestures toward the Dardanelles and the Soviet-Turkish border.

Spain

The strategic importance of Spain in the Second World War centred on the control of Gibraltar. The German General Staff saw that if Spain could be brought into the war on the Axis side, General Franco would open his border to German forces and allow them to pass through to drive the British out of Gibraltar and severely restrict Allied access to the Mediterranean. Fearing that by allowing Spain to enter the war it would re-open the still-raw wounds of the Spanish Civil War, Franco was not willing to allow his country to become involved militarily in 1940, despite the threat of German occupation if he resisted. His strategy was to assure Germany of his willingness to join the Axis as a co-belligerent but, at his meeting with Hitler at Hendaye Plage on 26 October 1940, he set a list of conditions he knew Hitler would not accept. As a compromise, he provided Germany with valuable assistance in the form of allowing German pilots to photograph Allied shipping from Iberian airliners and by permitting German naval and merchant vessels to use the Spanish ports of Santander, Vigo, and Cadiz and harbours in the Canary Islands for refuelling and resupply. No doubt Franco was also able to argue that the threat of having humanitarian aid cut off by the U.S. who, although not yet at war, were anxious to promote Spanish neutrality, would result in the starvation of the Spanish population on a massive scale and total collapse of internal order.

A second element which was important was tungsten (known to the Germans as wolfram), a rare super-strong metal. With the highest melting point of any metal, the highest tensile strength and the least expansion when heated, its main use was in hardening steel to make machine tools, filaments and armour. Among its multiplicity of uses was the production of gun barrels and artillery shells, and Germany was the first nation to use wolfram in the production of armour-penetrating ammunition. As wolfram combines hardness with a relatively light weight, it is also used in the production of aeroplane engines and propellers. It is estimated that Germany imported some 3,500 tons annually from Spain and Portugal, which satisfied the whole of the German war requirements for this critical material in 1942-1943, and about half the total in 1944, the last full year of the war. To illustrate the importance of the Iberian trade to Germany, the Portuguese dictator António de Oliveira Salazar went as far as to say that to deny wolfram to Germany would inevitably reduce its capacity to continue the war. In 1940 there was no evidence that Britain had any interest in wolfram at all and their motivation in trying to curtail its export to Germany was simply because it was clear that Germany valued it highly and obviously used it extensively. In 1941, Britain began to import it but only to the extent of taking about 4 per cent of Spain's total production.[11]

Almost all sections of the Spanish chemical and pharmaceutical industry came under the control of I.G. Farben. It controlled many Spanish firms such as Sociedad Electro-Quimica de Flix and Quimica Commercial y Farmaceutica S.A. Farben Unicolor S.A. represented sixteen German firms having interlocking directorates with several large Spanish chemical companies. There were also two prominent German-owned banks in Spain and the Spanish Civil War had given Germany a strong foothold there. In November 1943, an agreement was reached in which Spain acknowledged a $1 billion debt to Germany. Several payments were made, in free credits. One payment was of $60 million to be used by the Germans to buy Spanish property, finance goods, and sustain the German diplomatic staff in Spain. In July 1944 the balance due had been brought down to $40 million, and by April 1945, Spain's debt was only $22 million, and it was being negotiated by German interests.

Spain's strategic location, however, gave it importance as a conduit for trade with North Africa and South America, which included industrial diamonds and platinum. Within Spain itself the production of wolfram was vitally important for the German war economy and made it the second largest producer of it after Portugal. Although

Spanish General Francisco Franco declared Spain neutral in 1939, he was openly sympathetic to the Axis powers, which helped bring him to power and only gradually abandoned his inclination to join the Axis. By 1943, however, Spain had gradually adopted a more neutral policy, largely in response to Allied economic warfare, the growing strength of Allied armed forces (especially in North Africa and the Mediterranean), and the reversals experienced by Germany from 1942 onwards.

The initial Allied strategy was to purchase enough of the ore to satisfy Spain's export demands and prevent it from increasing its trade with the enemy, but the Franco regime combined desultory trade negotiations with the Allies and secret agreements with Germany to ensure the continued delivery of critical war supplies. The British hesitated to act decisively against Spain for fear of driving Franco more fully into the Axis camp, a position that was roundly criticised by the U.S., but in January 1944 the Allies imposed an oil embargo on the country.

Negotiations ensued in which Britain was willing to see wolfram exports to Germany at the 1943 level, but the U.S. demanded a complete ban. When, in May 1944, Germany's defeat became more certain, however, Spain agreed to limit exports of wolfram to Germany, but senior members of Franco's cabinet cooperated with Germany in smuggling more than 800 tons in July 1944 in violation of the agreement. Spain's exports of wolfram to Nazi Germany ended with the closing of the Franco-Spanish border in August 1944.

In May 1945 the Western Allies issued a decree freezing all German assets in Spain believed to be worth about $95 million. Initial estimates put Spanish acquisition of German gold to be 123 tons, worth nearly $140 million. Eleven tons were taken directly from Germany and German-occupied territories, 74 tons from the German account at the SNB, and about 38 tons directly from the SNB, which the Allies believed included some looted gold. Some $100 million of this was estimated to be looted. Much of this gold was transported by truck from Switzerland to Spain to pay for Spanish goods exported to Germany. The German state-owned enterprise Sofindus (Sociedad Financiera Industrial), run by Johannes Bernhardt, is reputed to have received 83 tons in gold bars alone.

Portugal

During the war, Portugal tried to balance its trade with both the Allies and the Axis powers, and both sides tried to persuade the country to deal preferentially with them by a mixture of threats and lucrative trade deals. Britain's commercial ties with Portugal had a long history, which gave it an advantage, but António Salazar, Portugal's dictator, made no secret of his admiration for Hitler and openly modelled his country's social institutions on the fascist pattern. Portugal, however, was also dependent on the U.S. for petroleum, coal, and chemical supplies. Germany, on the other hand, with its conquest of France, now had direct overland routes along which it could boost its export trade and support the Portuguese economy if the Allies imposed a naval blockade. This was something that Britain in particular was not eager to do since it would inevitably draw Portugal into a much closer alliance with Germany and threaten supplies of raw materials, which would be strategically damaging to the Allied war effort. Britain, after all, was buying more from Portugal than Germany was. For its part, Portugal offered Britain very generous credit facilities to such an extent that, at the end of the war, Britain owed Portugal over $322 million. At first Portugal refused to trade on a credit basis with Germany, but trade increased significantly after late 1941 when exports were paid for through the BIS working through the Banco de Portugal and the SNB.

This competition between the belligerents for Portuguese raw materials proved to be hugely beneficial to Portugal's economy and generated huge profits for its businesses and banks. Portugal was an important source of wolfram, tin, manganese, mica, chrome, and antimony for the German armament industry, but the Portuguese were not prepared to accept Reichsmarks and insisted on payment in gold. Wolfram in particular was hugely important, and the pure metal was extracted at the rate of 1.5 grams for every ton of ore processed. The German military build-up in preparation for its invasion of the Soviet Union hugely increased its need of wolfram, the price of which had rocketed since the start of the war.

Portugal was ranked as second only to Switzerland in terms of the quantity of looted gold it received from Germany during the Second World War. Between 1939 and 1944, Portuguese domestic gold holdings increased sixfold. Estimates put the amount of gold delivered to Portugal from the SNB at some 123.7 tons. In addition to that, the partly Swiss-owned Banco Espiroto Santo was active in laundering looted gold to finance German purchases of Portuguese raw materials for war production. Before 1944 German investment in Portugal had been restricted to mining, but after this time it was redirected towards the purchase of property. While German firms had extensive interests in the country, companies such as I.G. Farben did not actually manufacture there but were involved with the marketing of pharmaceuticals through Bayer Ltd. in Lisbon and

Oporto. The most important German manufacturer in Portugal was the electrical firm of Siemens Companhia de Electricidad S.A.R.L., a division of the Siemens group of Germany. No German banks were established in Portugal.

Gold flowing into Lisbon from Germany at the beginning of 1942 was becoming so obvious and extensive that Montagu Norman, in his role of director of the Bank of England, notified the BIS that it would refuse to transact any further transfer of gold held in its vaults to Portugal. Unfortunately, this was not the crushing blow to German trade that it might have been because at around this time, the Germans were taking possession of the Belgian gold repatriated from West Africa. Portugal was quite happy to view this transfer as a legitimate transaction since it had been agreed to by the Vichy government, who controlled the gold on behalf of the Belgians, and it saw no reason for refusing to accept it as payment for its exports to Germany. The Portuguese, however, were careful to ensure that the gold did not come to them directly from the Reichsbank, but was first laundered through the SNB in three accounts, A, B and C. The Banco de Portugal sold escudos to the SNB in return for Swiss francs, which were deposited into account A, while private Portuguese banks did the same, depositing the Swiss francs in account B. The SNB deposited the escudos in account C and used them to buy gold from the Reichsbank. The SNB then sold on this gold to the Banco de Portugal, who paid for it in the Swiss francs from accounts A and B. The Germans then used the escudos to pay for Portuguese raw materials and Portugal became the legal owner of the gold. It has been estimated that over 20 tons of Belgian gold found its way into Portuguese reserves during 1943. This apparently was enough to settle the nerves of the Allies, who seemingly found that acceptable at first but began to raise objections in 1943.[12] At this point, the Banco de Portugal began divesting itself of German gold, selling as much as 45 tons by February 1945.

The Allies issued a warning on 22 February 1944, the Declaration on Gold Purchases, which stated that they would not recognise transfer of looted gold from the Axis powers and would not buy gold from any country which had not broken relations with them. The Portuguese claimed that up until that time all their gold transactions with Germany had been undertaken in good faith, but there is evidence that they continued trading up until 13 October of that year. On 5 June 1944, the Allies were able to compel Portugal to stop all wolfram shipments to Germany, at which point the Germans liquidated their mining assets and invested the proceeds in assets such as hotels, cinemas, and factories. The Portuguese would later claim that it was not their responsibility to return looted gold exchanged with Germany during the war for tangible assets.

Switzerland

By mid-1944, Germany had increased its trade with the neutral nations, and, with the exception of Portugal, which had major trade ties with Britain, became the major trading partner of all of them. Switzerland, entirely surrounded by Germany, had been drawn even more completely into Germany's trade orbit than the other neutrals, and by 1943 Germany absorbed nearly a third of all Swiss exports, which were primarily manufactured items that required small amounts of raw materials, large amounts of capital, and highly skilled labour. The most important products exported to Germany required the exceptionally high degree of skill and precision for which Swiss watch and machine tool industries were famous. In addition, Switzerland annually exported to Germany one-half billion kilowatts of electricity, or about 40 per cent of the total power supply of southern Germany, and Swiss hydroelectric power annually produced 16,000 tons of aluminium and aluminium products for Germany during the war. Moreover, the unprecedented use by Germany of the Swiss railway to move goods to and from Italy allowed large quantities of raw materials, foodstuffs, chemicals, and other materials to be transported.

The U.S. Secretary of State Cordell Hull warned on 9 April 1944 that '[The U.S.] can no longer acquiesce in these nations drawing upon the resources of the allied world when they at the same time contribute to the death of troops whose sacrifice contributes to their salvation as well as ours... we ask them only, but with insistence, to cease aiding our enemy.'[13] President Roosevelt went so far as to take steps to 'block the Swiss participation in saving the skins of rich or prominent Germans' and warned of serious consequences if the warning was ignored. In August 1944, Switzerland drastically reduced its exports of strategic items such as ammunition, locomotives, automobiles, diesel engines, and machinery to Germany, and negotiations in the autumn moved Switzerland towards a total ban on such exports. The Swiss also agreed to a ban on the transit of all war matériel between Italy and Germany, including various categories of loot.

Chapter 4

THE SWISS BANKS

'Our raw material is money – foreign money, whatever its source.'[1]

Swiss neutrality and independence had been agreed to by the European powers at the end of the Thirty Years' War in the Treaty of Westphalia, on 24 October 1648, and was later confirmed in the 1815 Congress of Vienna. Switzerland had remained aloof from the First World War, but its independence came under extreme pressure during the Second World War. One of the consequences of its independence, and one reason why neither side in the war was eager to challenge the country's neutral stance, was that it was one of the few places in Europe where activities of foreign intelligence agencies were tolerated within its borders. For instance, the U.S. Office of Strategic Services (OSS, forerunner of the CIA) had a presence in Bern at 23 Herrengasse, from where Allen Dulles and his deputy Gerry Mayer held nightly conversations with OSS headquarters in Washington. Later in the war, Dulles would hold talks in Bern with Hans Bernd Gisevius, the German vice-consul in Zurich, about the possibility of negotiating a secret peace agreement between the Allies and a German resistance movement led by Abwehr chief Wilhelm Canaris. Switzerland had also long been a cornerstone of British Intelligence operations in Europe ever since the First World War.

The Nazis had special reasons for wanting Switzerland and its banks to operate freely during the war. The Nazi Spy chief Walter Schellenberg maintained a close relationship with his Swiss counterpart, Colonel Roger Masson, which allowed him to channel funds to finance German Intelligence operations across the world through Swiss banks. Masson asked for and was given the green light to conduct liaisons with Schellenberg by the Swiss Federal Council, the executive body of the federal government of the Swiss Confederation, which serves as the collective head of state and government of Switzerland. The rationale for such cooperation was given as the need to avoid presenting Germany with any pretext for invading Switzerland, but the relationship continued to thrive long after the war had turned against the Axis powers and the threat of invasion had become almost non-existent. For his part, throughout the war the Reichsbank Vice-President Emil Puhl had a close, personal contact with the 'hidebound, pig-headed…custodian of the [Swiss] currency', Ernst Weber, president of the SNB, which allowed much business to be conducted on the basis of 'old pals' verbal agreements between the two men leaving no paper trail. Although the SNB was ostensibly a privately owned bank, its chief executives were all Swiss government appointees. When Weber washed his hands of association with contamination by looted gold, he was speaking for the Swiss government by saying, quite explicitly, that, 'It would be impossible to refuse to accept gold from one particular country. That would conflict with Switzerland's neutrality. The National Bank cannot have regard to the provenance of the gold that is sold by the Deutsche Reichsbank.'[2] Puhl was to become a star witness at the Nuremberg War Trials and contradicted Weber's assertion when he gave evidence against many of his wartime colleagues. Of Weber, he would say, when questioned about the Swiss involvement in the handling of looted monetary gold, that it had been 'the President of the Swiss National Bank', himself, who informed him that the Swiss 'were fully aware of the gold's provenance'.

Three quarters of Switzerland's population were native German speakers and there was a strong cultural bond between the two countries, but that would not deter the Nazis if they thought it was in their interests to invade the country. There had been even stronger links between Germany and Austria and the latter had been swiftly swallowed up into the Reich. There was little to say that Switzerland might not suffer a similar fate. As a measure of what he called the new political realities of Europe, in May 1940 the Swiss Foreign Minister Marcel Pilet-Golaz redefined his country's future policy as one that would be steered along lines defined by Germany. It was clear that if Swiss independence was to be maintained, there would be a price to pay. Switzerland's neutrality would be an 'ambiguous, expedient kind of neutrality' based more on self-interest than any abstract or moral principle.[3]

Soon Switzerland would be almost completely surrounded by Axis forces, which allowed the Swiss, when facing criticism for its 'shrewd, active, organised complicity with the Third Reich',[4] to argue that they had little choice but to collaborate economically with Germany or face a catastrophic economic blockade or worse. This argument is weak given that a German invasion would have thrown into doubt the legitimacy of the Swiss franc, the only currency apart from gold that was acceptable to neutral trading partners, and that would have had an extremely damaging consequence for that trade. As early as October 1940, U.S. newspapers were carrying stories about the Nazis trading gold with the Swiss in return for Swiss francs to purchase war materiel, since neutral countries were refusing to accept Reichsmarks in payment. Clearly it was vital for Germany to have a close partnership with the Swiss banks at the same time as giving the rest of the world an excuse to turn a blind eye by colluding in the false perception of Swiss neutrality. Germany became entirely dependent on the Swiss, and the Swiss, for their part, were tied up with a trade agreement dated 18 July 1941 in which they 'committed [themselves] to making continuing deliveries to the Reich on credit only'. This, in the German Foreign Office's opinion, meant that by running up huge deficits 'Switzerland simply could not escape whether or not she wished to do so'.[5] There was never any serious attempt by the Nazis to annexe the country.[6] Indeed, after the German invasion of the Soviet Union in 1941, when the war front moved far to the east, the Swiss sense of security against invasion was significantly increased.

The German government took it for granted that Germany would exert even greater control over Switzerland after winning the war and assumed that it would become little more than another vassal state. At the start of the Second World War, Switzerland was seen as a useful source of much-needed supplies at a time when Germany had exhausted its foreign exchange reserves and the Swiss were prepared to extend massive credits to the Germans for their purchases. It is the case, however, that Germany started planning the invasion of Switzerland on 25 June 1940, the day France surrendered. The final plans were drawn up for Operation Tannenbaum in October, but never put into action. It may well have been little more than a staff exercise in planning to occupy the Wehrmacht while it clicked its heels waiting for the order to move against the Soviet Union. Hitler himself had never seemed interested in an invasion and had remarked in the summer of 1940 that Switzerland was 'far more valuable' as a foreign exchange turntable and 'must not be attacked under any circumstances'.[7] Hitler's own personal bank account was held in the Union Bank of Switzerland in Federal Square, Bern.

The idea that Switzerland could be of more use to Germany as a source of goods and banking services, especially in relation to other neutrals such as Portugal and Spain, overcame the strategic benefits of conquest and occupation. Faced in 1941 with proof that the gold it was purchasing from Germany had been looted from Austrian and Czech vaults, the Swiss government and banks, unable now to deny the gold's provenance, adopted the view that looting during war was legal. If a country invades another country, they said, it is acceptable to assume legal title to its gold reserves and private property, and if this gold is transferred to financial institutions in Switzerland, such deposits may then legitimately be used to make purchases inside Switzerland or in other neutral countries.[8] Such arguments might have had some weight, but when it became clear, later, that 'victim gold' looted from Jewish communities and concentration camp inmates was being traded, there was nowhere for the Swiss to hide.

Throughout the war, much of the world continued to trade as normal. Underneath the slaughter and devastation of the fighting war was another extremely complex trade war. Germany in particular was always reliant on the purchase of munitions from outside the German sphere of influence. The whole of its manganese requirements, essential for steel manufacture of gun barrels, came from abroad, mostly Spain. Another metal, wolfram (tungsten), used in the manufacture of aircraft, of which 4,000 tons were imported in 1943 alone, came from Portugal. Turkey supplied stainless steel, Sweden iron ore, South America diamonds and Romania oil. All these materials had to be paid for in foreign currency or gold, and almost all Germany's stock of both had been exhausted by the end of 1939.

Since this was well known by Swiss bankers, they must have known that the gold it was handling on behalf of Germany was looted gold. Allied intelligence networks were kept well informed about gold movements in and out of Switzerland and were aware that most gold transactions were conducted through the Reichsbank Bern depository, opened in May 1940. By 1940, Switzerland had been integrated de facto into the greater German Reichsdeutsch economic area.[9]

Portugal, Turkey, Sweden and Spain sold war matériel to Germany but were unwilling to accept payment in Reichsmarks. Instead, they took payment in Swiss francs then used the francs to purchase the very same gold the Germans had originally used to purchase the francs. For these and similar transactions, the Swiss bankers charged handling fees. Assets stripped from subjugated countries had to be laundered so that they could be used to pay for goods on the world market. The same applied to gold looted from private individuals. It was the Swiss banks who performed this role.

An Allied economic intelligence document dated 5 February 1946 entitled 'Allied Claims against Swiss for Return of Looted Gold' stated that at least $398 million ($6.5 billion in 2022) of gold was shipped to Switzerland by the Reichsbank during the war. This was only part of the estimated total of $648 million ($10.7 billion in 2022) looted between 1938 and 1945. Of the £398 million, some $280 million was sold to the Swiss National Bank, £20 million went into other Swiss banks and around $100 million was laundered to pay for German imports from Spain and Portugal. By its own admission, between 1939 and 1945 the SNB accepted German gold to the value of 1.7 billion Swiss francs,[10] the last delivery being on 6 April 1945. Up until 1944, the SNB had requested no proof from the Reichsbank that it was the legal owner of the gold, and even after 1944, gold was accepted as legal simply on the word of Walther Funk and Emil Puhl.

The first gold deliveries to the Deutsche Reichsbank deposit account with the SNB was on 14 January 1940. This account was legally assigned to the BIS. Looted gold crossed into Switzerland on the German border at Basel then transferred to the subterranean vaults in Bern. Sometimes it would be exchanged for Swiss francs and other times it would be used by Nazi purchasing agents to pay for German imports. Some of the gold was taken in payment for Swiss exports, but overall, the gold deposits were never enough to cover the total cost of German imports. By 1945, the Nazis would accrue debts amounting to some 1 billion Swiss francs.

The plunder of monetary gold by Germany was well understood by the Allies right from the start, but little was done to counteract it until 1942 when, in July of that year, the Allies issued a warning to the Axis powers and neutral countries that they would not recognise the transfers of property taking place in territories occupied by the Axis, whether these transfers appeared to be legal or not. This was formalised into a declaration, signed by seventeen nations, on 5 January 1943: the 'Declaration on Forced Transfers of Property in Enemy-Controlled Territory', better known as the 'Inter-Allied Declaration Against Acts of Dispossession'. The signatories could declare invalid 'transfers of or dealings with property, rights and interests of any description whatsoever' presently or formerly situated in territories under Axis control or belonging to residents of those territories. 'This warning applied whether such transfers or dealings have taken the form of open looting or plunder, or of transactions apparently legal in form, even when they purport to be voluntarily effected.'[11] The hope was that this declaration would create uneasiness in the minds of neutrals who were trafficking in German gold. At this time, however, the Nazi grip on Europe was still very strong and tended to outweigh other considerations for neutral countries.

By mid-1943, Swiss bankers, as managers of Europe's key financial centre, would have been aware that all German pre-war gold stocks had been used up so any further gold purchases from Germany would be of looted gold. Indeed, huge quantities of Belgian gold found its way into the vaults at Bern at this time, indicating that Allied warnings were generally being ignored. In July of that year, the SNB bank committee met to discuss whether to continue accepting Nazi gold. They consulted the Federal Council and were informed that they should continue to do so, but were advised that 'gold dealings [should take on] more modest proportions in the future'.[12] It is clear from a memo sent to Ribbentrop on 3 June 1943 by Carl August Clodius, the special representative for the conduct of trade negotiation between the Third Reich and Switzerland, that gold-laundering services were of vital importance to Germany's ability to prosecute the war. In this long memo he wrote:

> Switzerland represents our only means of obtaining freely disposable foreign exchange [and Funk] could not, even for two months, forgo the possibility of effecting [such] foreign exchange transactions in Switzerland…The Ministry of Munitions stated that [the loss of] arms contacts [for] special technical equipment awarded to Switzerland would seriously affect the German tank and remote-control programme.[13]

Their 1943 warning having been largely ignored, the Allies again tried to call a halt to the trading of looted gold with a new 'Gold Declaration' on 22 February 1944, which formally declared that the U.S. 'does not and will not recognise the transference of title to the looted gold which the Axis…has disposed in world markets'.[14] The fear was that Nazis were hoarding gold in neutral countries, especially Switzerland, in the hope of financing a post-war safe haven for themselves, and this prospect of a German military revival would be opposed by all means possible.

In March 1945, Emil Puhl was moving in and out of Switzerland from Konstanz in southern Germany, trying to sell Nazi gold to the Swiss banks in Bern and the Bank for International Settlements in Basel. However, the BIS president Thomas McKittrick told him that the BIS was no longer able to accept German gold and suggested instead that the SNB buy it. Puhl wrote about how pleasing it was to see 'how strong the cultural ties [were] that connect [Switzerland and Germany] even if…political opinion…is not in our favour'.[15] It was not possible, however, to move the gold from Konstanz before the war ended.

After the war the Swiss initially opposed returning any Nazi gold on the pretext that it had been purchased in good faith and had been acquired legitimately by Germany as war booty in accordance with international legal principles. The 1946 Allied-Swiss Washington Accord, however, forced the Swiss to transfer $58 million of gold to the Tripartite Commission for the Restitution of Monetary Gold, also called the Tripartite Gold Commission (TGC). This did not include some $120 million in gold held on accounts for other countries.

In 1983, Hans Ulrich Jost, of Lausanne University, exposed to the world what the Swiss had been doing during the war and, for his troubles, was subjected to abuse from Swiss bankers and put under constant police surveillance. Switzerland fulfilled an important function in the gold market, he claimed. Most countries, including Portugal and Sweden, refused to accept German gold in payment for exports of strategic raw materials to Germany. Taking refuge behind the argument that it was acting as a neutral country, Switzerland took the gold without question. 'The profits from Nazi gold...have been invested and reinvested, laundered, and relaundered...converted into real estate and portfolios under new names.'[16]

Chapter 5

THE BANK FOR INTERNATIONAL SETTLEMENTS

'I hope that we can all agree that the most important test for any country today is not what it did or failed to do in the past, but what it is doing now and will do in the future to face the past honestly.'
Stuart Eizenstat in his opening address to the
London Conference, 2 December 1997

Even before 1914 there had been occasions when central banks had found it useful to cooperate with one another in order to facilitate international settlements. Then, after the First World War, monetary and political authorities soon became interested in the idea of substituting such ad-hoc and temporary associations for a more permanent system of cooperation, especially in relation to the problem of reparations owed by Germany. To achieve this, the Bank for International Settlements (BIS) was set up by the National Bank of Belgium, the Bank of England, the Bank of France, the Bank of Italy, and the Reichsbank, and by two banking groups, one acting in the place of the Bank of Japan and another formed by three United States banks; J.P. Morgan and Co., the First National Bank of New York, and the First National Bank of Chicago, designed to promote cooperation and make financial settlements easier.

The governors of the founding central banks and representatives of an American banking group met in Rome to create the BIS, which began operations on 17 May 1930. Its dual role was to:

- Promote the cooperation of central banks and to provide additional facilities for international financial operations

- Act as trustee or agent in regard to international financial settlements entrusted to it under agreements with the parties concerned.

The BIS was free to process international transactions with all countries in time of war. Its Constituent Charter stated that the bank, its property and assets and all deposits and other funds entrusted to it were immune in time of peace and in time of war from any measure such as expropriation, requisition, seizure, confiscation, prohibition or restriction of gold or currency export or import and other similar measures. The bank could 'buy, sell, exchange or hold gold for its own account or for the account of central banks, make advances to or borrow from central banks, discount, re-discount, purchase or sell, with or without its endorsement, bills of exchange and other short-term obligations of prime liquidity'.[1] In effect, all warring nations had signed up, ensuring that the BIS could never be closed down or have its assets appropriated. It was therefore 'virtually untouchable before the war and nothing could be done to restrict its actions'.[2] It was also written into the statutes that operations of the BIS must be in conformity with the monetary policy of the central banks of the countries in question. Before carrying out an operation on any market or in any currency, the BIS must give all the central banks directly concerned an opportunity to dissent. It had no direct contact with the public, having neither counters nor tills nor strong rooms. Its gold, funds, and its securities were kept at the central banks, which were its correspondents. It should be remembered also that the BIS was not actually a Swiss bank, even though it was based in Switzerland and enjoyed close cooperation with a number of Swiss banks, including the SNB.

One of the fundamental reasons for the formation of the BIS was to assist with implementation of the Young Plan, which had been designed to manage Germany's reparations after the First World War. This inevitably involved the bank in making a high level of investment in the German economy in amounts corresponding to the long-term deposits placed at its disposal by the various creditor governments. These investments included interest-bearing funds held at the Reichsbank and bills and bonds of the German Treasury and the German Railway and Postal Administrations. The bank's interventions in the form of purchases of Reichsmarks and of investments on the German market, although technically at short term, were in fact for an indefinite period since the date of the termination of these operations depended on the German foreign exchange situation. In this way, the BIS's investments in Germany became considerable. At least three-fifths of its start-up capital went into investments inside Germany.[3]

From 1931 onwards, the BIS took an active part in the attempts made to counteract the effects of the financial crisis. While German reparation payments were never formally cancelled, they were temporarily suspended in 1931 during the international financial crisis and the bank's priorities shifted to further developing banking services offered to its central bank customers, which included the expansion of its role as a clearing house in gold transactions between nations. Since it was assumed German reparations payments would resume at some future date, the bank was obliged to maintain a high level of investment in German industry in accordance with the Young Plan. The sort of transactions in which the bank was most commonly engaged were:

- Carrying out transfer orders from or between central bank deposit accounts held with the BIS
- Foreign exchange transactions with or for the account of central banks
- Gold transactions with or for the account of central banks
- Carrying out transfer orders from or between central bank gold accounts held with the BIS.

After the Munich Agreement of 1938, the BIS was faced with many difficult problems. To avoid becoming embroiled in political questions, it chose to adhere meticulously to the technical character of the bank and strictly disregard all political considerations in reaching the necessary decisions. The bank wanted to ensure that there should be no diminution of the special privileges it possessed, in time of war as in time of peace, and proclaimed its intention 'to refrain from any business transactions involving the currencies or markets of two countries at war with each other, and [avoid making] any transactions which might be judged reproachable'.[4]

From June 1938 to August 1939, the bank was instrumental in shipping well over 100 tons of gold from Europe to the U.S. for the account of its members' central banks. A further 29 tons were then shipped between September 1939 and June 1940. In the winter of 1939-1940, where the central banks of a number of countries not yet involved in the war desired to transfer a substantial part of their monetary reserves to places overseas, especially to New York, the BIS was able to handle a considerable part of these transfers. Moreover, certain central banks with deposits at the BIS gave it a standing order to transfer these deposits overseas immediately if their country became involved in the war. It was not possible for the BIS, from a legal point of view, to refuse to receive any payments made in accordance with the contracts entered into under the Hague Agreements of 1930, which governed the implementation of BIS instructions to central banks, and any such refusal would moreover have been prejudicial to the interests of the creditor countries, especially France and Great Britain.

After the German occupation of the rump of Czechoslovakia in March 1939, however, the BIS could not rule out the possibility that, despite declarations to the contrary, the gold it was transferring might have been looted, in one form or another, from either Austria or Czechoslovakia. After a careful examination of the questions involved, however, the bank prevaricated by deciding to accept gold in respect of all transfers legally due to it and to take steps to ensure that at some future date an enquiry could be made into the origin of all gold bars it had received. This was the sort of decision now more commonly referred to as 'kicking the can down the road'.

Thomas Harrington McKittrick was president of the BIS from May 1939 to June 1943, under the chairmanship of Otto Ernest Niemeyer (May 1937 – May 1940) and Ernst Weber (Dec 1942 – Nov 1945). A U.S. citizen, McKittrick started out as a lawyer with little experience of banking. That changed, however, when he was appointed to the German Credits Arbitration Committee in 1931 and came under the tutelage of fellow committee member, Marcus Wallenberg, of Sweden's Enskilda Bank, who taught him all about the intricacies of international finance and how to negotiate the delicate path between the opposing European powers. Wallenberg would go on to play both sides against the other during the war and reap enormous profits.

McKittrick had close ties to Germany. The BIS general manager was a Frenchman, Roger Auboin, and the assistant general manager was the German Nazi Party member, Paul Hechler. Wartime directors of BIS included Reichsbank directors Emil Puhl, who became a close, personal friend of McKittrick, and Walther Funk. Throughout the war, British staff at the BIS worked alongside Nazi Party members. McKittrick was put up for re-election to the presidency in 1942 by the Germans, who viewed his personal opinions as 'safely known'.[5] Throughout the war, McKittrick would travel from his base in Switzerland to New York, unhindered by the Axis powers. He was a close family friend of Allen Dulles, who lived in Switzerland during the war as Swiss director of the OSS and would later become the first director of the CIA, and his brother, John Foster Dulles, the future American Secretary of State. Together, the Dulles brothers would play leading roles in the 5412 Committee of the CIA, which took on responsibility for clandestine operations during the early part of the Cold War.

When he travelled to New York in December 1942, McKittrick was feted by executives from many prominent U.S. banks and industries such as the New York Federal Reserve, the National City Bank, the Bankers' Trust, General Electric, Standard Oil, General Motors, J.P. Morgan, Brown Brothers Harriman, several insurance companies, and Kuhn Loeb, in what Adam LeBor described as 'probably the greatest single gathering of America's war profiteers'.[6] He was not universally popular in U.S. financial circles, however. Henry Morgenthau and his aide, Harry Dexter White, at the U.S. Treasury were scathing about 'an American president [of the BIS] doing business with the Germans while our American boys are fighting the Germans'.

While in the U.S., McKittrick was extensively debriefed by U.S. Intelligence, and was eventually cleared to return to Switzerland where he held regular clandestine meetings with Dulles and kept him informed about Herman gold transactions at the same time as negotiating with Nazi industrialists about the structure of post-war German industry and 'preserve the industrial substance of the Reich'.[7] For Morgenthau this was nothing short of treason. His plans for post-war Germany were to strip it of its industrial power and return it to an agrarian society to prevent any resurgence of militarism.

During each year of the Second World War, the BIS paid out dividends of several million Swiss francs to its owners and part of these payments were funded by German interest payments on investments in Germany, around 10-12 million Swiss francs, which in turn had been made with looted gold from Belgium and Holland laundered through Switzerland. It is an example of how international finance operates in quite bizarre ways during wartime, when it is clear that looted Nazi gold found its way into the vaults of Allied belligerents, including the Bank of England, and went some way towards part funding the British war effort.

The outbreak of war had brought a sudden and sharp decline in BIS activity, with a significant reduction in profits. During this time German interest payments constituted the bulk of BIS income and were instrumental in maintaining the bank's liquidity. The following table illustrates this:

Year	Interest earned in Reichsmarks	Other earnings	Net profit
1937/1938	8,979,900	7,340,700	9,012,000
1939/1940	8,565,400	4,725,600	7,962,100
1942/1943	7,234,000	1,852,100	4,508,900
1944/1945	6,878,000	1,474,300	0

A sizeable portion of the money paid to the bank by Germany was also returned in the form of dividends. For many in the Allied camp, the BIS was seen to serve the economic interests of the Nazis over those of the Allies and amounted to treason.[8]

On the day Germany launched its attack against Poland, 1 September 1939, the Reichsbank had four gold deposit accounts with the BIS in Bern (numbered 5, 7, 10 and 11), which held a total of 1,861.70292 kg of fine gold. During the war the Reichsbank transferred gold at regular intervals to the SNB, which was credited to the numbered accounts at the BIS. In the summer of 1941, it was suggested that Germany was trying to buy some of the BIS shares belonging to the French, Belgian, Netherlands, and Norwegians in an attempt to gain control of the bank. A U.S. study of 1945 claimed that the Reichsbank had a 'remarkably close and solicitous relationship with the [BIS] throughout the war [which gave] advantages...to the Reichsbank and to the German Reich in general from their relationship with the BIS [and raises] serious questions as to the legitimacy of much of the wartime business of the BIS'.[9]

By 1942, however, when the bank's annual report (and McKittrick's debriefing in New York) revealed the extent to which it was working closely with the Reichsbank, both Britain and the U.S. lodged strong objections and threatened to withdraw membership. It was not until 1944, however, that measures were taken to prevent Nazi leaders from using the BIS to move looted gold into countries such as Argentina, to which they planned to escape at the war's end. Norway tabled a motion to liquidate the BIS and launch an investigation into the extent to which the bank had allowed itself to be manipulated by Germany, but this was opposed by a number of very powerful U.S. bankers such as Leon Fraser of the First National Bank of Manhattan, himself a former president of the BIS, who argued that the BIS had an important role to play in the reconstruction of European economies after the war.

The U.S. Treasury Department collected evidence in June 1945 that the BIS had received re-smelted looted gold from the Reichsbank and demanded an immediate inspection of all gold owned by or in the possession of the bank and all relevant books, files, and records. In December of the same year, a preliminary assessment of BIS wartime activities was made and concluded that the BIS accepted looted gold, aided the Reichsbank in salvaging assets threatened by blocking in neutral countries, was dominated by Axis interests, continued to pay dividends to occupied countries despite inevitable confiscation by the Nazis, and furnished financial intelligence to the Reichsbank.

The following is a breakdown of the 13,452.21892 kg of fine (almost pure) gold delivered to the BIS by the Reichsbank during the Second World War:

- 3,701.24774 kg of monetary gold looted by the Germans from the central banks of Belgium and the Netherlands
- 5,012.88208 kg of pre-war minted gold bars deemed by the Tripartite Gold Commission to have been 'very unlikely' looted monetary or non-monetary gold
- 1,391.56773 kg of gold bars delivered before 26 August 1942, which seems to indicate that it did not include gold looted from Holocaust victims
- 3,437.52137 kg of gold bars and gold coins, which may or may not include looted Holocaust gold.[10]

Records show that gold delivered to the BIS by the Reichsbank was distributed as follows:

- 3,893.46171 kg was transferred to the National bank of Romania
- 3,138.28017 kg was transferred to the National Bank of Yugoslavia
- 1,118.55459 kg was sold to the National Bank of Bulgaria
- 799.27177 kg was sold to the Banco de Portugal
- 699.38898 kg was exchanged with the SNB against gold held in New York.

This meant that it still held 3,893.26170 kg on 1 February 1947 as follows:

- 2,367.64140 kg at the SNB, Bern
- 417.98290 kg (in gold bars) at the Reichsbanknebenstelle, Konstanz
- 1,107.63740 kg (in gold coins) at the Reichsbanknebenstelle, Konstanz.

On 24 June 1948, 2,785.62430 kg of this was transferred to the Bank of England as part of a total payment of 3,740 kg, in accordance with the terms of the Washington Agreement of 13 May. The remaining 1,197.63740 kg was sold, which meant that by 1 October 1948, all the gold transferred to the BIS by the Reichsbank had been disposed of.

Chapter 6

USTAŠE GOLD AND THE VATICAN

> 'The [Ustaše] organisation had its own army that terrified the countryside with a brutality that shocked even Heinrich Himmler.'[1]

The story of Ustaše (Ustasha) gold is not directly linked to the looting of gold by the Nazis during the war, but it is significant in a number of ways and links into the overall narrative of Nazi gold. It does so not least because the Ustaše, a Croatian fascist organisation, was installed as a puppet of the Nazis and the gold it looted during the war was later channelled to South America, where it funded neo-Nazi organisations that harboured Nazi war criminals.

Immediately prior to the outbreak of Second World War, the National Defence Council of Yugoslavia sent a major part of its gold reserves to the Bank of England and the Federal Reserve Bank in New York. In May 1939, the first consignment of the gold reserves, comprising 980 chests containing 3,379 gold bars, was transferred to England on the Yugoslav destroyer *Beograd*. The National Bank of the Kingdom of Yugoslavia in London already had 225 gold bars, so that reserve was increased to 44,886.61 kg. A further 14,168.16 kg of Yugoslavian gold was shipped from Switzerland through Athens to New York in the summer of 1940.

In November 1940, the National Bank of the Kingdom of Yugoslavia packed up its remaining gold reserves and stored them in a specially constructed vault in the city of Užice. Desperate to remove the estimated 120 tons of gold remaining in the country in early 1941, the Yugoslavs sent 22 tons to Argentina and Brazil and another 17 tons to New York. Gold held at the BIS in Basel was converted into U.S. dollars and the money deposited in the New York Federal Reserve on 5 April. After the

German attack in April 1941, the remaining 12 tons of gold was moved again; first to Mostar, Cetinje and Herceg Novi and then, on 15 April, to Nikšić, where it was hidden in caves in Trebjesa Mountain.

In the wake of the German attack on Yugoslavia, King Peter II fled the country, taking with him six cases of gold. The Yugoslavian state was dismembered and replaced by the so-called independent state of Croatia on 10 April 1941, which was run by members of the Fascist Croat Ustaše political movement, headed by Ante Pavelić, and supported throughout the Second World War by both Italian and German occupation forces. Based on a blend of Roman Catholicism and fascism, the group had no qualms about using genocide and terror against Serbs, Jews, and Sinti-Romani peoples living in Croat-controlled territory to reach its ultimate goal of creating an independent and purely Croatian state, free from Yugoslavian influence. In August 1941 the U.S. State Department Balkan Desk described the Ustaše regime as following a 'comprehensive policy of extermination of the Serb race in the Independent State of Croatia'.[2]

It is estimated by U.S. Intelligence that Ustaše leaders at one time had at their disposal more than 350 million Swiss francs' worth of gold coins, much of which had been looted from Jews, Serbs, and Sinti-Romani, all victims of the Ustaše ethnic cleansing campaign which had started with the internment of most of the 35,000 to 45,000 Croatian Jews in the spring and summer of 1941. As many as 700,000 victims, most of them Serbs, would be killed at the Ustaše death camps at Jasenovac and elsewhere. Croatian Catholic authorities condemned the atrocities committed by the Ustaše but remained otherwise supportive of the regime.[3]

In 1944 the Ustaše regime began to move assets into Swiss bank accounts for safekeeping. On 12 May 1944 the Croatian State Bank received 358 kg of gold from Germany and exported it on 31 May to the SNB, where it was deposited in a newly created Croatian State Bank deposit account without the requisite permit. Another 980 kg was illegally transferred to the same account 'for safekeeping' to the SNB on 2 August 1944 by 'patriotic officials' of the so-called Croatian State Bank, but again this transaction was completed without regulation permits.[4] This Croatian gold appears to have been the same 980 kg taken by the Croatian authorities from the Sarajevo branch of the National Bank of the Kingdom of Yugoslavia in 1941. Along with the gold came 25 tons of silver bought by the SNB to mint coins. In October 1944 representatives of the Croatian puppet government sought to persuade the SNB to allow the transfer of gold in the Croatian account to Germany, but were unsuccessful. In December 1944 the SNB refused the Croatian request for the return of the gold to Zagreb, and the Swiss Federal Council froze all Croatian assets in Switzerland.

On 7 May, thirteen boxes of gold weighing some 290 kg were removed from the Croatian State Bank onto two trucks and a car. The car, driven by Dr Mirko Puk, was waylaid by partisans who made off with two boxes of gold. The remaining eleven boxes made it to the Wolfsberg Franciscan monastery, where Major Josip Tomlienović distributed the contents of nine boxes among refugees, while the last two boxes were taken to Rome by Dr Krunoslav Draganović. Unconfirmed rumour has it that these two boxes ended up in the Vatican. The thirty-two cases of gold left over in Zagreb at the Franciscan monastery of Kaptol were handed over to the National Bank of Yugoslavia in February 1946.

Although the general German surrender took place on 9 May, the Ustaše and their murderous Serb nationalist Chetnik allies held out for a further six days. This gave the leaders of the Croatian regime time to escape with some of the Ustaše treasury through Austria to Italy. It is believed that Ante Pavelić, along with a party of up to 1,500 Ustaše fighters, took some 500 kg of gold into the British zone of occupation of Austria, where it was seized by the British authorities.[5] Pavelić was released with half the gold after being held in British custody for two weeks, but the rest of the gold he was carrying was confiscated and his companions were turned over to the Yugoslav authorities. A CIA report of April 1952 alleged that, at the end of the war, Pavelić sent twelve cases of gold and jewels to Austria, which were then hidden near Salzburg. According to this report, Pavelić arranged for the recovery of this loot in 1951 and in 1952 sought to sell 200 kg of gold in Buenos Aires.[6] The gold was hidden there until it was recovered and used in part to finance anti-Communist activities aimed at Yugoslavia, and in part to maintain Pavelić in exile in Argentina. The British occupation authorities in Austria did not acknowledge recovery of any monetary gold or non-monetary gold originating with the puppet Croatian Ustaše regime.

U.S. Intelligence reported that the College of San Girolamo degli Illirici (San Girolamo dei Croati) located just outside the walls of the Vatican in Rome, provided living quarters for Croatian priests studying at the Vatican during and after the Second World War, and was a centre of Ustaše covert activity and a Croatian underground that helped Ustaše refugees and war criminals to escape Europe after the war. British Intelligence identified San Girolamo as the church for the Ustaše managed by a brotherhood of Croatian priests, the 'confraternita di San Girolama'.[7] This brotherhood issued identity cards with false names to the fugitive Ustaše, allowing them to evade arrest or detention by the Allies. Monsignor Juraj Madjerec was head of the college, but the main Ustaše supporter was the secretary, Father Dr Krunoslav Dragonović; an Ustaše colonel and former official of the Croatian Ministry for Internal Colonization, the agency responsible for the confiscation of Serb property in Bosnia and Herzegovina. Father Dragonović helped Ustaše fugitives emigrate illegally to South America by providing temporary shelter and false identity documents, and by arranging onward transport, primarily to Argentina. He was also reportedly entrusted with all the valuables brought out of Croatia by the fleeing Ustaše.[8] Later, in 1951, Draganović organised the escape of the Nazi war criminal Klaus Barbie to South America. When his protector Pope Pius XII died, Dragonović, was ordered to leave the College of San Girolamo.

Ante Pavelić arrived in Rome in 1946 disguised as a priest with a Spanish passport and spent the next two years living at San Girolamo, where the U.S. Army Counter-Intelligence Corps (Army CIC), which had responsibility for tracking down war criminals, kept him under surveillance. In late July 1947, Pavelić was reportedly living in a particular Vatican-owned building in Rome and U.S. and British plans were laid to extradite him to Yugoslavia, although these were soon shelved in order not to lose support among Catholic and anti-Communist émigrés. U.S. military intelligence agreed on the grounds that Pavelić's arrest would alienate the Croatians loyal to the Ustaše cause, who were being increasingly employed as informants by U.S. Intelligence agencies. U.S. Intelligence reports portray the Croatian underground in Rome as making use of a considerable quantity of gold, probably including victim gold, that the Ustaše sent or brought out of Croatia between 1943 and 1945. In November 1948, Pavelić emigrated to Argentina on the Italian motorship *Sestrire*. Following an assassination attempt, he moved to Spain in 1957 and died there two years later.

Chapter 7

SAFEHAVEN

'The Safe Haven Programme, or project, was organized as one of the chief instruments by which the United States Government meant to defeat Germany's aim to rebuild its strength outside of Germany. The fundamental purpose was to frustrate Germany's attempt to penetrate foreign economies, to transfer internal assets beyond reach of the Allies, to evade payment of reparations by having no apparent resources, and to avoid any share in the rehabilitation of Europe.'[1]

After 1943, concern mounted over the prospect of Germany hiding gold and other assets abroad so they would not be impounded as war reparations and would be available to rebuild Axis strength in the post-war period. To confront this issue, the Safehaven Programme was launched at the United Nations Monetary and Financial Conference held at Bretton Woods, New Hampshire, in July 1944. Resolution VI of the conference was intended to block Germany from transferring assets to Switzerland and other neutral nations as it contemplated military defeat. The preamble to the conference accused Axis leaders, enemy nationals and their collaborators of transferring assets through and to neutral countries for the purpose of concealing them, and of thus maintaining Axis power, influence, and ability to plan future aggrandisement. It named loot, transfers of assets of occupied and neutral nations accomplished by threat and transfers of Axis property by use of blinds and cloaks as the kinds of wealth Germany found it useful and easy to conceal. It also took note of the parts played by puppet governments for future reference.

The aims of the programme were to:

- restrict and prevent German economic and cultural penetration outside of Germany
- block Germany from transferring internal assets to neutral countries

- ensure that German wealth would be administered by the Allies so German payment of war reparations would be assured
- make certain that Germany's resources would be available for use in the rehabilitation of Europe
- make possible the return to legal owners of properties looted from countries once occupied by the Germans
- prevent the escape of strategic German personnel to neutral havens
- implement plans for lasting peace by helping to make it impossible for Germany to start another war.[2]

The term 'Safe haven' was originally coined to describe the action of exploring the nature and extent of the German plan to hide assets, but was soon adopted to describe the counter-plan to preserve all intelligence on looted and flight capital and German assets generally. All communications regarding the said operation were now to contain the code word 'SAFEHAVEN'.

Between 16 August and 10 October 1944, Samuel Klaus, an official of the U.S. Foreign Economic Administration, led a group of officials to London, Stockholm, Lisbon, and Madrid to assess the possibilities and problems in perfecting the Safehaven Programme. In his final report of October 1944 Klaus said:

> [the] most important aspect [of Safehaven] is the use of neutral countries as bases for maintaining the assets, skills and research necessary for the conversion of Germany to a war basis at an appropriate future date. ... the presence of I.G. Farben personnel in Spain, the expansion of Siemens production in Sweden or the presence of German military technicians in Argentina are of more far-reaching significance and constitute as well the most difficult Safehaven activities.[3]

On 6 December 1944, the U.S. State Department discussed ways of presenting the issues of looted gold and enemy property to the neutrals without jeopardizing the negotiation of war trade agreements, but a row erupted over how to balance the war trade agreements with the basic requirements of the Safehaven Programme, namely, the adherence to Bretton Woods Resolution VI and to the Gold Declaration. While the U.S. had for all practical purposes assumed responsibility for the Safehaven Programme, the Swiss infuriated them by 'continuing their assistance to the enemy's war economy to the bitter end [by] collaboration with Germany on financial matters [and] the purchase of Axis gold'. The Allies set out to isolate from the world's gold market those countries which had purchased looted Nazi gold.[4] Britain and

France were more conciliatory than the U.S. in their approach, but all agreed to talks, which were held in Bern. The Swiss, however, despite agreeing to extensive restrictions on all German-held assets, resisted all calls to stop gold purchases from Germany and refused point blank to discuss historical gold purchases, except to say that it would be willing to return any gold that could be shown to have been looted, but that the burden of proof for this would rest with the Allies.

Reports of movements of German-origin gold were still reaching Washington and Switzerland, along with other neutrals, who were resisting U.S. pressure to adopt a gold policy in line with Resolution VI. The UN expressed 'concern over the possible flight of Axis capital for the use of war criminals and other dangerous persons and other Axis manipulation of assets located abroad to the detriment of both the peace and security of the post-war world and the welfare of the country in which such assets were located'.[5] While the war was still being prosecuted, Safehaven objectives of finding and restoring looted assets, preventing the escape into the neutral nations of German assets, and preventing the resurgence of Nazi Germany became mingled with continuing efforts to halt the trade of the neutrals with Nazi Germany.

Jurisdictional disputes dogged the operation right from the start. Nobody seemed to know where authority lay, but 'everyone wanted to participate in it [resulting in] confusion, jealousies, misunderstandings and waste'.[6] A row erupted between various Allied personnel over proposals for restitution of the German economy after the war. In September 1944, U.S. Treasury Secretary Henry Morgenthau had put forward his plan for a punitive programme for a defeated Germany through partition and de-industrialisation, with a radical downscaling of its economy. The U.S. Secretary of War Henry Stimson, however, feared that such a drastic imposition would only foster lingering resentment in Germany in the way that the Treaty of Versailles had done in 1919 and create the sort of conditions that would encourage new waves of radical political parties, potentially laying the foundations for another war. The State Department also opposed Morgenthau and called for a system of controls, but ones that, crucially, would allow Germany to rebuild a modern economy and take its place as an equal in the post-war international economy.

Emil Puhl visited Zurich soon after the Bern negotiations to see just how much damage had been done to Swiss-German relationships. He met representatives of the Kreditansalt, the Bangesellschaft, the Bankverin, the Eidgenössiche Bank and the Basler Handelsbank, all of whom 'did not lack to pay [him] personal attention' and were anxious to avoid a total cessation of dealings with Germany. As a result, Puhl was able to reach an agreement that allowed continued trade in a number of important areas for which 'local German firms may be thankful to the Reichsbank'.[7] As a result, 3 tons of gold went to the SNB, 1.5 tons to the BIS and 1.5 tons to the German Legation from the Reichsbank branch in Konstanz. Puhl, in celebratory mood, told Funk on 6 April 1945 that he had 'absolutely circumvented the Allied payment blockade [and concluded] a gold transaction [which was] certainly very unagreeable to our opponents'. Weber at the SNB had 'repeatedly and strongly advised me to continue my endeavours', he said, 'which would be of far-reaching importance beyond [1945]'.[8]

When the Allies became aware of these transactions, they immediately labelled the gold as 'looted' and subject to military seizure, but they mistakenly thought it was still at Lörrach, in Germany, awaiting transfer. When the French later occupied the town in April 1945, they were unable to locate any gold there. At the same time, the BIS president, Thomas McKittrick, insisted that the forty cases of gold Puhl had allocated to his bank was not looted gold at all. Since there were no stamps on the gold bars it was impossible to verify this, but the gold was held at Konstanz and could not be moved while Morgenthau repeated demands to have the BIS wound up.

An essential component of the Safehaven Programme was control of German assets after the war, but the Swiss rejected Allied demands that it should include assets outside the country. 'The actual occupation of German territory', they said, 'can hardly have any effect beyond German borders.'[9] The British and French were not eager to pursue the matter and risk damaging an already fragile relationship with the Swiss, and many in the U.S. maintained that Switzerland performed certain indispensable services in regard to U.S. prisoners of war in Germany and Japan. Eventually, though, the U.S. pushed through Public Law No. 5, designed to promote international peace and collective security by the elimination of the German war potential. This law stipulated that all foreign German assets were to be administered by a body to be called the 'German External Property Commission'.

Before negotiations between the commission and Swiss delegates could start, however, the story of looted Nazi gold in Switzerland hit the world's headlines and the Swiss were backed into a position of denial and obfuscation, while the U.S. and its allies hardened their position on a full investigation. The Swiss reacted by challenging the legitimacy of Public Law No. 5, rejecting Allied claims about the quantity of gold that had passed to Switzerland from Germany during the war and claiming that the issue of looted gold was one that the Swiss alone should decide. They reiterated their assertion that

Puhl had categorically assured them none of the German gold they had purchased was looted. The Swiss delegate, Walter Stucki, had distinguished himself by negotiating the surrender of the French Vichy government and was later instrumental in brokering the surrender of Japan, meaning he was a seasoned negotiator. He eventually suggested a compromise whereby the Swiss would agree a 50/50 split of all German assets found in Switzerland and contribute 250 million Swiss gold francs towards Europe's restoration programme, but this was still some way short of recognising the figure for looted gold estimated by the Allies. Nevertheless, exhausted Allied negotiators accepted the deal, despite Belgian objections that the Swiss had refused to recognise that some of their gold looted by the Nazis had found its way to Switzerland and should be repatriated.

Chapter 8

THE RED HOUSE DOCUMENT

'Ever since the collapse of the Third Reich in 1945, a spectre has haunted western life—the spectre of resurgent Nazism.'[1]

For years prior to the outbreak of the Second World War, Germany had been establishing an extensive network of agents across the U.S. through organisations such as the Friends of the New Germany and the German American Bund. One of the objectives was to reinforce U.S. isolationist opinion and encourage links with German ex-patriate business communities in South America. U.S. Intelligence agencies were well aware of these movements and had infiltrated them with their own agents, but Germany had been careful to link U.S. banks and businesses with their South American counterparts through neutral intermediaries, especially in Switzerland. These Swiss middlemen would transfer ownership of German companies to Swiss and American names, thus allowing them to continue trading throughout the war by channelling goods and currency to the Nazis. Swiss banks in New York such as the Swiss Bank Corporation, the Swiss American Corporation and Crédit Suisse were used to front Nazi economic interests in the U.S., actively aiding the Third Reich under the pretence of neutrality having been 'unduly influenced by Germany's apparent success in establishing a new European order'. A memo dated 2 June 1942 sent to U.S. Treasury Secretary Henry Morgenthau claimed that 'representatives of these banks participated actively in the affairs of Swiss-German industrial concerns [and are a camouflage] for German interests'.[2]

After the defeat of German forces in the Falaise Pocket in August 1944, at a secret meeting at the Maison Rouge Hotel (Hotel Rotes Haus) in Strasbourg on 10 August, Nazi officials and an elite group of German industrialists made plans for Germany's post-war recovery. Details of this meeting were contained in U.S. Military Intelligence report

EW-Pa 128, dated 27 November 1944, also known as the Red House Document. They were supplied by an agent of the French Deuxième Bureau, who was vouched for by a Commandant Zindel. The meeting was presided over by SS Obergruppenführer (honary rank) Dr Johann Friedrich Scheid, the director of the Heche (Hermandorff & Schonburg) Company. Others present were:

Dr Kaspar, of Krupp

Dr Tolle, of Rochling

Dr Sinderen, of Messerschmitt

Drs Kopps, Vier and Beerwanger, of Rheunmetall

Captain Haberkorn and Dr Ruhe, of Bussing

Drs Ellenmayer and Kardos, of Volkswagen

Engineers Drose, Yanchew and Koppshe, of various factories in Posen, Poland (Drose, Yanchew and Co., Brown-Boveri, Herkuleswerke, Buschwerke and Staftwerke)

Captain Dornbuach, head of the Industrial Inspectin Section at Posen

Dr Meyer, an official of the German Naval Ministry in Paris

Dr Strossner, of the Ministeru of Armament, Paris.

It is worth mentioning at this stage that Gerald Steinacher, a research Fellow at the Centre for European Studies at Harvard University, claims that 'not a single piece of evidence has turned up to support this incredible story…to plan the emergence of the Fourth Reich'. Steinacher also refutes the suggestion made in some quarters that among those attending the Maison Rouge meeting were coal tycoon Emil Kirdorf, Georg von Schnitzler of I.G Farben, Gustav Krupp, Fritz Thyssen, and banker Kurt von Schroeder. Kirdorf, he said, had died in 1938, and Thyssen was, by that time, being held captive in Sachsenhausen concentration camp.[3] Note that none of these three names are listed in the original document so it is not clear how they came to be associated with it in the first place.

Apart from Steinacher, there has been lively debate over the authenticity of the Red House Document. Among those who challenge it is Alexander Peter d'Erizans of the Department of Social Science, Borough of Manhattan Community College, who says that:

> the alleged civilian chairman of the meeting, a Dr Schied, was indeed a ceramic industrialist and leading official in Albert Speer's ministry, but he would have been a poor choice of an individual who could have

brought the SS into the plan. Having experienced immense difficulty himself in obtaining membership in the Nazi Party, he never even became a member of the SS.

Heinz Schneppen, in his book *Odessa und das Vierte Reich: Mythen der Zeitgeschichte,* seriously questions whether a conspiratorial meeting could have actually taken place only weeks following the 20 July attempt on Hitler's life. He argues that the idea of any substantial capital transfer of funds out of Germany seems highly improbable, especially in light of the increasingly restrictive rules concerning financial transactions with Nazi Germany that the Allies were imposing at the time upon neutral states, like Switzerland, and a transfer of capital to Argentina could therefore simply not have taken place.[4]

However, the chairman of the subcommittee of the Committee on Military Affairs of the United States Senate on 25 June 1945 said:

> Senator Kilgore released a press story of a recent interview with the manager of the Krupp Works obtained by an American newspaperman, and a number of hitherto confidential documents which came to the attention of the subcommittee in the course of its investigations of German economic warfare. Senator Kilgore pointed out that these documents - a report on the postwar plans of the Krupp Armaments Works, a statement on the connections of its Essen manager, Eduard Houdremont, with the Nazi Government, and a memorandum on a secret meeting of German industrialists in August 1944 to discuss the post-defeat military revival of Germany - are evidence of how German industry worked hand in hand with the Nazi Party to unloose against the world a war of aggression.

In his book *Hitler's Secret Bankers,* Adam LeBor says of the report that, when he was given access to it, it carried declassification number NND765055 dated 05/06/1966. Its structure and writing style, he says, appear authentic. Copies of the report were sent to the U.S. and British Political Advisers SHAEF. Evidence for the existence of the report, however, does not guarantee accuracy of its contents.

According to the document, Dr Scheid began the meeting by declaring that the war could not be won by Germany and from that moment on German industry must take steps to prepare a post-war economic plan for Germany. The first objective was the immediate evacuation of all industrial material from France to Germany. Then each industrialist was to make contacts and alliances with foreign firms but individually rather than at company level and without attracting attention. One essential was to lay the groundwork for finance by making arrangements for massive borrowing from foreign countries after the war. Scheid quoted as examples of the kind of preparations required the fact that patents for stainless steel belonged to the Chemical Foundation, Inc., New York, and the Krupp Company of Germany jointly, and that the U.S. Steel Corporation, Carnegie Illinois, American Steel and Wire, and National Tube, would be under an obligation to work with Krupp. He also cited the Zeiss Company, the Leisa Company and the Hamburg-American Line as firms which had been especially effective in protecting German interests abroad and gave their New York addresses to the industrialists at this meeting.[5]

Soon afterwards, another, smaller, meeting took place presided over by Dr Bosse of the German Armaments Ministry and attended only by representatives of Hecho, Krupp and Rochling. Bosse told the meeting that the German government would allocate large sums to industrialists so that each could establish a secure post-war foundation in foreign countries and build a strong German economic empire. In cooperation with the industrialists and to avoid exposure, certain Nazi Party leaders would be placed in important positions with various German factories as technical experts or members of its research and designing offices. These factories would then create small technical offices or research bureaus which would be absolutely independent and have no known connection with the factory. These bureaus would be furnished with all the most up-to-date research documents, which they would need to continue their research. Much of Germany's economic reserves would be transferred to neutral countries where they would be beyond reach of the wartime Allies. All government controls over the export of wealth (money, patents, scientists and administrators) were to be relaxed immediately, and the transfer of these national assets becoming an official policy of the Nazi state. Highlighting the importance of Switzerland as a Nazi banking centre, export of capital would be arranged through Schweitzerische Kreditanstalt in Zurich (Crédit Suisse) and Basler Handelsbank. As soon as the Party had become strong enough to re-establish its control over Germany, the industrialists would be paid for their effort and cooperation by concessions and orders.[6]

In 1946 the U.S. Treasury Department reported that some 750 companies were set up all over the world by the German industrialists following the Strasbourg meeting. Their listing noted 112 in Spain, 58 in Portugal, 35 in Turkey, 98 in Argentina, 214 in Switzerland, and 233 in various other countries. Ownership was disguised by the use of bearer bonds. Total German assets in neutral countries had been estimated by the U.S. State Department in July 1945 to be Switzerland $600 million,

Sweden $51 million, Turkey $51 million and Portugal $35 million.[7] On the strength of the intelligence report of the House meeting, U.S. Treasury Secretary Morgenthau became a powerful advocate for the post-war de-industrialisation of Germany.

According to Adam Lebor in an article for MailOnline dated 9 May 2009, a highly educated, intelligent lawyer and economist called Otto Ohlendorf, who was hanged at Nuremberg, was transferred to the German Ministry of Economics in the winter of 1943 and given responsibility for preserving the SS's massive pan-European economic empire after Germany's defeat. Ohlendorf used as his template a document written by the German economist Ludwig Erhard on the transition to a post-war economy. Erhard, financed by I.G. Farben, said that to avoid hyperinflation that would wipe out the value of any funds, the post-war priority was rapid monetary stabilisation through a stable national currency, which was achieved in 1948 and made Germany, once again, an attractive trading partner and so kick-started the German economy. By 1948, despite six years of war, the capital stock of assets such as equipment and buildings was larger than in 1936, thanks mainly to the armaments boom which allowed the German industrial conglomerates to rapidly rebuild their economic empires across Europe.

Erhard had suggested that the German industrial base could expand its reach across the shattered European continent through a voluntary surrender of national sovereignty to an international body such as the European Coal and Steel Community (ECSC), established in April 1951 by six European states to create a common market for coal and steel which it regulated. This set a vital precedent for the steady erosion of national sovereignty.

Historian Dr Michael Pinto-Duschinsky says that 'The continuity of the economy of Germany and the economies of post-war Europe is striking. Some of the leading figures in the Nazi economy became leading builders of the European Union…For many leading industrial figures close to the Nazi regime, Europe became a cover for pursuing German national interests after the defeat of Hitler.'[8] The two most powerful Nazi industrialists, Alfried Krupp of Krupp Industries and Friedrich Flick, whose Flick Group eventually owned a 40 per cent stake in Daimler-Benz, were released from prison after serving barely three years.

Like Krupp and Flick, Hermann Abs, post-war Germany's most powerful banker, had prospered in the Third Reich. He became one of the most important figures in Germany's post-war reconstruction and was put in charge of allocating Marshall Aid – reconstruction funds – to German industry. By 1948 he was effectively managing Germany's economic recovery. He was also a member of the European League for Economic Co-operation, an elite intellectual pressure group set up in 1946. The league was dedicated to the establishment of a common market, the precursor of the European Union. When Konrad Adenauer, the first Chancellor of West Germany, took power in 1949, Abs was his most important financial adviser.

In 1957, the six members of the ECSC signed the Treaty of Rome, which set up the European Economic Community. The treaty further liberalised trade and established increasingly powerful supranational institutions, including the European Parliament and European Commission. Like Abs, Ludwig Erhard flourished in post-war Germany. Adenauer made Erhard Germany's first post-war economics minister and in 1963, Erhard succeeded Adenauer as Chancellor for three years.

Chapter 9

THE MERKERS MINE AND THE FOREIGN EXCHANGE DEPOSITORY

> 'If these were the old free-booting days when a soldier kept his loot, you'd be the richest man in the world.'
> General Omar Bradley to General George Patton, 12 April 1945

During late 1944 and early 1945, as American bombing of Berlin increased and the Allies closed in on the Reich from both east and west, some 20 tons of the Reichsbank gold reserves were dispersed to branch banks in central and southern Germany. Then, on 3 February, the U.S Eighth Air Force dropped 2,000 tons of bombs on Berlin and virtually demolished the massive bunker-like Reichsbank building. At the same time, Soviet forces were closing in from the east with a keen interest in getting hold of the Reichsbank gold for themselves. In January, the Reichsbank boss Walther Funk had requested Hitler's permission to move the Reichsbank gold out of Berlin but was refused. Hitler feared that such a move would undermine the full and normal operations of the Reichsbank, which were essential for a proper functioning banking system in the country. After 3 February, however, when the printing presses at the Reichsbank were utterly destroyed, there was no longer a sound argument against Funk's plan and he was given the green light to go ahead to move the gold.

His choice of location for the gold was founded on the assumption that the German forces, now retreating on all fronts, would consolidate in a 'fortress' area or National Redoubt stretching from Bavaria to northern Italy, where they would hold out until a negotiated peace could be struck. Having the gold reserves there would create a basis for the economic revival of the country after the war. As a first step, Funk planned to set up the new banking headquarters at Erfurt, in the heavily fortified, forested area of Thüringen. Valuable documents and books from the State Library in Berlin had already been secreted in a number of salt mines in that area. The library of the Prussian State Opera, as well as the Library of Fine Arts, had sent its books, and municipal centres such as Bremen and Rostock had stored their public records in mines around the village of Merkers. Many of the mines, including the one at Kaiseroda, 2,000 feet underground with up to 30 miles of tunnels now commandeered by the Reich, had been owned by the Wintershall chemical company, the leading German producer of potash, synthetic fuels and rock salt. It was here that Funk decided to transfer the gold bullion, along with gold, silver and jewellery taken from concentration camp victims that had arrived too late to be processed at the Frankfurt firm of Degussa (Deutsche Gold- und Silber-Scheideanstalt, the German Gold and Silver Separation Institute) for re-smelting.

A week after the bombing of the Reichsbank, a special train with twenty-two trucks left Berlin, accompanied by Dr Witte of the Reichsbank and Albert Thoms, head of the Reichsbank's Precious Metals Department. A second train left Berlin on 11 March but with only four trucks this time. Ironically, with all this gold under his control, Thoms was unable to stay in Merkers because he had no ration coupons with which to buy food. He returned to Berlin and brought another shipment by road on 23 March, picking up Dr Werner Veick, the head cashier of the Reichsbank's Foreign Notes Department, and Dr Otto Reimer, the chief cashier of the Reichsmark Department in Berlin, at Erfurt. The last gold shipment arrived at Merkers on 3 April, one day before units of the U.S. Third Army arrived in the village.

On 1 April, currency was in short supply and so Reichsbank officials decided to move the Reichsmark notes back to Berlin for distribution to other places in the Reich. On 2 April, Thoms, Reimer and Reichsbank Director Frommknicht arrived and started loading about 200 million Reichsmarks and some fifty packages of foreign currency into a 2.5-ton truck, which set off for Magdeburg and Halle, while the foreign currency was destined for Berlin. The proximity of U.S. forces, however, forced them to abandon those plans and they started to offload the currency back into the mine, just as U.S. soldiers arrived in the village.

Early on the morning of 4 April, Frommknicht and Thoms fled Merkers, while Veick and Reimer, along with their Polish workers, continued taking the currency back down into the mine. Meanwhile, Frommknicht and Thoms were overtaken by vehicles of the U.S. Army and fled into the forest. Frommknicht got away, but Thoms, who was much less mobile after being injured in a bombing raid in 1944, was captured and brought back to Merkers for questioning.

On 22 March 1945, units of General George Patton's U.S. Third Army had crossed the Rhine and advanced towards Gotha. On 4 April the Third Battalion of the 358th Infantry Regiment, 90th Infantry Division, passed through the village of Merkers. Intelligence officers questioned a number of displaced persons employed as forced labour for the Germans in the area, who told them of rumours that gold shipments had arrived from the Reichsbank in Berlin and had been placed inside the Wintershal AG's Kaiseroda potassium mine. Orders were issued prohibiting all civilians from circulating in the area of the mine while investigations were carried out.

When Lieutenant Colonel William A. Russell, an intelligence officer of the 90th Infantry Division questioned other displaced persons in the vicinity of the mine, he was told that works of art were also stored there and that Dr Paul Ortwin Rave, curator of the German State Museum in Berlin and assistant director of the National Galleries in Berlin, was on site charged with caring for the paintings. Russell soon discovered that gold and valuable art treasures were stored in the Merkers mine and other mines in the area. Russell was staggered when Veick, under questioning, told him that the gold in the mine constituted the entire reserve of the Reichsbank in Berlin. Russell immediately called for the 712th Tank Battalion and Military Police to proceed to Merkers and stand guard at the mines. Arrangements were made for power generators to be brought up to give light so that the mineshafts could be examined. The First Battalion of the 357th Infantry Regiment was brought up as extra security when it was discovered that Merkers had at least five entrances.

The mines at Merkers, Kaiseroda, Leimbach, Springen, and Dietlas were now guarded by three companies of the First Battalion, with the assistance of one platoon of heavy machine guns and two sections of light tanks. Special guards were placed on essential operating installations such as electric plants, transformers, and elevator mechanisms. On 7 April, Russell, with other U.S. officers and Rave, descended the 2,000 feet via lift and immediately found 550 bags of Reichsmarks. Moving down the tunnel, they found the main vault which was sealed off with a brick wall 3 feet thick and 100 feet wide, in the centre of which was a large steel door, complete with combination lock and timing mechanism. When Russell returned to the surface, Veick told him that the gold was behind the brick wall. When Patton was told, he ordered that the door be blown open by army engineers.

This was accomplished on the following day, opening up the vault known as Room No. 8, which was approximately 75 feet wide by 150 feet long, with a 12-foot-high ceiling. A small-gauge railway track ran down the centre of the vault. On either side of this, stretching to the back of the cavern, were more than 7,000 bags, stacked knee-high, laid out in twenty rows with approximately 2.5 feet between each row. All the bags and containers were marked, and the gold bags were sealed. Baled currency was found stacked along one side of the vault along with gold balances and other Reichsbank equipment. At the back of the cavern, occupying an area 20 by 30 feet, were 18 bags and 189 suitcases, trunks, and boxes. Each container bore a packing slip showing the contents and a tag bearing the name 'Melmer'; victim gold.

An initial inventory indicated that there were 8,198 bars of gold bullion; 55 boxes of crated gold bullion; hundreds of bags of gold items; over 1,300 bags of gold Reichsmarks, British gold pounds, and French gold francs; 711 bags of American twenty-dollar gold pieces; hundreds of bags of gold and silver coins; hundreds of bags of foreign currency; 9 bags of valuable coins; 2,380 bags and 1,300 boxes of Reichsmarks; 40 bags containing silver bars; 63 boxes and 55 bags of silver plate; 1 bag containing 6 platinum bars; and 110 bags from various countries. As a result, security at the mine was boosted and the whole 357th Infantry Regiment moved its headquarters to Merkers. The Army, meanwhile, decided that Merkers had become a political issue and handed over control of the mine complex to Colonel Bernard D. Bernstein, who served as the financial adviser to General Eisenhower. When Bernstein questioned Thoms, the German initially claimed that the gold and silver was not stolen and that those items that had come from the economic department of the SS had only just started arriving recently. Thoms would remain vague and evasive throughout the whole of his interrogations.[1]

Bernstein realised that leaving the treasure at Merkers was not an option because, according to the decision of the Committee on Dismemberment of Germany at the Yalta Conference (4-11 February 1945), that particular part of Germany would be in the Soviet sector of occupation after the war. Immediate plans were drawn up to move everything out of the mines to Frankfurt, which was to be the headquarters of Eisenhower's staff and the headquarters of the U.S. Group Control Council when they got to Germany. Eisenhower ordered that Bernstein would be responsible for making a complete inventory of the entire contents of the mine and would arrange with the Third Army for the movement of the treasure to other areas when, and if, deemed advisable. Bernstein chose to have everything moved into the Reichsbank building in Frankfurt. This building, on the corner of Taunus-Anlage and Mainzerlandstrasse, had been requisitioned on 10 April by Lieutenant Colonel Henry D. Cragon, head of the Currency Branch, Supreme Headquarters, Allied Forces Europe (SHAEF) and was established as the Foreign Exchange Depository (FED), whose function was to receive, hold and supply occupation currency for Allied Armed Forces and Military Governments. By the end of 1945, this depository would contain the second largest single collection of wealth in the world after Fort Knox.

Patton and Eisenhower went to Merkers on 12 April to inspect the contents. On seeing the gold, Patton wanted to have it recast into medals to be awarded to each and 'every son-of-a-bitch in the Third Army'. Later, descending by lift, Patton remarked on the single cable saying that if it broke 'promotions in the United States Army would be considerably stimulated'. Eisenhower was not amused and basically told Patton to cut out the wisecracks until they were 'above ground again'.[2]

Early in the morning of 14 April, thirty-two 10-ton trucks arrived at Merkers from Mainz and the process of extracting the treasure began. Jeeps and quarter-ton trailers were lowered into the mine, along with ten officers of the 357th Infantry Regiment, soldiers, medics, tank crew members, and other support personnel. The treasure was taken out of the vault and loaded onto the trailers by two crews of fifty men each in alternating shifts. The gold on the trailers attached to the Jeeps was then driven to Shaft No. 2, where the trailer was detached and sent to the surface by lift. Shaft No. 1 was used for loading currency bags and miscellaneous objects. Here the material was unloaded from the trailers into mine carts and sent up in the lift.

An officer and a soldier stood at the door of the vault and recorded the contents as they were taken out and loaded into Jeeps. Each consignment was given a number and the names of the driver, assistant driver and recording personnel with army numbers were noted for that consignment. The whole was inventoried again at the surface. This inventory recorded, among other things: 3,682 bags and cartons of Germany currency; 80 bags of foreign currency; 4,173 bags containing 8,307 gold bars; 55 boxes of gold bullion; 3,326 bags of gold coins; 63 bags of silver; 1 bag of platinum bars; 8 bags of gold rings; and 207 bags and containers of SS loot. Once the inventory was completed, the treasure was loaded onto the trucks. During the whole time a continuous air patrol was begun over the area, and it would continue until the move was completed.

The convoy, code-named Task Force Whitney, set off for Frankfurt the next day. Two companies of the 474th Infantry Regiment were sent on ahead to Frankfurt to establish a perimeter around the Reichsbank building, while another two were joined by elements of the 785th Military Police Battalion. The whole 85 miles of road to Frankfurt was cleared and all intersections blocked off. Two M8 armoured tanks led the convoy, which consisted of two separate but identical blocks of vehicles. The sequence of all vehicles in each of the two identical columns was as follows:

- 2 military police on motorcycles
- 1 quarter-ton military police truck
- 1 M-20 tank
- 1 quarter-ton truck with infantry
- 2 mobile anti-aircraft guns
- 5 10-ton trucks loaded with gold
- 1 M8 tank
- 5 10-ton trucks loaded with gold
- 1 M8 tank
- 1 2.5-ton truck with infantry
- 1 mobile anti-aircraft gun
- 5 10-ton trucks loaded with gold
- 1 M8 tank
- 2 2.5-ton trucks with infantry
- 1 quarter-ton military police truck
- 1 three-quarter-ton truck with infantry
- 1 mobile anti-aircraft gun
- 2 military police on motorcycles

Following the second unit came:

- 3 wreckers
- 2 spare 10-ton trucks
- 2 M8 tanks
- 1 ambulance
- 1 2.5-ton wrecker

All vehicles proceeded under air cover of a Piper Cub observation aircraft and P-51 Mustang fighters. When the convoy arrived in Frankfurt, some 700 combat infantry troops were patrolling the Reichsbank building and the whole of the Merkers treasure was unloaded, after which another inventory was carried out. Bernstein monitored the whole operation 'like the bride's mother at a wedding'.[3]

Valuables at other locations were also on Bernstein's mind. He proposed to search for other Nazi gold and foreign exchange assets after the move of the treasure from Merkers, since everything, he wrote:

> confirms previous intelligence reports and censorship intercepts indicating that the Germans were planning to use these foreign exchange assets, including works of art, as a means of perpetuating the Nazism and Nazi influence both in Germany and abroad... Many of these caches have not yet been uncovered and should be ferreted out as soon as operations permit...In order to prevent further transfer or movements of Germany's foreign exchange assets and works of art to more secure places in southern Germany or in neutral countries such as Switzerland and Sweden, it is essential to locate and protect these assets.[4]

The next day Bernstein returned to Merkers to supervise the movement of art treasures which was undertaken in a second convoy of twenty-six 10-ton trucks, two of which were loaded with POWs, and two empty for use in the event that a transfer of loads became necessary. This convoy was called Task Force Hansen and had approximately the same strength security guard as the gold convoy, with the exception that fewer aircraft were used.

In a report sent back to Washington it was noted that a large quantity of the loot appeared to have been taken by the SS from victims and suggested that proper agencies be contacted to send representatives to review the loot in terms of being evidence in war crimes proceedings. At the same time, Bernstein learned from Thoms about gold deposits at other locations and recommended a full-scale reconnaissance of Germany for other caches of loot. Alongside other military officers including Lieutenant Commander Joel H. Fisher and Lieutenant Herbert G. DuBois, Bernstein set out with a small team, known as Task Force Fisher, which arrived in Halle on 20 April. In the vault of the Reichsbank building there they found sixteen wooden boxes, each containing four gold bars belonging to Dollfuss Mieg of Meulhausen, Alsace, bearing seals of the Société de Banque Suisse at Le Locle, two large wooden chests containing foreign currency meticulously itemised with names of owners from which it was looted, and seven bags of gold coins. Despite the fact that the owners of the gold bars were identifiable, some 25,862.530 troy ounces of it were deposited in the Bank of England in the account of the Tripartite Gold Commission. (One troy ounce of gold = 31.1034768 grams, making 1 kg of gold = 32.1507466 troy ounces.)

Task Force Fisher then moved on to Plauen, where they had to blast open the vault and found thirty-five bags of gold coins that had been

The Swiss National Bank building in Bern.

Frankfurt Reichsbank building.

Fort de Médine, Kayes, where the French and Belgian gold was kept.

Ruins of the wolfram (tungsten) mines of Regoufe in Portugal.

Ante Pavelić greeting the Croatian parliament in February 1943.

Nazis and Catholic bishops giving the Nazi salute.

Interior of the church of San Girolamo degli Illirici, Rome.

Meran (Merano), c.1945.

Wedding rings looted by the Nazis.

The extraction of dental gold straight after prisoners had been gassed at Auschwitz concentration camp.

Hermann Pook, the SS dentist in charge of sending all gold from the death camps to the Reichsbank.

U.S. soldiers guarding the Hungarian gold train at Werfen.

Stacks of looted gold at the Merkers mine.

Dwight Eisenhower, Omar Bradley and George S. Patton at Merkers.

Maria Eva Duarte Iburguren (Eva Perón).

Daily Express headline, 25 November 1972.

deposited in the name of Heinrich Himmler in April 1944. Again 25, 296.075 troy ounces of this gold was deposited in the Bank of England in the account of the Tripartite Gold Commission. At the small town of Gera, Fisher found documents relating to forty-one bags of gold that had arrived there on 3 April 1945, but had subsequently been moved to Zwickau, then to Aue, which was still under German control. Everywhere they went, Fisher's team found evidence of gold being sent to the National Redoubt, where the Nazis were planning to make their last stand.

Next came Magdeburg, which Fisher reached on 28 April, where he found large quantities of Hungarian silver in the Reichsbank vault. At Eschwege, forty-one bags of gold were uncovered and were recorded as having been deposited in August 1943. The Eschwege gold was identified as Belgian gold that had been taken from France. At Coburg, bank officials had buried bags of gold on a farm; some under a chicken coop and others under a pile of manure and this, too, was subsequently shown to be Belgian gold. Of the gold found at Eschwege and Coburg, 65,549.567 troy ounces were deposited in the Bank of England in the account of the Tripartite Gold Commission. At Nuremberg, Fisher found thirty-four bags of gold which apparently had come from Holland. Of the Nuremberg gold, 43,588.203 troy ounces were deposited in the Bank of England in the account of the Tripartite Gold Commission, along with a further 32,637.948 found in the Reichsbank at Zwickau.

Officials from several countries, including Belgium and France, went to the FED in Frankfurt to see if they could identify any of the gold as that which had been looted from their treasuries and which should therefore be restored to its legal owner. They took lists of markings, weights, and box numbers of to identify the gold, but most of it had been melted down and remoulded into new bars with fake markings. The U.S., however, did not want to get into any detailed discussions while the situation was 'fluid' and 'evidence so incomplete' and claimed that it was 'premature...to attempt to determine title [to the gold]'. The French knew perfectly well what was in the Merkers mine since they had taken Puhl into custody. Even Italy, who had fought on the Axis side, claimed title to some of the gold since the Germans had cleared out their vaults in 1943, but they were treated with some disdain and told bluntly that their request could not be considered at that time and they would be informed 'if the position changes'.[5] The Soviets took note and were ready to make reparation claims on any German gold, but lost interest when it became clear that the bulk of the Merkers gold had been looted.

Altogether the Allies recovered 98.6 per cent of the $255.96 million worth of gold shown on the closing balances of the Precious Metals Department of the Berlin Reichsbank. In mid-August 1945, experts from the United States Treasury Department and the Bank of England completed the job of weighing and appraising the gold, gold coin, and silver bars that had been captured. Bernstein's final 'Report on Recovery of Reichsbank Precious Metals' recorded $238.5 million in gold at Merkers and $14 million at other locations. There were a small number of allegations of looting by U.S. soldiers at Merkers, but no charges were ever brought.

Apart from the Merkers shipments, another seventy-five were received by the FED throughout 1945, mostly from the U.S. zone of occupation. When a team arrived in June, all the gold bars were logged and stacked in piles of thirty. Each bar was identified by bar number, the date received by the Reichsbank, the name of the original smelter, the name of the assayer, weight and fineness of the gold and the information was recorded in the 'Howard Report'. By this time, it was becoming clear that the volume of material coming in would quickly fill the Reichsbank vaults and so various other locations were used within the U.S. zone. Extensive security arrangements were put in place.

The Frankfurt building now housed the German Foreign Office gold, called the Ribbentrop Gold, the Hungarian monetary gold and the crown jewels of the Hungarian, Hesse and Hohenzollern dynasties, as well as 200 suitcases of looted SS valuables and 300 kg of gold fillings extracted from concentration camp victims. The gold deposits were categorised as monetary gold belonging to national treasuries, non-monetary gold looted from institutions or individuals, returnable gold which was identifiable and earmarked for return to its rightful owners, and German gold that had been looted under German Military Law 53, which had ordered all Germans in the U.S. Military Zone of Occupation to deliver all gold and silver coin or bullion to the nearest Reichsbank branch in return for an official receipt.

Records of the Reichsbank's Precious Metals Department, consisting of seventy reels of microfilm, were discovered on 1 April 1997 and are now available for research at National Archives at College Park, Maryland. These documents conclusively show how much of the looted German gold acquired by the Allies was composed of non-monetary gold, that is gold that came from victims of Nazi persecution, including such things as gold teeth. However, not all the original documents were photocopied. All the originals had been handed over to Albert Thoms, who was working for the successor bank to the Reichsbank. These records have subsequently disappeared in Germany.

Chapter 10

MELMER GOLD

> 'The 8,307 gold bars seized with the Reichsbank holdings at Merkers may, after proper assay and expert consideration, be determined to represent melted down gold teeth fillings.'
> Livingston T. Merchant, Minister-Counsellor for Economic Affairs at the United States Embassy in Paris, July 1946

Lying in one area of the Merkers mines were 18 bags of silver and gold alloy bars and 189 parcels, boxes, suitcases, and trunks containing jewellery; gold and silver articles such as watches, wedding rings, cigarette cases, compacts, spectacle frames, candle sticks, and Passover cups; hundreds of pounds of gold dental crowns and fillings; and gold and silver coins. Albert Thoms, who was captured at Merkers, identified this hoard as part of the Melmer account belonging to the SS. This loot was the latest manifestation of a programme that had been ongoing in Germany since 1934 and had gained significant importance for the German war effort after 1943, when they had looted all the monetary gold available to them from European banks.

The scarcity of foreign currency led the German state to tap private resources from 1936 onwards. Initially, the Reich sold large parts of German property abroad to acquire foreign currency, especially foreign shares from private stocks. Apart from increasingly strict measures against capital flight from 1934 onwards, plans were made in 1936 for the appropriation of the very last precious metals reserves owned by individuals, including German property abroad and privately owned gold coins, wedding rings and jewellery, which were to be transferred into foreign currency. Jewish emigrants were stripped of their valuables as they fled the country in a programme run by Reinhard Heydrich, head of the Devisenfahndungsamt (Foreign Currency Investigations

Office). Heydrich had acquired considerable influence on legislation, as well as on the operations of subordinate financial authorities.

On 12 August 1942, Funk informed Puhl of an agreement between Reichsführer Heinrich Himmler and Reich Finance Minister Lutz Schwerin von Krosigk, whereby the Reichsbank was to receive shipments of confiscated valuables that had been 'deposited' in the 'eastern occupied territories'.[1] He emphasised the utmost secrecy in the handling of these shipments: nobody was to know they had originated from the death camps at Bełżec, Sobibór, Treblinka and Auschwitz. All instructions were conveyed verbally, and nothing was put down in writing. The cash proceeds from the conversion of these shipments would be used to finance SS industrial enterprises. Puhl, who was told by Funk to 'ask no other questions',[2] made the necessary arrangements for these shipments with Oswald Pohl, head of the SS Economic Administrative Main Office (SS-WVHA) who appointed Herr Frommknecht, the Reichsbank director for cash and vault, and his subordinate, Albert Thoms, chief of the bank's Precious Metals Department.

SS Hauptsturmführer Bruno Melmer, the head of the Finance Office in the Troop Administration Department (Amtskasse-Hauptabteilung A/II/3) of the SS-WVHA, was instructed by Pohl to make the first shipment to Thoms on 26 August 1942, and other deliveries quickly followed. Testifying at the Nuremberg War Trials, he reported that the SS had made a total of seventy-six deliveries of valuables into an account designated 'Melmer', after which the Reichsbank sorted and inventoried the deliveries and distributed them to the Prussian Mint or the Municipal Pawnshop in Berlin. Gold and silver bars and currency were bought by the bank at full value from the SS and small items like gold rings were sent to Degussa for re-smelting. Jewellery and larger items were sent to the Municipal Pawnshop, which sold the better items abroad for foreign currency. The gold was sold back to the Reichsbank and credit for the proceeds was deposited in the SS 'Max Heileger' account at the Reichshauptkasse (Reich Main Accounting Office) in the Reich Ministry of Finance. Once added to the Reichsbank's holdings, the victim-origin gold was indistinguishable from gold Germany had either acquired legitimately or had looted from occupied nations.[3] Max Heileger was a fictitious name concocted to disguise the true identity of the account holder. The name Heileger was derived from the German 'Heilig', meaning holy, and is considered to have been a cynical Nazi joke.

By 1946, the U.S. Military Government knew from available records and from interrogations that, beginning in August 1942, the Reichsbank was receiving and converted gold and other valuables the SS had looted from Jewish victims in Poland and from Jewish and non-Jewish concentration camp inmates. In fact, Puhl's role in arranging for the receipt, classification, deposit, conversion, and disposal of properties taken by the SS from victims exterminated in concentration camps formed the basis for his indictment in 1946 before the U.S. Military Tribunal at Nuremberg, which subsequently sentenced him to five years' imprisonment. The origin of the gold and other valuables in these shipments was clear from the 'Reinhard' designation of the file in which Melmer kept the correspondence relating to his deliveries.

The small private firm of Friedrich Roessler Söhne had been purifying gold and silver since 1871 and had quickly become a public company handling all the government's metal purification when it changed its name to Degussa. It was able to purify gold to almost 100 per cent, after which it handed it over to the Prussian Mint for marking with the Reichsbank stamp, a serial number and a date (often backdated to hide its origin). Much of the Dutch and Belgian monetary gold, as well as the Melmer gold, went through Degussa before being sold as German bullion. The surviving Degussa smelting ledgers only identify gold by its gross weight, receipt date, and the originating agency, with indication of whether the gold consisted of personal possessions. Similarly, the smelted gold Degussa sent back to the Reichsbank is identified only by date and the weight of the entire amount being sent, so that it would appear to be impossible to match up a particular delivery of gold to Degussa with a subsequent amount of smelted gold sent to the Reichsbank. A few documents, however, refer to 'Jd', evidently referring to the gold confiscated from German Jews and clearly indicating the Degussa company was aware at the time that it was receiving gold illegally seized from Jews.

Although the Melmer deposits provided the most direct evidence that the Reichsbank received gold robbed from individuals persecuted and murdered by the Nazis, the SS was not the only agency from which the Reichsbank received gold taken from private individuals and enterprises. In a statement on 19 September 1945, Thoms explained the Reichsbank's role in the confiscation of the personal property of German Jews to his U.S. interrogators. According to a decree of 21 February 1939, German Jews had to turn in their valuable personal property to the Municipal Pawnshops, some of which came to the Reichsbank, which had its own pawn office. This material included gold coins and gold bars. While the Reichsbank acquired the gold coins and bars taken from German Jews, the German Foreign Office assisted in liquidating the gems and jewellery confiscated both from German Jews and from individuals and businesses in the countries conquered by Germany by exchanging them abroad either for commodities essential to the German war effort or for the foreign currency needed to buy them. The Foreign Office regularly transferred packages of jewellery specifically referred to as Judenschmuck, or Jewish jewellery, to its legation in Bern via diplomatic pouch. The packages were given to a German agent in Bern, who exchanged them for industrial diamonds, described as vitally important to the German war effort, despite the fact that the sale and export of industrial diamonds was banned under Swiss law. In at least one instance, the German Foreign Office arranged for gem diamonds to be sold to a Swiss citizen in Bern for Swiss francs.[4]

All the correspondence from the period 1942-1943, when the Reichsbank began sending articles from SS loot shipments to Degussa to be smelted, has apparently been destroyed. One significant letter remains, however, written on 8 February 1945 by the head of Degussa's Berlin branch plant, who reported that he was in the process of destroying the confidential records of the Sonderring, a special group within Degussa's Berlin organisation established in 1942 to deal with precious metals. This letter shows that records of the processing of victim-origin precious metals by Degussa for the Reichsbank were intentionally destroyed, once again indicating that Degussa was aware that some of the materials it had been processing had not been legitimately obtained by the Reichsbank.

The Reichsbank used the gold it acquired from the SS shipments in the same way it used the gold looted from the central banks of the nations it occupied: it was sold to domestic and foreign banks in order to acquire foreign currency needed to finance Germany's war effort. Records show that most of the melted-down gold was sold by two German banks, Deutsche Bank and Dresdner Bank. Deutsche Bank was Germany's largest private financial institution, which from the early days of Nazi rule had adopted a policy of Aryanisation and still held 3.6 tons of looted gold in its vaults at the end of the war. The Dresdner Bank, known to be Himmler's favourite bank, bought a total of 5.8 tons of gold from the Nazis and made substantial profits by selling it on to countries such as Turkey. During the war it swallowed up a number of European banks, including the Bohemian Discount Bank of Prague, Societa Bancara Romana of Bucharest, Handels-und-Kreditbank of Riga, Kontinentale Bank of Brussels and Banque d'Athens. In May 1945 it still had 4.2 tons of Nazi gold in its vaults.

The Reichsbank then returned a statement to Melmer that gave the value of each shipment and reported that the equivalent value in Reichsmarks had been paid to the Reichshauptkasse. Among the records was the receipt for the first three Melmer deliveries on 26 August, 4 September, and 7 September 1942, valued at 1,184,375.59 Reichsmarks, which the Reichsbank paid to the Reichshauptkasse on 27 October 1942. After 1943, some of the consignments carried stamps clearly stating they had come from Lublin and Auschwitz, which were known at the time to be locations of death camps.

Will Burger, the administration chief at Auschwitz concentration camp from June 1942 until April 1943, testified at Nuremberg that while he was stationed at Auschwitz, an order came from the SS-WVHA to send all dental gold and such valuables as jewellery, rings, and watches to Melmer. In late 1943, an order was issued to all concentration camps besides Auschwitz to send dental gold and valuables to Burger's department, which delivered them to Melmer. Auschwitz, however, continued to ship them directly to Melmer because the number of valuables it collected was so large.

Melmer kept all correspondence relating to deliveries to the Reichsbank in a file designated 'Reinhard', which referred to Operation Reinhard, the SS programme for exploiting Jewish property and labour and murdering millions of Jews in killing centres in Eastern Poland. Some of the Operation Reinhard documents also revealed how gold and other valuables robbed from murdered Jews passed from the Lublin camps and Auschwitz via the SS Economic Administrative Main Office to the Reichsbank. In February 1943 Odilo Globocnik, the SS and Police Leader in Lublin and head of Operation Reinhard, reported that 1,775.46 kg of gold bullion and coined gold currency valued at 843,802.75 Reichsmarks was delivered, and his final report listed 2,909.68 kg of gold bullion valued at 8,147,104 Reichsmarks and minted gold currency valued at 1,736,554.12 Reichsmarks. In total there were seventy-eight 'Melmer' deliveries, of which about forty-three were fully inventoried by the Reichsbank. Gold taken from dead Jews outside the death camps arrived at the Reichsbank independently of the Melmer deliveries.

On 24 July 1998, German officials acknowledged that twenty-six crucial, secret files containing records of gold stolen from Jews in concentration camps had mysteriously disappeared from German archives. These files had been discovered in 1945 by American troops in eastern Germany and shipped to the United States, where some were microfilmed. But sections, apparently including the twenty-six Melmer files, were not. The documents were handed back to the German authorities in 1948 and left in the care of the Bank Deutscher Lander, the forerunner of the present German central bank, the Bundesbank. The *New York Times* reported on 'the possibility that they had been deliberately destroyed to cover the tracks of former Nazi banking officials entrusted by the Allies with high offices in post-war Germany'. It went on to say that, 'The German report chronicled lapses by German and American officials in safeguarding the documents [which] to outside observers it will seem incomprehensible that documents so closely linked to the crimes of Nazism could be distributed so carelessly and finally lost'.[5]

In April 1945, the Melmer account still held 207 containers of unprocessed SS loot which had been taken to the Merkers mine in their original containers. These containers, some of which held hundreds of pounds of gold teeth and dental fillings, represented part of the contents of twenty-one SS shipments. The Bergier Commission concluded that a total of $2.5 million in gold had been deposited in the Melmer account. German sociologist Hersch Fischler, however, concluded that the value of the gold in the SS shipments totalled $3 million, while U.S. researcher Sidney Zabludoff's report for the World Jewish Congress put the total value at $4 million. (Figures cited are in wartime values, when the price of gold was set at $35 per ounce.) The total amount credited to the SS for the gold in its loot shipments to the Reichsbank can be very conservatively estimated as at least $4,652,606.48, but it should be borne in mind that this estimate refers only to the amount that the Reichsbank apparently credited to the SS for the gold in its loot shipments. This figure appears somewhat low in view of the fact that SS and Police Leader Odilo Globocnik reported in 1944 that he had shipped $3,986,953.66 in gold bullion and coins to the SS in Berlin to be forwarded to the Reichsbank as part of Operation Reinhard. The gold shipped by Globocnik, which was deposited in the Melmer account, did not include the gold looted by the SS from its victims at Auschwitz and at the concentration camps and slave labour camps outside Lublin District in Poland.[6]

It should also be borne in mind that the gold in the SS shipments to the Reichsbank may well have represented only a fraction of the gold looted from individual victims, many of whom had been robbed of most of their valuable possessions before their arrival at the camps. Nor was the SS the only source of gold received by the Reichsbank. Since 1939, Jews in Germany and in areas occupied by Germany had been forced to turn in jewellery and other personal items containing gold to the Berlin Municipal Pawn Shop, which made deposits into the 'J' account, signifying that it was sourced from Jewish victims.

Gold also came to the Reichsbank from non-German inhabitants in the areas of Poland annexed by the German Reich. According to the head of the Haupttreuhandstelle Ost, Funk and Schwerin von Krosigk had ordered that all the confiscated valuables, including significant quantities of gold, be delivered to the Reichsbank. The Reichsbank Berlin instructed its office in Katowice to accept smelted gold as long as it met the purchasing requirements of the Reichsbank.

It is clear that just as it received and incorporated looted monetary gold into the Reich's reserves, so did the Reichsbank receive and incorporate gold looted from individuals persecuted and murdered by the Nazi regime. If the gold looted from individuals was not already in a negotiable form, it was re-smelted into bullion and was therefore visibly undistinguishable from monetary gold. The need to determine how much gold Germany looted from European central banks and how Germany disposed of such gold led to a study of captured records of the Reichsbank Precious Metals Department and the Prussian Mint made available by the Soviets in Berlin. Analysing these records with the assistance of Albert Thoms, the French had succeeded in tracing the looted Belgian monetary gold the Belgian government had sent to France for safekeeping at the start of the war and that the Germans had subsequently confiscated. This encouraged speculation that the records would also reveal the fate of looted monetary gold belonging to other nations and deposited in the Reichsbank. Certain specific Degussa smelting operations were identified during the course of this investigation. For instance, one Prussian Mint operation in which Dutch guilders were smelted into gold bars shows that 37 kg of gold acquired by the Reichsbank from the Melmer deliveries were traded to the SNB, the Banca d'Italia and the Banco Commerciale Italiana.

Among the many deeply disturbing issues of looted gold was the one concerning 'dental gold'. On 23 September 1940, SS Reichsfürher Heinrich Himmler had given SS doctors orders to collect 'Zahngold'(golden teeth) from the mouths of the dead, and also 'the golden teeth that cannot be repaired' from the mouths of the living. A second decree of 23 December 1942 ordered that this be carried out systematically on all concentration camp inmates. In 1940, the dentist Wiktor Scholz wrote a doctoral dissertation in Strzelin, lower Silesia, which was highly commended by the Medical University of the Stomatology Institute in Breslau. Scholz stated that extracting dental gold from the dead was vital for the economy of the Third Reich.

On 21 September 1943, a directive went out for the attention of the commandants of the concentration camps of Dachau, Sachsenhausen, Buchenwald, Mauthausen, Flossenbürg, Neuengamme, Auschwitz, Gross-Rosen, Natzweiler, Riga, Stutthof, Lublin, Ravensbrück, Herzungen, and Bergen-Belsen:

A special case leads us to bring you further details on the Reichsführer's order dated 23/09/1940, according to which dental gold collected from the dead must be sent each month to the chief of the dental health service at the Waffen-SS sanitary inspection (now SS-FHA– service group D department 14– in Berlin W 15, Knesebeckstraße 43/44). According to this order, dental gold collected in concentration camps must not be sent to the families of the victims. The general security service of the Reich advises you to answer any request from a family of a victim, as follows: 'died in this camp, the corpse has been cremated…which makes it impossible for us to send you back the dental gold.'[7]

When a prisoner arrived at a concentration camp, a medical examination was performed. Gold teeth were extracted and their anthropometric descriptions were immediately written on the inmates' medical records or imprisonment cards. Later, crowns were also extracted in some camps from the mouths of living inmates. Dental gold was also extracted from dead bodies before they were cremated, the bodies being marked with a blue cross or with a short thread tied on a toe. A receipt was written for each inmate detailing what had been extracted.

At Auschwitz concentration camp, straight after the gas chambers, a Sonderkommando team usually opened the mouths of the dead and extracted all the metals they could get. The teeth were then put into zinc buckets filled with sulfuric acid to remove fragments of soft flesh and bones which were still attached. A gold foundry was created in Crematorium III, at the end of 1943, where the metal was melted in graphite moulds and shaped into bars of a given weight. Every fortnight, an ambulance came to take delivery of the collected gold. Customary German efficiency and attention to detail, along with a penchant for meticulous record-keeping, meant that a receipt with the odontogram was written for each dead inmate detailing which teeth had been extracted. When they were sent to Berlin, a monthly receipt recapitulated the weight of dental gold which was thus sent. Gold was delivered to Berlin at the heart of the SS-WVHA by Dr Hermann Pook, an SS dentist in charge of centralisation and sending all gold from the camps to the Reichsbank. After the war, his affiliation to a criminal organisation and a conviction of crimes against humanity brought him a ten-year prison sentence, of which he only served five years and nine months. In 1959 he was given a licence to practice again by the West Berlin Health Department, who said that proof of serious offenses had not been presented.[8]

On 28 April 1945 investigations at the Buchenwald concentration camp led to a spot where two tunnels had been excavated to make air raid shelters. The entrance to the tunnels had been blocked with rocks, which were removed to reveal suitcases containing gold coins, rings, diamonds and gold tooth fillings. A second tunnel was found to contain valuables that eventually filled nine 2.5-ton trucks and was taken to the FED in Frankfurt. This discovery is mentioned here, although, strictly speaking, it was not classed as Melmer gold since it was never deposited in a bank.

Chapter 11

DEGUSSA

'The Degussa corporation played a pivotal role in the processing of plundered precious metals in Nazi-occupied Europe and controlled the production and distribution of Zyklon B, the infamous pesticide used to gas the inmates of Auschwitz and Majdanek concentration camps during the Third Reich.'

Peter Hayes, 'From Cooperation to Complicity: Degussa in the Third Reich' abstract

The Nazi regime had permanent control of all economic resources from as early as 1933 and utilised them for the purposes of its politically determined economic goals and rearmament. Their demands, however, continuously outstripped the country's resources and by 1939 they had started to tap into private property; a process that was extended to all countries that were subsequently occupied. The robbery of precious metals from private sources became a fundamental part of economic policy, but grew from a series of ad hoc measures that solidified into procedures.

The scarcity of foreign currency available to the Nazis led to confiscation of privately owned gold coins, wedding rings and jewellery from 1936, when the state sold much of it abroad to acquire foreign currency. Much of this was confiscated from Jewish emigrants after the appointment of Reinhard Heydrich as head of the Foreign Currency Investigations Office in 1936. It was Heydrich who directed the foreign currency and customs authorities towards an anti-Jewish policy and went on to oversee the confiscation of precious metals during the occupation of the Reich Protectorate of Bohemia and Moravia and the invasion of Poland.

Seizures of privately owned precious metals continued when Austria was annexed to the Reich. In March 1938, Austrian Nazi organisations plundered Jewish properties, particularly precious metal objects, on a large scale. This plunder was formalised in Göring's 'Decree for the Reporting of Jewish-Owned Property', which came in just weeks after the Anschluss on 26 April and required all Jews in both Germany and Austria to register any property or assets valued at more than 5,000 Reichsmarks which, at the time, was equivalent to $2,000. Jewish property was to be used not only to finance the rearmament of Germany through Göring's Four Year Plan, but also to replenish the Reich's foreign currency reserves. The significance of the scarcity of foreign currency for the plundering of Jewish precious metals even before the war is also shown by the so-called 'Pawnshop Action' in March 1939, when German and Austrian Jews had to consign their gold, silver and platinum objects to pawnshops. The 1.3 tons of gold derived from the pawnshop policy was not distributed but sent to the Berlin Pawn Institute (Berliner Zentrale Pfandleihe) and was later refined by Degussa and fifteen smaller companies. Following the outbreak of the war, the gold was used for industrial production in Germany. This haul of gold and silver was important because imports had been made difficult by the Allied economic blockade. Silver and platinum were important for industrial processes in the armament industry and the gold was sold to acquire foreign currency.

An examination of the actual looting of precious metals in the occupied territories between 1939 and 1945 immediately reveals that quite different measures were taken in each territory. It should be noted that as well as state robbery of private assets, a great deal of precious metals was taken by individual German officials, soldiers or SS members in cases of corruption and individual embezzlement, which was ubiquitous, though rarely documented. Only those who took too much or too often were prosecuted. The full extent of such pillaging is impossible to determine.

It is also clear that in the case of stolen precious metals, the methods employed in the East were carried out with significantly greater criminality, often resulting in the death of the victims. In the West, the looting was more circumspect, often employing modern financial and administrative methods. It both East and West, however, looting was undertaken at local levels with no central guidance and even in occupied territories there were usually a number of different organisations responsible for the theft of precious metals. Among them were the Devisenschutzkommando (Currency Protection Squads), Wehrerfassungskommandos (Military Requisition Squads), the Einsatzgruppen in the Soviet Union, the Haupttreuhandstelle Ost (Main Trustee Office East, HTO), the Ahnenerbe (Office for Establishing Arian Hereditary Background), the ghetto administrations, the

German administration in the occupied territories, police battalions, and, finally, the SS.[1]

Around the middle of October 1939, Himmler and the head of the HTO, Mayor Max Winkler, agreed that precious metals were not to be confiscated and processed by the HTO, but by the General Trustee for Securing German Cultural Property (GTH). All precious metals not considered to be works of art were to be handed over to the state-owned Utilization and Management Company (Verwaltungs- und Verwertungsgesellschaft mbH, VVG,) for further processing. Several organisations, including the currency protection squads, customs authorities, army units, several SS organisations, and the civilian administration were all expected to take part in the collection process. The precious metals confiscated from the Łódź Ghetto by the ghetto administration, the criminal investigations police in Łódź, the HTO and the customs authorities, were sent directly to the Berlin central pawn authority. In the Polish occupation administration, the Department of the Trustee Administration with the Government (Treuhandstelle), and its subsidiary, the Trustee Administration Company (Treuhand Verwertunggesellschaft mbH), as well as the Special Commissioner for the Registration of Works of Art and Cultural Assets, Kai Mühlmann, the police force, the army, and the SS, also stole massive amounts of precious metals from Jews and Poles.[2]

Currency Protection squads were set up to operate in Poland under the guise of customs and tax authorities and began their work in the first days of September 1939. Their primary task was to secure desperately needed foreign currency reserves in Polish banks. Secondary targets were pure gold and other precious metals, precious stones and jewellery. In many places, the foreign currency protection squads appointed the Deutsche Bank and other banks to take possession of the looted treasure.

The stolen precious metals and valuables were received by different organisations such as the Reichshauptkasse Beutestelle (Reich Main Treasury Booty Office), the Reichssicherheitshauptamt (Reich Security Main Office), the Haupttreuhandstelle Ost, the Reichsbankhauptkasse (Reichsbank Treasury), the Wirtschaftsverwaltungshauptamt of the SS (SS Economic Administration Office), the two state enterprises Wifo and Roges, the Wehrwirtschaftsrüstungsamt (Military Economic Armament Office), the Reichsstelle für Edelmetalle (National Agency for Precious Metals) or the Four Year Plan Authority.[3]

All through the war, the vast majority of the stolen gold was used to purchase war matériel from neutral and friendly states, while other precious metals were made use of in German industry. Silver was used by the armament industry in the production of silver solder and electrical contacts, as well as for x-ray radiographs and aerial reconnaissance photography. Platinum was used as a catalyst in the manufacture of nitrogen, in the production of artificial silk, and also for special rhodium mirrors used in anti-aircraft searchlights.

From February 1941 through to 1944, Degussa took delivery of old and fragmented gold and silver, but because the records are fragmentary, only a few deliveries can be verified and the exact amount is not known. The Łódź Ghetto administration sent at least 6.6 tons of silver fragments, amounting to approximately 4.9 tons of pure silver, to Degussa, where it was processed and used in German industry. Degussa received substantial quantities of gold and silver fragments taken from Polish and Jewish possessions. Furthermore, Degussa established a branch in Warsaw that cooperated with the trustee authority of the government and received stolen precious metals from there.

It is likely that Degussa, and presumably others, had a suspicion about the origin of all the valuables made of precious metals, especially dental gold, by 1942. Even so, the companies of the precious metals sector went along with the system at a point when they knew about the rapacious nature of the metals' procurement and knew that the gold was tainted with blood. Records show that Degussa melted down 2,260 bars of looted gold, most of it from Italy, Belgium and the Netherlands.[4]

Chapter 12

HUNGARIAN GOLD TRAINS

> 'Hungarian Jewry suffered immeasurable losses in human lives and property owing to Fascistic inhumanity. 600,000 Hungarian Jews lost their lives in Nazi concentration camps. The remaining valuables of the 200,000 Hungarian Jews, who survived, are on the "Train of Gold" and we think that the greatest injustice would befall these people if they could not get back even their remaining few valuables after what they have been through.'
>
> Letter of the Central Board of Jews in Hungary and the
Autonomous Orthodox Israelitic Religious
Bodies in Hungary to the U.S. Legation
in Budapest, 26 February 1947

Hungary was late to the Second World War. It was invaded by Germany in March 1944 before being systematically looted by the SS of privately held valuables, including gold. The Fascist government of Ferenc Szálasi, which came to power on 16 October 1944, was little more than a Nazi puppet state and proceeded to issue a discriminatory decree against the Jewish population obliging them to deposit their gems, their golden jewels ornamented with gems, and generally all their valuables made of gold, including wedding rings, with the authorities. On 23 January 1945, a 'Gold Train' carrying 32 tons of monetary gold left Fertőboz on the Hungary-Austria border to travel west ahead of Soviet advances east of Hungary. The cargo also included the Crown of St Stephen, a large amount of foreign currency, valuable documents such as the Corvina books of King Matthias and the scientifically important platinum master bar of the metre. Moreover, there were gems, diamonds, pearls, watches, approximately 200 paintings, Persian and Oriental rugs, silverware, chinaware, furniture, fine clothing, linens, porcelains, cameras, and stamp collections on the train, many of which were taken from the Jewish families in Hungary.[1]

The train was taken over by Patton's Third Army when it entered Spital am Pyhrn and returned intact, apart from St Stephen's Crown, to Hungary in August of that year.

As Allied forces approached, Szálasi had looted valuables loaded onto a second Gold Train consisting of forty-four cars and had them shipped westward under military escort on 29 March 1945. This train was seized by U.S. forces at Werfen in May by the U.S. troops of occupation and pushed into a railway tunnel at Boeckstein. According to reports, among a large quantity of other valuables, the hoard contained ten cases of gold having an average weight of 45 kg; one case containing 100 kg of gold coins; eighteen cases of golden jewels with an average weight of 35 kg; and thirty-two cases containing golden watches of weight varying from 30 to 60 kg.[2] Part of the train remained in U.S. hands and was taken to Salzburg in Austria and stored in the in the Military Government Warehouse, while the remainder was transported into the French zone where it was seized by French troops in St Anton. The French recorded thirty-one cases with markings of gold, two cases containing golden coins and three cases containing gold watches.

The U.S. government and military authorities decided that it was not possible to identify the ownership of the property recovered from the Gold Train and determined that it should be given to the Intergovernmental Committee for Refugees. On 20 December 1945, however, the Temporary Managing Committee of the Central Bureau of Hungarian Jews wrote to the U.S. Legation in Budapest insisting that these valuables were considered, even in terms of the Nazi-decrees, as Jewish deposits, and had never ceased to be the undoubted property of their original owners. The U.S. refused to send anyone to examine the valuables. In July 1946, Nikolaus Nyaradi, the Hungarian minister of finance, visited Berlin in an attempt to convince American authorities not to dispose of the property found on the Gold Train, but the U.S. authorities refused to change their mind.

Hungarian Jewish leaders continued to argue that at least a portion of the assets were identifiable and feared that auctioning the valuables for whatever cause would create a bad precedent. They worried that if the U.S. auctioned the valuables found in Werfen, the French government would follow suit with that part of the Hungarian treasure they controlled. Despite this, some contents of the Gold Train were auctioned in New York by the Preparatory Commission for the International Refugee Organization (PCIRO) in July 1948. The Department of State wrote to the U.S. Legation in Budapest explaining the U.S. position saying, 'The basis for this action was the decision of this government to apply to so-called non-monetary gold found in Austria the principles of Article 8 of the Paris Repatriation Agreement of December 1945 and of the Five Power Agreement of June 1946 for the implementation of this provision'.[4]

It is indisputable that the conduct of the American forces occupying Austria was less disciplined than that of the American forces occupying Germany. On 13 July 1945, Major General Harry J. Collins, Commander of the 42nd ("Rainbow") Division in western Austria, took possession of property for his headquarters identified as U.S. Government Property (from Hungarian Train, Military Government (MG) Warehouse) including different objects made of onyx, five rugs and eight paintings. He also requisitioned valuables from the Gold Train for his home including chinaware, silverware, and glassware 'of the very best quality and workmanship available'. The property control officer responded to this request by taking these items from the MG warehouse in which the Gold Train properties had been stored. Subsequent requisitions by Major Collins for Gold Train property included twelve silver candlesticks and eleven carpets, two rugs to decorate his railway car, and thirteen rugs for the decoration of his villa, Maria Theresien Schloss.[5] Property Control Office records show that numerous other high-ranking officers of the American Forces in Austria, including General Laude, General Hume, General Howard and Brigadier General Linden appropriated Hungarian Jewish treasures found on the Gold Train for the decoration of their residences.

In addition to requisitions by U.S. forces and sales through the Army Exchange, property on the Gold Train was also subject to outright theft. In one case, the property control officer reported that two small suitcases of gold dust had disappeared from the warehouse. He declared that the Property Control Warehouse had been robbed by military guards when the subject gold dust was stolen. Further complications of identification of ownership arose when the property was repacked and the original containers and labels indicating country and names of owners were lost.

Crates with Jewish property from the Gold Train labelled 'unidentifiable as to ownership' started to arrive at Staten Island in the middle of December 1947, with the initial sales due to take place at the Parke-Bernet Galleries in New York in June 1948. The *New York Times* reported on 22 June 1948 that the 'ownerless assets' of tinted and cut-glass goblets and liqueur glasses, decorative porcelain vases, Bohemian-cut sapphire blue and ruby glassware, Meissen, Dresden, Herend, Rosenthal, and Vienna porcelain statuettes and figure groups, eighteenth and nineteenth century continental pewter flagons and tureens were sold for a total of $152,850.

By the start of 1945, many Nazi leaders who were in a position to do so began frantically grabbing what valuables they could and hiding them either to finance their escape or to be recovered after the war. Joachim von Ribbentrop had eighty-one sacks of Italian gold placed in the cellars of the Schloss Fuschl, while more were hidden in a factory at Gaissau Hintersee, both of which were near to Salzburg. Not one to put all his eggs in one basket, Ribbentrop hid more gold in the Liebenau Monastery at Worms and a castle in Mühlhausen and finally had 2 tons of gold coins hidden in the area around Hamburg. It was here that Ribbentrop, masquerading as Herr Reiser, was arrested on 14 June 1945. He would later be found guilty of war crimes at Nuremberg and hanged on 16 October 1946.

The SS Deputy Leader, Ernst Kaltenbrunner, who was by now the commander of all German forces in southern Germany, had set up his headquarters at Altaussee. It was from Berlin to this town that a special gold train took his personal loot at the end of March 1945. Like Ribbentrop, Kaltenbrunner, calling himself Dr Unterwegen, was never to benefit from this gold. Arrested with his mistress Countess Gisele von Westrap on 12 May in a remote cabin in the Totes Gebirge mountains near Altaussee, he went to trial at Nuremberg, was convicted of war crimes and crimes against humanity, and hanged with Ribbentrop on 16 October 1946.

Chapter 13

EAGLE AND JACKDAW

'An Eagle, swooping down on powerful wings, seized a lamb in her talons and made off with it to her nest. A Jackdaw saw the deed, and his silly head was filled with the idea that he was big and strong enough to do as the Eagle had done. So with much rustling of feathers and a fierce air, he came down swiftly on the back of a large Ram. But when he tried to rise again he found that he could not get away, for his claws were tangled in the wool. And so far was he from carrying away the Ram, that the Ram hardly noticed he was there. The Shepherd saw the fluttering Jackdaw and at once guessed what had happened. Running up, he caught the bird and clipped its wings. That evening he gave the Jackdaw to his children. "What a funny bird this is!" they said laughing, "what do you call it, father?" "That is a Jackdaw, my children. But if you should ask him, he would say he is an Eagle."'

The Eagle and the Jackdaw, *Aesop's Fables*.

While much of the Reichsbank gold deposits had been moved out, gold continued to flow into Berlin from towns across Germany that were in imminent danger of being overrun by Allied forces, but it was clear that the capital was no longer a safe place to store it. For some months, leading Nazis had developed the idea of retreating into southern Germany and northern Austria to establish a last National Redoubt or fortress from which they would negotiate the final surrender, and it was here that plans were drawn up to move all the remaining gold from Berlin. Lieutenant Colonel Friedrich (Fritz) Josef Rauch had been a member of the Nazi Party since the Beer Hall Putsch of 1923 and had served in 1st SS Division Leibstandarte SS Adolf Hitler, seeing action in Bulgaria, Greece, Romania and Yugoslavia before being appointed SS Sturmbannführer of the Schutzpolizei (Security Police). In April 1945, he was adjutant to Hans Lammers, the head of Hitler's Reich Chancellery and formulated a plan to remove the gold and all remaining currency and printing plates at the Reichsbank, together with assorted looted valuables in the war chests of Göring and Himmler. On 13 April 1945, after many days of continuous bombing of Berlin, Lammers finally persuaded Hitler, now crushed, half-crippled and quite insane cowering in his bunker beneath the Chancellery, to give his approval.

The valuables, comprising 25 boxes and 365 bags of gold, millions of dollars' worth of foreign currency, 500 million Reichsmarks and 34 currency printing plates, were loaded onto two trains, codenamed 'Adler' (Eagle) and 'Dohle' (Jackdaw) at Berlin-Lichterfede West freight yard, under the direction of Hans Alfred von Rosenberg-Lipinsky. Eagle was to take the Reichsmarks to Munich, where the lack of German currency was an acute problem, while Jackdaw would travel on with the gold to the beautiful Alpine town of Mittenwald, once described by the poet Göthe as a 'living picture book', on the Austria-Germany border.[1] For 2,000 years, Mittenwald had been an important transit point across the Alps, most notably during the sixteenth and seventeenth centuries when it had been used by Spain to send treasure to the Netherlands to pay its troops and mercenaries in the Eighty Years' War.

Getting to their destination, however, was going to be far from easy, with Allied forces closing in from both sides. The Western Allies were approaching the Elbe River, forcing the trains to cross into Czechoslovakian territory after passing through Dresden. After two days of slow progress, often under the gaze of Allied reconnaissance aircraft and always under threat of bombing, the trains reached Pilsen, where eleven bags of currency, including Swiss francs, were offloaded onto a truck for speedier delivery to the Reichsbank branch at Regensburg. On the way their identification tags were removed. It was another four days before Eagle chugged back into German territory at Eisenstein, where another sixty bags of foreign currency and 100 million Reichsmarks were loaded onto trucks to join a convoy of five or six Opel-Blitz trucks belonging to the Berlin Police. These trucks had left Berlin on 14 April in the charge of Police Lieutenant George Krüger and were accompanied by Lieutenant Colonel Rauch. At further stops along the way, more currency was unloaded onto trucks and delivered to various Reichsbank branches for distribution. On 22 April, Rosenberg-Lipinski took some fourteen sacks of foreign currency to Lindau, at the eastern end of Lake Constance, and returned with twenty-five boxes of gold bullion which had been stored in the Konstanz Reichsbank.

Meanwhile, Funk and August Schwedler had travelled down in a car driven by Bernard Miesen. The 25 boxes of gold, 364 bags of gold (one of the original tallies was missing) and currency printing plates had passed through Munich and arrived at Mittenwald, where Funk, now a broken man who was 'drunk much of the time',[2] was waiting for it in his mountain hideaway at Bad Tölz. Funk and Schwedler met up with Lammer, who had travelled down separately, and all three spent days touring the area around Mittenwald looking for suitable places to hide the gold. Several locations were looked at as suitable depositories, but the first choice, a lead mine at Peissenberg, was prone to flooding and the gold was instead to taken to the barracks of the elite Mountain Infantry School, which was run by Colonel Franz Wilhelm Pfeiffer. When Rosenberg-Lipinski arrived at Peissenberg to join up with the main body, he found that they had already left, with no indication of where they had gone.

The cargo could clearly not stay where it was with Allied forces closing in, so at the end of April, Rauch was charged with finding a suitable place to hide it, while Funk and others waited to be arrested. One of the German soldiers, Captain Hans Neuhauser, was the son of the chief forester of the Walchensee area and it was in this man's house in the woods, 10 miles north of Mittenwald, that the 700 gold bars and other valuables were stored in a shed at the rear. Two days later, the whole 17 tons of valuables were loaded onto mules and taken to a remote location near the hamlet of Einsiedel, where they were buried in six different pits, three of which contained the gold bars. The pits were then laid with makeshift booby traps. The Reichsmark printing plates were obviously going to be worthless after the war and were dumped in nearby Lake Walchen.

On 9 May, the day after the German surrender, Lieutenant Herber G. DuBois and his Task Force Fisher, the reconnaissance mission that had set out in April to locate looted gold, went off in search of Eagle and Jackdaw. In Munich DuBois discovered a large quantity of foreign currencies and then at Mittenwald, they questioned residents and soon discovered that the gold had been taken to Neuhauser's house, which was in a forested area reputed to be swarming with armed German soldiers. DuBois questioned Funk, who was now at the U.S. Seventh Army Interrogation Centre in Augsburg, but he had no more idea than they did where the gold had been buried. Only after three weeks of investigation and questioning of residents in the area did DuBois return to Mittenwald and resume the search. It was known that the gold had been moved by mules, so he followed animal droppings and hoof marks into the woods and finally, using metal detectors, found the first gold deposit. Fortunately for the searchers, the booby traps failed to explode and when the excavation was complete, the haul consisted of bags of gold and currencies, jewellery and the 364 bags of gold bars. When compared to the inventory carried out in Berlin on 13 April, it was estimated that about a half ton of gold, all the Swiss francs and a quantity of U.S. dollars were still unaccounted for.

On 23 June, Captain Hans Neuhauser gave himself up to Lieutenant Chatel of the U.S. 574th Antiaircraft Battalion and said that he had information pertaining to a large cache of gold at Mittenwald and would lead Chatel to it in return for official army discharge papers and the release of his father, who was being held as a POW. He told Chatel that on 28 April, while he was at his father's house, a Reichsbank official and an SS officer had shown him papers authorising them to inspect the hidden treasure. When they had done that and left, Neuhauser went up to the area and, because of recent snowfall, saw that some of the pits had been disturbed and new ones dug some distance away. When he took U.S. officers to the spot, they found that three large holes had been dug and the area was littered with chewing gum wrappers and U.S. ration boxes. Nearby, however, Neuhauser was able to locate new areas which, when excavated, delivered twenty boxes later found to contain gold coins which were sent to London.

Rauch, meanwhile, had kept a low profile, but a few days after Neuhauser's excavation, he saw an opportunity to ingratiate himself with the Allies and made contact with them through Helmuth Groger, an interpreter working for the 512th Military Police Battalion. Rauch told the U.S. authorities that he knew of a large cache of twenty boxes of gold, each containing 50 kg as well as gold coins and currency, in the woods around Mittenwald, and would take them to it in return for certain unspecified favours. When they arrived at the scene, however, Rauch found only two bags of gold coins plus twenty-three bags of U.S. and Norwegian currency. He was apparently unaware that DuBois and troops from the 10th Armoured Division had taken most of it away. U.S. troops came up and helped excavate a wider area and uncovered more bags of currency and four bags of gold coins, which were shipped to London and deposited with the Tripartite Gold Commission.

Rauch should have been automatically arrested due to his SS rank, but he was not interned until 27 November, when a special Counter-Intelligence Corps agent seized and interrogated him at Tegernsee city gaol. Rauch was then, inexplicably, transferred to a Civilian Enclosure at Stephanskirchen and released the following year. In February 1948 Rauch and his wife emigrated to Argentina with the direct help of the Croatian Roman Catholic priest Krunoslav Draganović, where he became José Federico Rauch. Rauch soon became a partner in a metallurgical firm by the name of Exact SCL, a company formed by Germans and based at Santa Rosa in Buenos Aires. Colonel Pfeiffer, from the Mountain Infantry School, was also living in Argentina at that time and was a partner in the same company. Both men later returned to Europe and would die there.

Chapter 14

THE GOLD POT AND THE PARIS REPARATIONS CONFERENCE

> 'German assets in those countries which remained neutral in the war against Germany shall be removed from German ownership or control and liquidated or disposed of in accordance with the authority of France, the United Kingdom and the United States of America, pursuant to arrangements to be negotiated with the neutrals by those countries.'
> Article 6 of the Paris Reparations Agreement

As soon as the Merkers hoard was discovered by the Allies, France and Belgium were ready with detailed records and requested access to the mines to identify any gold that had come from their vaults and claim it in accordance with the UN declaration of 5 January 1943, rather than leave it to be classified as U.S. war booty. The French had a fair idea of what was in the mines because they had captured and interrogated the Nazi economist, Emil Puhl. The U.S., however, was determined to retain total control of the gold and would not allow any outside inspection until they had time to decide what their policy was going to be. If the French were given access, then there was no way that other countries, even Italy, could be denied the same, and this would then present unnecessary administrative problems at a time when the war was still raging. To counter arguments put forward by claimants, the U.S. chose, as a negotiating strategy, to suggest that it might, after all, claim all the gold for itself as war booty in accordance with Article LIII of the Hague Regulations of 1907, which stated that 'if material is actually in use by the enemy forces or is helping its operations it is liable to confiscation' and since the gold was clearly being used by the

German state at the time of its capture, it could legally be claimed as war booty.[1] This gold might then be allocated to the reconstruction of the German economy or used to buy wheat to feed the starving German population. This assertion seemed to fly in the face of U.S. commitments to the U.N. declaration on looted gold made in 1943 and was never advanced as a serious argument, but remained in the background as a warning to countries who made unreasonable demands of the 'Gold Pot'. It also deterred liberated nations from reneging on existing debts to the U.S. and acted as a brake on French demands for the return of all identifiable Belgian gold to Paris.

Already, post-war politics were starting to cloud the issue. Allies would soon become enemies, and Allied aims were reappraised and reinterpreted in the light of the new political climate. U.S. policy in regard to the Gold Pot would become inexorably influenced by geopolitical considerations. Soviet forces occupied most of eastern Europe and half of Germany and had their own plans for reparations, which basically involved stripping all occupied countries of the whole of their industrial infrastructure and hauling it away to the Soviet Union. At the Potsdam Conference in July 1945, President Harry Truman, British Prime Minister Clement Atlee and Soviet leader Joseph Stalin agreed that the reparations programmes for the Soviet Union and the other Allies would be kept separate. Essentially, the Soviets were given a free hand to extract reparations from the part of Europe it dominated, while the Western powers were to deal with reparations from their own occupation zones and take responsibility for all German external assets in the neutral nations. They reached agreement on a common policy for the disposition of the monetary gold found in Germany, as well as the gold Germany had sold abroad to finance its war machine. They adopted an American proposal to establish a Gold Pot into which the Allies would collect all the looted monetary gold from Germany and from the neutrals and distribute the resulting amount to the former occupied nations from whose central banks it had been looted.

Stalin had initially claimed a third of all gold found at Merkers but seemed to lose interest when it was revealed that most of it was looted gold. He surprised everyone by abandoning all claims to the gold found by his Western Allies saying, 'The Soviet Government makes no claims to gold captured by the Allied troops in Germany'.[2] As with much of Stalin's machinations, the reason for this in not clear. It is believed, however, that the Soviets were much more interested in stripping Germany of its industrial assets and waived its claims to the gold in order to claim a bigger share of those. It was not clear, either, how they viewed claims made by countries such as Austria and Hungary, which now found themselves in the Soviet zone of influence. At the Paris Reparations Conference in November and December 1945, the Allies further agreed to distribute looted monetary gold to countries from which it was looted 'without reservation, condition or encumbrance'[3] under the auspices of a Tripartite Gold Commission for the Restitution of monetary Gold (TGC), located in Brussels.

Britain and France were not convinced that the U.S. was being totally honest about the amount of gold it had recovered from Merkers, but talks began on formulating a policy to deal with it. There were three issues:

- Whether SS looted gold from the concentration camps, Melmer gold, should be included along with the looted monetary gold
- Whether the governments of Germany's Axis partners should have entitlement to a share
- Whether the looted gold that had been sold to Switzerland should be added to the pot.

It was agreed that no claims from Poland should be considered since that country was now under the control of the Soviet Union, who had renounced all claims to the Gold Pot. The general principle adopted was that:

> All the monetary gold found in Germany by the Allied Forces and [any monetary gold which may be recovered from a third country to which it was transferred from Germany]…shall be pooled for distribution as restitution among the countries participating in the pool in proportion to their respective losses of gold through looting or by wrongful removal to Germany [and] without prejudice to claims by way of reparation for unrestored gold, the portion of monetary gold thus accruing to each country participating in the pool shall be accepted by that country in full satisfaction of all claims against Germany for restitution of monetary gold.[4]

There followed the setting up of the Inter Allied Reparation Agency (IARA), which represented all claimants.

Restitution of gold to its original owners proved problematic in the case of gold that could be traced back and gold that had lost identification marks through re-smelting. It had been agreed that all claimants would receive the same proportion of their claim, but restitution of identifiable gold might result in some countries getting more than this share. Therefore, as a general principle, maritime law was applied. Simply put, this stated that, 'if A and B both ship cargo on a particular vessel and during a storm or fire A's cargo is jettisoned to save the ship, B's cargo, when it arrives safely in port, must bear a proportionate share of the loss suffered by A'. Both Britain and France began to suspect that the U.S. was not being entirely forthcoming about the details of the Merkers gold, particularly regarding identification marks, and this was exacerbated by Eisenhower's financial advisor, Colonel Bernstein, whose obdurate attitude, influenced by Washington, was found by the British to be 'most discourteous'.[5] However, Bernstein was soon to be relieved of his responsibilities as U.S. policy shifted in favour of greater leniency towards Germany in the face of the Soviet threat.

It is understandable that in the 'fog of war', recording of gold and precious metals finds were not rigorously documented and there was no clear understanding of the need to classify finds as monetary gold or Melmer gold. It was only later, when the scale of the systematic theft from private citizens and Holocaust victims became known, that administrators came across the problem of which gold should be repatriated to national banks and which should be distributed to survivors or their descendants. Evidence shows that some mixing occurred at the FED where 'American troops failed to follow orders from Washington to analyse chemically the assembled gold to determine its provenance'.[6]

In the light of the new relationship between the U.S. and the Soviet Union, a special judgement was made in the case of the gold taken by Patton's Third Army from the Hungarian train when it entered Spital am Pyhrn in August 1945. For one thing, the whole consignment was easily identifiable and secondly, the Soviets made it clear that the gold was desperately needed to rebuild the Hungarian economy. To avoid a confrontation with the Soviet Union, the Paris Conference chose to exempt the Hungarian gold from being swallowed up in the Gold Pot and justified the decision by saying it had not been seized by Patton's troops but merely delivered to them, presumably for safekeeping, and ironically to keep it out of the hands of the Soviets. The U.S., however, was loath to release it until both the Soviet and Hungarian governments made a great fuss and, eventually, 2,669 gold bars and 49 bags of gold were loaded onto a train pulled by an engine originally built by the Germans as a gift for Mussolini.

Almost before the TGC could start its work, its operations became mired in the growing tensions between the Western Allies and the Soviet Union that would eventually result in the Soviets blocking all roads, canals and railways into Berlin from the British, French and U.S. zones of occupation in Germany on 18 June 1948. The U.S. Department of Defence, in anticipation of the deepening hostilities, had, in January 1948, instructed the FED to transfer all the monetary gold held in Frankfurt to the vaults of the Bank of England and deposit it in two accounts in the name of His Majesty's Treasury. One account would hold gold bars and the other gold coins. Between 19 and 26 January, 820 boxes of gold coins were packed up in Frankfurt and over the following weeks, 732 boxes of gold bars were likewise boxed up. The first idea to transport all the gold in one shipment on a fast passenger ship without insurance cover was vetoed, and the contact was instead awarded to Pan American Airways, which was actually the highest bidder, charging $800 for each flight. Once agreement was reached on the documentation and security of the operation, flights began out of the Rhein-Main air base near Frankfurt and continued daily until the last flight was made on 28 July. It was during transfer of this last consignment that one gold bar went missing and was never found, despite extensive investigations. There is little evidence that the Bank of England ever received 'personal' gold.

Upon receipt of the gold, the Bank of England conducted a full inventory and came across a number of problems. Much of the Prussian minted gold was not 'good delivery' bars. For gold to be classified as 'good delivery' it required a minimum fineness of 99.5 per cent, with bars of specified dimensions weighing between 11 and 13 kg marked with a serial number, refiner's hallmark, fineness and year of manufacture. The Prussian gold was therefore melted down and reformed into 'good delivery'. Gold coins which were deemed not to be of numismatic value were also melted down and made into bars. Charges for storing the gold amounted to over half a million dollars in 1948 alone, and when challenged, the Bank of England was obliged to refund a significant portion of this to the TGC.

Ten nations made claims upon the TGC: Albania, Austria, Belgium, Czechoslovakia, Greece, Italy, Luxembourg, the Netherlands, Poland, and Yugoslavia. It was no surprise that claims against the monetary Gold Pot greatly exceeded the amount of monetary gold recovered, and so the TGC established a proportional redistribution system under which each country would receive approximately 65 per cent of its recognised claim. Most of the gold in the pot was redistributed to claimant countries in the 1940s and 1950s, but in 1997 a total of 5.6 metric tons of monetary gold remained in the TGC's accounts at the Federal Reserve Bank of New York and at the Bank of England.

The governments of France, Britain, and the U.S. formally dissolved the commission on 9 September 1998. A closing statement showed that a total of 336,446.97 kg of gold had been collected into the Gold Pot, but at the same time remained mindful of the possibility that additional Nazi-looted gold could yet come to light. The three governments envisaged that any such gold would be handled in a manner consistent with the Paris process.

In August 1945, the American government requested the right of ownership or control of all German assets in Switzerland. The authority over all enemy assets was to be held by the Allied Control Council as the de facto government of Germany. The Swiss Federal Council declined the request, which according to the council had no legal foundations. In October 1945, the Allied Control Council passed a regulation which established a German External Property Commission, which was granted all titles and rights to German property outside of Germany, owned by German citizens. However, the Swiss Federal Council further refused to recognise the rights of ownership or control of the Allies over German property in Switzerland. Early in 1946, the United States, Britain, and France invited Switzerland to send representatives to Washington to discuss the issues flowing from the Paris Reparations Conference. In spring 1945, an Allied delegation had demanded the freezing of German assets in Switzerland, the cessation of exports and of all gold trade with the Reich, and the termination of the transit between Germany and North Italy. On 8 March 1945, Switzerland largely agreed to the conditions stipulated by U.S. chief negotiator Lauchlin Currie, but this 'Currie Agreement' left many questions unresolved. Following on from the Paris Reparations Agreement, in the spring of 1946, representatives of the U.S., Britain and France, came together in Washington to meet those of the Swiss government in the first of a series of meetings with the states that had remained neutral in the war. The Swiss were looking to negotiate the release of frozen Swiss assets in the U.S. and bring an end to the Allied boycott of companies that had traded with the Axis powers during the war. The Allied delegation wanted discussions to cover reparations and restitution of looted property, as well as the elimination of the threat of a post-war Nazi resurgence financed by hidden assets that might facilitate espionage, sabotage, and propaganda. While elimination of German external assets could be taken for granted in Allied nations, those in neutral countries needed to be addressed. Essentially, discussion centred on ownership and of the right to recover looted property. It would be the enactment of Public Law No. 5 that became the foundation of the Allied claim to German private external assets in the neutral countries.

The Swiss negotiators, from the very start, adopted a confrontational approach and asserted that, 'On the matter of Swiss Sovereignty,

[they] will in no way be haggled with'.[7] With breath-taking contempt for proceedings, the head of the Swiss delegation, Walter Stucki, a 'competent, rather chilly, difficult person' who displayed 'an astonishing degree of arrogance and self-righteousness'[8] began by saying that Switzerland's war record during the war years was above reproach and that Switzerland had long opposed Nazism. He clearly saw his role as adversarial by seeking 'an agreement with the Allies... that reflects Swiss juridical principles and interests whilst also being apt to dispel the atmosphere of distrust vis-à-vis Switzerland still predominant among the Allies [and diminishing] the demands step by step, up to the demolishing of the basis of the allied claim'.[9] When the Allied side reminded Stucki that they had fought for years at immense cost in lives to free Europe from totalitarianism, he countered with the preposterous argument that by confronting Bolshevism, Hitler had pursued the same ends as the Allies and that the end justified the means. He made a speculative and provocative reference to the possible argument by Hitler that his cause was a 'good faith' attempt to achieve the benefits of a unified Europe and many influential Swiss bankers felt that banking transactions with Germany were within their clear rights as neutrals, if not indeed their duty as custodians of international monetary stability.[10] Stucki emphasised that traditional Swiss neutrality had permitted trade useful to the Allies as well as to the Germans. The Swiss delegates strongly objected to the ACC Law No. 5 and denied that it could be applied to the title of German assets outside Germany or give the Allies use of them or their proceeds for reparation purposes. Pursuing economic rather than moral arguments, they argued that Germany had incurred large commercial debts to Switzerland during the war, and that the clearing arrangements required German assets in Switzerland be applied to their satisfaction. The U.S. pressed for inclusion of the fate of the substantial assets placed in Swiss banks by persons who had perished, leaving no known heirs, and called for these to be used for the relief and resettlement of survivors or their successors. The Swiss argued that compliance on their part would violate the very foundations of the Swiss banking industry, which was based upon absolute secrecy and confidentiality.

Allied negotiators, led by Randolph Paul for the U.S., Mr F.W. McCombe for Britain, and M. Paul Charqueraud for France, claimed that German assets in Switzerland were theirs, 'not from a legal, but from a higher, moral point of view'. Switzerland, they said, had been saved by the Allied war effort and 'as a privileged state [was] obliged to make these resources available to [the Allies]'. The U.S. bluntly told Stucki that if he and the Swiss delegation did not change their negotiating stance, they might as well pack up and go home, something that Stucki considered to be 'a scandalous insolence'.[11] The Swiss intransigence was paying dividends for them, with the U.S. unable to break them down and negotiations were on the point of collapse when a weak compromise was reached whereby the U.S. was able to claim that they had achieved their objective without compelling the Swiss to violate their principles. The Swiss agreed that they would give 'sympathetic consideration' to the issue of heirless assets, which was fairly meaningless, but at least they acknowledged that the issue had substance and could no longer be denied. With that the Washington Accord was confirmed by an exchange of letters dated 25 May 1946. It was clearly a successful outcome for the Swiss since the Allies were to receive only 50 per cent of the German assets in Switzerland for the reparations. The other 50 per cent was to repay Swiss creditors for the supplies and services that they had furnished to the Germans, right up to the day of the final surrender. Furthermore, the rights conceded to Allied investigators gave them little scope for detailed examination of Swiss files and scant supervision of the process of identifying assets, which left the clear impression that the Swiss were owning up to a very much smaller quantity of gold the Allies knew had passed through Swiss banks. The Swiss had gambled that a stonewall approach would exhaust the U.S. desire for justice in a post-war world in which Swiss banking experience and facilities would be an essential component of economic recovery for a Europe bracing itself for confrontation with the Soviet Union.

The question arises as to why the Swiss were treated with such leniency when the Allies had such control. The Swiss bankers played a strong hand throughout the negotiations and gave ground only grudgingly on all issues. They had little choice given that there was considerable political opposition in the Swiss Parliament towards any concession offered. Obstacles of all description were placed before the small team of Allied investigators trying to implement the agreement. The U.S. negotiators had also come up against opposition from Britain and France in particular, who strongly argued for a swift return to normal relations with the Swiss. This, they said, was essential for implementation of plans not only in reconstruction but in financial and monetary stabilisation to oppose Soviet post-war domination of Europe.

Probably the most important issue coming out of the agreement was the commitment to identify, liquidate, and distribute the proceeds of German holdings in Switzerland. The Swiss skilfully drew out the arguments with prevarication and obfuscation, endlessly bringing up such issue as the rate of exchange to be used for each separate currency. A full and complete census of German-owned properties, they said, was nigh on impossible, which was disingenuous at best given the almost obsessive propensity for detailed record-keeping of both the Swiss and Germans. The Allied delegation were outflanked at every turn and eventually, exhausted, they agreed to a bulk settlement into the reparations account of an amount generally conceded to be grossly inadequate. By this time the Marshall Plan, providing financial aid for the economic recovery of Europe, had been adopted and the U.S., especially, was feverishly engaged in rebuilding, rather than eliminating, German economic and industrial power. The fear of German military resurgence was a fading memory. The U.S. was pouring resources into Germany in amounts that dwarfed possible reparation payments based on German external assets. As far as the issue of looted gold, the Washington Accord did reach an agreement but one that was known to be inadequate by all sides right from the start. Stucki's proposal for a Swiss payment of $58.1 million for what he called 'Switzerland's voluntary contribution to the reconstruction of Europe',[12] was accepted by the U.S. government even though it was only a quarter of all known gold that had been looted from Belgium alone and was well below their own estimations of $276 million overall.[13]

The Washington Accord was signed off on 25 May 1946 but came under severe criticism in the Swiss press and parliament. The national press was indignant and accused the U.S. of treating Switzerland as 'a defeated country'. In a session held in June 1946, Swiss politicians called the agreement 'shameful', 'disgraceful' and 'the most profound humiliation'. The bankers, however, realised that they had got off lightly and were eager to put the whole issue behind them, but they could not resist boasting later about how they had outsmarted the U.S. negotiators. In a letter dated 28 May 1948, Stucki wrote that the Allies 'could accuse us [with some justification] of having deceived them'. On 27 December that same year, another member of the Swiss team, Charles Bruggmann, wrote about Swiss 'deliberate non-cooperation [which had not aroused] disapprobation [and] we shall... be exceptionally happy to have acted as we did'.[14]

The way in which the Swiss authorities handled the implementation of the provisions of the agreement and the subsequent attitude they displayed towards dealing with its wartime economic conduct reopened a debate on the moral ambiguity of Swiss neutrality during the Second World War, and opened the door to Holocaust-related claims supported by powerful politicians within the U.S. Senate and the Clinton Administration in the 1990s. Holocaust-related claims came to the fore as a result of the dissolution of the Soviet Union, when new freedoms allowed people who had been trapped behind the Iron Curtain to make their voices heard in the West.

This resurrected the issues of dormant accounts which had been left at the disposal of Swiss banks and the subject of looted gold. Again, the concept of banking secrecy was fundamental to the understanding of the controversy. By agreeing to pay a lump sum of 250 million Swiss francs in gold to the Allied Reparations Fund whilst refusing to recognise any legal basis for the Allied claims, Switzerland deftly circumvented discussion of the validity of the whole concept of looted gold. Claims on dormant accounts were easily deflected by demanding that heirs to the assets produce a death certificate, the name of the depositor's bank, and a bank account number, three things that, under the circumstances, were nigh on impossible to find.

In October 1996, two class action suits were filed against the Swiss investment bank UBS and the U.S. announced its own investigation, led by Stewart Eizenstat and William Slany, into the matter of dormant accounts and Nazi gold. As a reaction to this, the Swiss parliament established an Independent Committee of Experts, under the chairmanship of Swiss professor and historian Jean François Bergier, with the aim of providing detailed findings on the involvement of the SNB and Swiss banks in international gold transactions, currency trade, flows of goods, looted goods and art dealings during the Second World War.

Chapter 15

THE TRIPARTITE GOLD COMMISSION (SEPTEMBER 1946)

'New alliances had forged new partnerships and the power to make the decisions on the restitution of millions of dollars of gold was far too powerful to ignore as a political and economic weapon.'[1]

At the end of the First World War, Germany had been obliged to make reparations in gold in a process that proved to be so complicated, little if any was ever actually paid. After the German defeat of 1945, the Allies decided that this time compensation would be in kind, which would simultaneously discharge its debts and eliminate German war industries to prevent a post-war resurgence of militarism in the country. Part III of the Paris Reparations Agreement required that, 'All the monetary gold found in Germany by the Allied Forces and [any monetary gold which may be recovered from a third country to which it had been transferred from Germany] shall be pooled for distribution as restitution among the [entitled] countries...in proportion to their respective losses of gold through looting or by wrongful removal to Germany.'[2] The Tripartite Commission for the Restitution of Monetary Gold, also known as the Tripartite Gold Commission, was established in September 1946 and proceeded to work with absolute secrecy without any sort of public scrutiny. Among the first things the commission did was to define monetary gold as 'all gold which, at the time of its looting or wrongful removal, was carried as part of the country's monetary reserve'. The Commission chose not to elaborate on the meaning of 'looting or wrongful removal'.

Three countries, France, Britain and the U.S., established the headquarters of the Tripartite Gold Commission on 27 September 1946 in the Residence Palace, 155 Rue de la Loi, Brussels and defined its mandate as to:

1. Receive detailed submissions supported by verifiable data from claimant governments for the right to participate in the division of recovered gold.
2. Scrutinise claims and determine the share of each claimant.
3. Announce, in due course, the total value of the pool of monetary gold.
4. Announce, in due course, the share of the pool available to each entitled claimant country.
5. Assist in the subsequent distribution of the gold.

It was clear that the commission was only interested in governmental claims and claims from private individuals. Commercial banks or companies, however well documented they may be, would not be considered and would be covered by other parts of the Paris Agreement. Neither was it the function of the commission to become involved in the recovery of any gold which would remain the responsibility of governments. Indeed, it would have been quite unable to attempt any such thing given that the commission rarely had more than a dozen full-time or part-time staff. The gold the commission would go on to distribute came initially from the Swiss in June 1947, but the bulk of it had been collected at the Frankfurt Exchange Depository, most of which had come from Merkers.

The first problem the commission came up against was that, despite the definition, countries argued about what was and what was not monetary gold. For instance, did it include gold that had been deposited in a country's central bank by individuals or organisations and then subsequently looted along with gold belonging to the state? The central banks of Austria, Belgium, Yugoslavia and the Netherlands had continued to function after German occupation and had collected gold from private individuals in accordance with new laws imposed by the occupation forces. This gold had then been transferred to the Reichsbank in Berlin and was now claimed as looted monetary gold by the four countries concerned. Furthermore, the fineness of looted gold had to be determined to assess its value and the exact monetary character (bars or coins). The exact factual circumstances of its looting also had to be provided. It was clearly a massive task for such a tiny organisation.

The whole issue of reparations was further complicated by geopolitical realignments that now had former enemies allied and former allies alienated. While France, Britain and the U.S. debated the protocols of any arrangements, the Cold War between East and West was brewing and 'The Allied decision to accept and ultimately to respond to the claimants is illustrative of their intent to interpret wartime declarations in support of post-war policies.'.[3] War reparations came to be used by the West as a tool of Cold War diplomacy and while claims of non-communist states were dealt with fairly quickly, the same could not be said for those from countries under the Soviet yoke. Of particular concern were claims by Austria and Italy, who had been on the German side during the war, and Poland, which was now under Soviet occupation. Eventually, Austria was granted a claim on all gold looted after 12 March 1938, whilst a similar agreement with Italy differed only in the date set at 3 September 1943. It was decided that Italy's claim should be recognised but that a portion should be withheld in anticipation of claims against Italy by France and Yugoslavia. Britain, in particular, was in no hurry to meet Italian claims in full until agreement had been finally reached on peace terms, but the U.S. vigorously opposed this strategy, perhaps because of fears of Italy falling into the communist camp. Assessment of Polish claims was delayed, causing the Poles to fear that by the time an agreement was reached, there would be no gold left at the commission. Clearly governments were having a huge influence upon the way the commission was operating. The Polish ambassador in Washington argued that 'an impression of political discrimination' had been created and demanded that distribution of the gold should be postponed until the claims of all countries concerned had been established. The U.S. responded coolly by referring all complaints to the Tripartite Gold Commission in Brussels.[4]

The Polish monetary gold, of course, had been sent to Canada from West Africa in 1944, and the bulk of Polish claims, which amounted to 138.7 tons, were in regard to victim gold looted by the Nazis which the Poles now claimed had been included in the Gold Pot and to which they had a legitimate claim. However, the Poles stubbornly refused to sign up to the protocol under its current form. As a result, two new categories of gold were added to the protocols of the commission. One covered gold that had been surrendered by individuals in occupied countries that was still in its original identifiable form. This was called 'restitutable gold', which should be returned to its rightful owners or heirs. In regard to the Polish claim, only 6.3 tons was considered to be in this category, the rest being outside the commission's remit. Under the Paris Agreement, gold of this type recovered in Germany was under the administration of the Intergovernmental Committee on Refugees and was to be used in the rehabilitation and resettlement of non-repatriable victims of Germany action. The other category was called 'German gold', which could not be categorised as either monetary gold or non-monetary gold under the declared definitions and should be returned to Germany to be used in support of the German economy under the supervision of the Allied authorities.

On 17 October 1947, the commission decided to make a preliminary distribution to alleviate distress and contribute towards the post-war economic recovery of Europe even before assembly of the Gold Pot had been completed. Initially, allocations were made in those cases where the commission felt the claims had met no legal impediments and were supported by full, verifiable data. At this time, the Allies were continuing their negotiations with neutral nations for the recovery of additional monetary gold for the Gold Pot and promised further allocations in due course. Security of all gold movements was made the responsibility of the FED. Personnel were responsible for handling, weighing, recording, and scaling at all stages of gold movements. The first consignment left Frankfurt on 19 November, when 88 tons was taken to the Bank of France in Paris on eighteen railroad cars. At the same time the commission set aside 26,187 kg for Austria and 3,805 kg for Italy, pending the completion of negotiations regarding their entry into the Gold Pot.

A claim by Albania was complicated by a counterclaim by Britain and Italy. Britain had sued Albania in the International Court of Justice for an amount exceeding that which Albania had claimed from the Gold Pot as compensation for damage caused to two of its ships in the Corfu Channel in 1946. Italy's claim was deemed spurious, while the British claim was side-lined as Albania was allocated 49,804.149 troy ounces on 29 October 1987 and a further 1,574.543 troy ounces on 13 July 1998, along with a sum of £2,106.24 from the Bank of England. In total, Albania received 0.47 per cent of the Gold Pot.[5]

Austria received a number of allocations over the years, including five in 1948. On 2 February it received 152, 630.007 troy ounces, 244,211.408 troy ounces on 7 March, 330,862,199 troy ounces on 17 August, 358,434.052 troy ounces on 14 October and finally 197,725.755 troy ounces four days later. It eventually received a final payment of 26,697.741 troy ounces and £23,000.32 on 25 June 1998. These payments, along with credits for gold that never left the Salzburg vaults, amounted to 1,640,079.339 troy ounces or 15.16 per cent of the Gold Pot.[6]

Belgium received 2,925,742 troy ounces as a first payment, a second of 803,805.64 troy ounces on 19 September 1954, another of 237,416.797 troy ounces on 1 July 1958 and a final distribution of 67,231.138 troy ounces on 30 April 1998, making a total of 4,169,686.986 troy ounces or 38.55 per cent of the Gold Pot.[7]

Belgium had bought gold in good faith from the Reichsbank in 1940, but later discovered that it had previously been looted by the Germans from Austria and Czechoslovakia. All three countries would submit claims for the same gold and in the end, an agreement on this issue was arrived at through governmental negotiations rather than through the commission.

The Czechs submitted their claim of 1,447,049.752 troy ounces, but there was serious disagreement over how much they would receive. The Gold Commission made an initial allocation of 1,224,626.017 troy ounces but Britain had outstanding claims against the Czechs and, after a first payment of 195,283.845 troy ounces on 17 May 1948, wanted those cleared up before agreeing to any further payments. Eventually, a further 591,573.190 troy ounces was agreed on in 1982, and then in 1998 payments to the Czech Republic and Slovakia brought the total to 797,342.610 troy ounces, or 7.37 per cent of the Gold Pot.[8]

France did not make any direct claims against the commission but received 463,644.348 troy ounces on 30 June 1948, drawn against Italy's allocation. This amounted to 4.29 per cent of the Gold Pot.[9]

Greece made a number of claims which were disputed by the commission because of the circumstances under which the gold had originally been acquired by Germany. Eventually, two small payments were agreed: one for 1,216.324 troy ounces and a second for 391.213 troy ounces on 29 June 1959. Later, on 26 June 1998, a final payment of 116.72 troy ounces brought the total up to 1,607.530, equating to 0.15 per cent of the Gold Pot.[10]

Whilst none of the negotiations over disbursement of the Gold Pot were easy, some were more difficult than others. Those with the Netherlands were complicated by Dutch claims that the Swiss had not made a sufficiently large contribution to the Pot. When a claim was duly submitted through the commission from the Netherlands against Switzerland for gold looted through Germany, the Allies suggested the claim should be made directly to the Swiss government, but the Swiss resolutely refused to discuss the issue. Two initial disbursements had been made for 1,153,906.527 troy ounces and 985,289.133 troy ounces, but a claim for the 307,714.795 troy ounces of gold that had gone down on Pilot Steamer No. 19 off Rotterdam on 11 May 1939 was rejected, since the commission considered this to have been salvaged by the

Germans rather than looted. Payment was made on the understanding that the Netherlands would give a written waiver of any further claims against the Allies, but the Dutch refused and retained a legal basis for future claims against the Swiss.[11]

Next came the issue of Italian gold that had been looted whilst the country was an ally of Germany and was then looted from them by Germany later in the war. France made a claim against Italy, although its justification for doing so was difficult to follow. However, the commission accepted the claim and France was allocated a share of the gold that had been awarded to Italy. Yugoslavia was also successful in claiming 269,841.177 troy ounces from the Italian allocation, which was paid on 23 September 1948. This left only 14,917.959 troy ounces for Italy out of its initial allocation, but a further two awards of 403,320.247 troy ounces on 7 July 1958 and 24,581.655 troy ounces on 25 June 1998 brought the total up to 442,820.446, which was 4.09 per cent of the Gold Pot.[12]

The claim from Luxembourg was fairly straightforward and it received an initial payment of 62,034.854 troy ounces, which was added to on 2 July 1958 by a further 24,113.056 troy ounces. A final allocation of 2,006.325 troy ounces on 26 June 1998 brought the total up to 138,941.668 troy ounces, or 1.28 per cent of the Gold Pot.[13]

By April 1948, however, none of the claims made by Poland, Czechoslovakia, Albania, Danzig or Yugoslavia, all of which were under Soviet control, had been met. Yugoslavia had entered a claim for 14,325.440 troy ounces of gold, part of a total of 68,208.375 extracted during the war by Germany from their Bor copper mines. They claimed a total of 394,326.470 troy ounces looted from the National Bank of the Kingdom of Yugoslavia and the National Bank of Serbia, some of which was looted by the Italians. The Yugoslavs were awarded part of Italy's share, as mentioned previously, plus another 6,919.813 troy ounces. Further allocations in 1950, 1958 and 1998 brought the total to 665,153.706 troy ounces, which was 6.15 per cent of the Gold Pot.[14]

Poland was not considered for an early interim payment because most of its gold had been whisked away to safety before the German invasion. In hindsight, it seems to have been a gross act of folly that the Belgians and French had not taken similar precautions. A claim submitted by the Free City of Danzig for 4.7 tons was upheld, but the commissioners had no intention of handing it over until the status of Danzig under communist control was clarified. It was only in 1976 that, since no other claimant had come forward, the Danzig gold was handed over to the Polish government in two lots of 50,237.827 and 29,327.197 troy ounces. In June 1998, Poland was granted a further

1,233.530 troy ounces, which made their total allocation to be 0.75 per cent of the Gold Pot.[15]

The Tripartite Gold Commission was wound up on 9 September 1998 with the following statement:

1. The Governments of France, the United Kingdom, and the United States today announce the closure of the Tripartite Commission for the Restitution of Monetary Gold. Consistent with the Agreement's goal of arranging "an equitable procedure for the restitution of monetary gold" which would be pooled and distributed among participants in proportion to their losses, the three Governments charged the Commission with receiving claims for looted monetary gold, adjudicating those claims, and making distributions from the monetary gold pool assembled by the Governments.
2. The Commission received claims from Albania, Austria, Belgium, Czechoslovakia, Greece, Italy, Luxembourg, the Netherlands, Poland and Yugoslavia. Following extensive deliberations conducted in accordance with its Terms of Reference, the Commission established as valid claims amounting to 16,527,422.101 troy ounces/514,060.2909 kgs of gold. In reaching its determinations, the Commission treated its adjudicatory responsibilities with the utmost care and diligence, and each claim received the Commission's close and deliberate attention. In accordance with the Commission's Terms of Reference, the costs of running the Tripartite Commission were deducted from the Gold Pool. The total gold deducted for this purpose was 43,880.424 troy ounces/1,364.8337 kgs, some 0.406% of the gold pool.
3. With one exception, all distributions from the gold pool have now been concluded and waivers of claims have been received from each of the recipient countries. A small remaining share of gold and currency allocated to the successor states of the former Yugoslavia has not yet been distributed, but will be held by the three Governments pending agreement among those successor states on its disposition. The Commission has delivered a final report on its work to the three Governments, which have in turn arranged for its delivery to each of the parties to the Paris Agreement. Accordingly, the Commission's work is now completed, and its archives have been transferred to Paris, and will be made available to the public.
4. The Tripartite Commission was able to meet about 64% of the validated claims on the gold pool. The three Governments had assembled the gold pool from various sources found on territories previously under the control of Nazi Germany and from certain

THE TRIPARTITE GOLD COMMISSION (SEPTEMBER 1946)

third countries to which gold had been transferred from Germany. Through these combined efforts, the Governments were able to assemble a monetary gold pool amounting to 10,817,021.139 ounces / 336,446.97 kgs.

5. In the view of the three Governments, it is appropriate under the circumstances that prevail today–over 50 years after the conclusion of the Paris Agreement–to consider the process of collecting gold for the gold pool complete. At the same time, the three Governments remain mindful of the possibility that additional Nazi-looted gold could yet come to light. The three Governments envisage that any such gold would be handled in a manner consistent with the Paris process.[16]

Chapter 16

ALLIED NEGOTIATIONS WITH NEUTRAL COUNTRIES

'One would assume that with the war over the victorious Allies would have little real difficulty in persuading neutrals to return the gold in question, but it was not to prove so easy for new alliances were being forged as war gave way to cold war.'[1]

Sweden

As early as 1944, the Allies had begun to draw Sweden into the Safehaven Programme. The Swedish Parliament (Riksdag) accepted some responsibility for post-war European recovery and voiced its support for the programme. In February 1945 it passed a series of laws to restrict the sale of German property, including German subsidiaries, and began a census of its gold and foreign exchange holdings to determine how much might be linked to German investors. Allied estimates of looted gold sold to Sweden by Germany ranged between $18.5 million and $22.7 million. In March 1946, British, French, and U.S. officials met to discuss Swedish gold transactions during the war and concluded that the Swedish gold reserves had increased, but they were unable to determine if this was due to looted gold. In at least one instance, the Germans had attempted to sell gold looted from Belgium to Sweden, but the Swedes had apparently refused to buy it.

Talks became stalled when Sweden refused to agree that the Allies had the right to claim or dispose of German assets and property outside Germany, and the Allies could not agree to the use of economic sanctions against Sweden to bring pressure to bear on them to negotiate. Appealing to the need for relief to relieve the desperate plight of a devastated Europe, the Allies persuaded Sweden to distribute more than $66 million in liquidated German assets as reparations, including a special $36 million fund at the Riksbank to forestall disease and unrest in Germany and to finance purchases essential for the German economy.

It also agreed to pay 7,155.32664 kg of fine gold to make up for the amount of Belgian monetary gold sold to Sweden during the war. Allied-Swedish negotiations regarding 638 bars of Dutch gold, however, could not be resolved, with the Swedish negotiators arguing that the gold had been acquired before the January 1943 London Declaration on looted gold. Eventually, in April 1955, the Dutch claim was proved conclusive, and Sweden transferred about $6.8 million in gold to the TGC (Tripartite Gold Commission).[2]

Portugal

From 1945 onwards, the Portuguese had shown little flexibility on the issue of looted gold, claiming that it was not their responsibility to return the gold they had exchanged with Germany during the war for tangible assets. On one notable occasion, officials at the Bank of Portugal tried to deny that '[any] gold whatsoever was ever shipped from Germany to Portugal between April 1938 and May 1945'.[3] Negotiations with Portugal for the restoration of looted gold and the disposition of German external assets began in September 1946 and eventually stretched into the late 1950s. The talks were held away from Washington and by the late 1940s were conducted on the Allied side by diplomatic representatives assigned to the embassies in Lisbon. Allied investigators estimated that there were $36.8 million in German assets in Portugal at the war's end, although this figure was considered tentative. They demanded the assets be liquidated and the proceeds delivered to them as reparations to help war refugees and rebuild Europe. In February 1947 the two sides eventually agreed on a division of the proceeds from liquidation, giving the first $4 million to the International Refugee Organization, $9.2 million to Portugal for its own wartime claims against Germany, and the remainder to the Allies as reparations. However, Portugal refused to implement the plan until the two sides could reach agreement on the restitution of looted gold. The plan's terms, however, would become the basis for all subsequent negotiations.

Based on Allied intelligence, it was believed that Portugal had received a total of 123,827 kg of gold from the Swiss National Bank, 20,117 kg of which was definitely thought to have been looted Belgian gold from the Reichsbank's deposit at the SNB. Of the rest, approximately 70,000 kg was suspected of being looted. The Allies therefore demanded the full 20,117 kg of looted Belgian gold, as well as the probably looted gold. As a first instalment, the Allies proposed that the Portuguese turn over 44,864 kg of gold they claimed was the amount the Portuguese had acquired from Germany after 1942, when it had become common knowledge throughout the world that Germany had expended its own gold reserves and was relying on looted gold. The Portuguese contested this assertion and claimed they had purchased all their gold in 'good faith', and it was no concern of theirs whether it had previously been looted or not. If they were to subsequently discover that they had, in fact, taken looted gold, they agreed they would hand it over to the Allies, but only after being compensated from any liquidated German assets. The Allies rejected this proposal, and a joint investigative Subcommittee on Gold was set up to review the Portuguese holdings and records at the Bank of Portugal.[4]

This committee issued a 187-page report on the amount of gold acquired by the Portuguese from the Germans between 1 January 1939 and 31 October 1945. The report included detailed evidence from captured German Reichsbank records showing where gold had been looted from and how it was re-smelted.

According to this report, the Portuguese had acquired 3,859 bars of gold (about 46 tons) but the Portuguese challenged this saying that only 2,246 bars met all the criteria of the Allies' evidence, 1,380 bars met most but not all the criteria, and 233 bars met none of the criteria. The Portuguese would only verbally confirm that the Bank of Portugal had in its possession bars bearing the identifying information provided by the Allies but refused to discuss the issue of whether or not the gold had been looted.

In 1949 the Portuguese did agree to begin liquidating German assets and keep the proceeds in a blocked account while the gold negotiations dragged into the 1950s and were soon complicated by the desire of the U.S. to make use of the Lagens air base on the Portuguese Azores islands, as Portugal effectively prepared for membership of NATO. The negotiations were further affected by the Allies' efforts to integrate West Germany into the Western alliance, which raised difficult issues over how Germany would honour reparations commitments made by the Allies after the war and handle Portuguese claims for wartime damages. Consequently, by July 1951, the State Department recommended accepting a Portuguese offer from July 1948 to turn over to the Tripartite Gold Commission 3.9 tons of Dutch gold for which Portugal would be fully reimbursed out of the proceeds of liquidation.

Intermittent negotiations continued for several years as Portugal demanded that West Germany be brought into the negotiations. In the interim, the United States, Britain, and France fulfilled Portugal's contribution to the $25 million Reparations Fund out of their portion of Switzerland's payments in implementation of its agreement with the Allies. Finally, in October 1958 the United States, Britain, France, Portugal, and West Germany reached an agreement, and in December 1959 Portugal delivered $552,000 to the Allies and 3.998 tons of gold to the Tripartite Gold Commission. In addition, Germany paid Portugal about $13.7 million to reimburse it for the gold and to cover its wartime damage claims, for which Germany received still-unliquidated German assets in Portugal.[5]

Spain

The Spanish economy was in a disastrous state after the Spanish Civil War, when the whole of its gold reserves had been evacuated by the Republican government to the Soviet Union, ostensibly for safekeeping. Yet the gold had been systematically swallowed up in hugely inflated charges for Soviet war matériel sent to the country between 1936 and 1939. On the other side, Franco's Nationalists, who prevailed in the conflict, had amassed some $212 million of debt to Germany for its military aid.

During the Second World War, Spain had pursued an active trading programme with the Nazis in goods and raw materials and Germany had invested heavily in the country. To prevent the dissipation of German assets, the Allies began negotiations with Madrid in April 1945 requesting Spanish adherence to Bretton Woods Resolution VI, intended to block Germany from transferring assets to Switzerland and other neutral nations, and the Gold Declaration of 22 February 1944. In particular they requested that Spain announce publicly its intention to adhere fully to the terms of the above agreements; immediately freeze all assets of persons of Axis or Axis-controlled countries; immobilise and facilitate the return of any looted assets; conduct a detailed census of all assets; provide the United Nations with full information concerning all persons in Spain with the nationality of Axis or Axis-controlled countries and all nationals who entered Spain since 1 January 1939; and establish effective controls with respect to any transactions with the Axis or Axis-controlled countries.[6] The Allied-Spanish negotiations were more intermittent and lengthier than the Allied-Swiss and Allied-Swedish negotiations which had preceded them. Spain proved to be every bit as obstructive to the Safehaven investigations as the other countries involved. Initially, Allied negotiators reported that Spanish implementation of the Decree Law of 6 October 1944, which regulated any and all transfers abroad of goods and assets from Belgium, had 'not been altogether satisfactory and the census has proved to be a complete farce'.[7] Nevertheless, having made a point and slowed down any momentum against them, in October 1946, Spain agreed to a much-reduced commitment by conceding to turn over to the Allies an estimated $25 million in official and semi-official German assets. The U.S. was singularly unimpressed and officially charged Spain with failure to implement Bretton Woods Resolution VI and the Gold Declaration and continued to block Spanish assets in the United States as a result.

The Allies also demanded detailed information on Spain's gold holdings, but Spain argued that such information was normally treated as confidential and would respond positively only if it was assured of Allied help in locating Spanish gold possibly looted by Germany after the Spanish Civil War, even though the whole of the Spanish gold reserves had been purloined by the Soviet Union in 1936. Some progress was made when, after two years of stalling and excuses, Spain finally provided records of its gold holdings from the Foreign Exchange Institute. These were thought to be riddled with discrepancies, but eventually a figure of 26.8 tons of fine gold was agreed as the amount traded through the SNB, the Bank of Portugal, and Banco Aleman Trans-Atlantico. The two sides agreed that Spain would return 101.6 kg of looted Dutch gold the Allies had identified at the Spanish Foreign Exchange Institute as having been bought directly from the Banco Aleman Trans-Atlantico. To satisfy Spanish pride, however, the Allies had to publicly acknowledge that Spain had not been aware at the time it acquired the gold that it had been looted, even though they knew that to be untrue.

In January 1948, negotiators agreed to deal with the issues of assets and gold separately when Spain reported that it had uncovered only 'very insignificant quantities [of looted gold]' and that therefore 'nothing practical would be lost if the [issue of looted property] was eliminated' from negotiations. Spain considered it an insult that they should be forced into an agreement over the gold issue when they were quite willing to return all looted property found in Spain voluntarily. The U.S. had a strong desire to clear the matter up so that the Spanish economy could be revived, and U.S. investors could extend what it called very substantial credits to Spanish industry. There was also the question of the feasibility of equipping three airfields in Spain to handle heavy bombers in emergency situations, but the strong anti-Franco sentiment in the U.S. convinced them that it was unwise to make any such an arrangement, even in secret. Instead, they looked forward to a resolution of the gold issue which might allow a privately financed civil aviation programme to make the necessary investment without political risk.

The Allied-Spanish negotiations had been fraught because they coincided with Allied efforts to ostracise the Franco regime and allow the Spanish people to freely choose a new government. By 1948, however, the U.S. had concluded that these attempts at isolating Spain were counterproductive and were detrimental to the Spanish economy. As a result, with the signing of the May 1948 agreements, the United States released over $64 million of Spanish assets frozen since the war and informed Spain that it would allow it to use its remaining gold as collateral for private loans. It was not lost on the Western Allies that, at a time when international relations were becoming ever more polarised between East and West that 'the primary objective of the U.S. policy towards Spain…is the reintegration of Spain politically, economically and militarily into the western European community of nations.'[8]

A final agreement on looted gold was reached on 10 March 1948 whereby Spain agreed to turn over 101.6 kg of fine gold identified as looted from the Netherlands and any other looted gold identified before 30 April 1949. In exchange, it reiterated its demands that the Allies agree that Spain had not been aware the gold had been looted. On 3 November 1948, the gold was deposited in the Foreign Exchange Institute, freeing Spain from the restrictions imposed by the Gold Declaration of February 1944.[9]

In 1950 the Federal Reserve Bank of New York held $50 million worth of gold, part of which was looted gold Spain had purchased from Switzerland and Portugal during the war, as collateral for loans by Chase National Bank of New York and National City Bank to the Spanish Foreign Exchange Institute. Both the State Department and the U.S. Treasury Department justified this by ruling that the gold was considered tainted only in the hands of the first purchaser. At the request of Citibank, as the National City Bank had been renamed, the looted gold Spain used to collateralise its loan was re-smelted into good delivery bars by the U.S. Assay Office. In 1951 Spain collateralised a $10 million extension of one of the loans using gold, including $2.6 million in looted gold, that it had bought directly from the German account at the SNB and had never revealed to the Allies. Both Treasury and State allowed the Federal Reserve to accept the looted bars, arguing that since Spain had negotiated the May 1948 Allied-Spanish accord on looted gold in good faith, they would not consider them looted.

Turkey

Turkey had been a neutral country up until February 1945, but joined the Allies for the last three months of the war. The Allies had accumulated evidence that the Axis countries had hidden assets in

Turkey during the war and used it as a centre of espionage. The U.S. also believed that the Nazi Ambassador to Turkey, Franz von Papen, had secreted gold in Turkey at the end of his tenure. The U.S. began pressing Turkey to implement Safehaven controls in 1944 and sent diplomatic notes to Turkey, warning that under the February 1944 Gold Declaration and Bretton Woods Resolution VI, it should neither acquire nor store any additional German gold and should preserve German assets for disposition in accordance with Allied policy. The Turks ignored this request. After several months of negotiations and revisions, the Allies presented their draft Safehaven accord to Ankara and six months later, Turkey issued its official response. While claiming it had already taken necessary measures to protect German assets and was happy to cooperate further, echoing the arguments put forward by other countries, Turkey demanded that it receive most of the proceeds from the liquidation of the assets and retain full sovereignty over the enforcement and control of these assets.

On 2 June 1947, the Turks agreed that they would adhere to the January 1943 Declaration, the February 1944 Gold Declaration, and Bretton Woods Resolution VI but maintained that because they had joined the Allies in the last months of the war, they were not bound by the Paris Reparations Agreement and so could retain the liquidated German assets. Allied investigators claimed that Turkey had purchased at least 3,047 kg of looted Belgian gold from Switzerland, but Turkey argued that it had purchased the gold in good faith, with no indication that it had been looted and was therefore not obligated to return it. On 12 August 1947, the Allies asked Turkey to return the property of Germany's victims, deliver to the Allies all monetary gold proven to have been looted by the Germans, place controls on German assets, and begin liquidating these assets. In January 1948, the Allies demanded the Turks hand over 249 bars of looted Belgian gold and investigate the origins of 32,000 gold coins and 243 kg of gold ingots believed to have been looted by the Germans. The Turks stalled claiming they were awaiting passage of a bill in their National Assembly, which they had submitted in November 1949, granting them the authority to negotiate a Safehaven agreement.[10]

The inevitable compromise loomed. By the spring of 1951 the Allies had agreed to relinquish their claims to German assets in Turkey in return for settlement of the gold issue. On 21 May 1952, the Allied governments transmitted a note to the Turkish Foreign Ministry in which it agreed to settle the gold issue for $1 million. In return the Allies would relinquish their claim to German assets in Turkey, remove Turkey from AHC Law 63, and consider justified Turkey's recompense to itself for the proceeds from liquidation of German assets. The whole negotiating process ground down to a halt and ultimately Turkey never turned over any monetary gold to the Tripartite Gold Commission.

Argentina

Despite the U.S. State Department's claim that Argentina had failed to control the transfer of German funds from Europe, negotiations on German external assets were never pursued with the Argentine government. Argentina had delayed adhering to the Gold Declaration until March 1945, which suggested that it might have acquired looted gold from either Germany or the European neutral countries. By the end of 1946, there was little hope the country could be brought into the Safehaven Programme and there was no expectation of the Argentine government coming forward with information about its gold acquisitions.

In May 1947 Argentina announced its intention to ship about $170 million in gold to the Federal Reserve Bank of New York, ostensibly to sell it to the United States. U.S. Treasury officials were concerned that this gold may have been German looted gold and insisted that it could not purchase Argentine gold without U.S. assay marks until it had verified that it was not looted, but some sections of the State Department believed that Argentina's acceptance of the Gold Declaration in 1945 should be sufficient to sanction the gold sale. The Treasury continued to insist that Argentina declare its wartime gold acquisitions at an interdepartmental meeting on looted gold on 3 October 1947, but Argentina gave only verbal assurances that it had not acquired gold from Axis or neutral countries and the gold complied with the Gold Declaration. On 11 October 1947, the Treasury Department gave up and weaselled out of the dilemma and concluded, based upon the reports from the embassy in Buenos Aires on its discussions with the Argentine Central Bank officials, that Argentina had not acquired any gold that had been looted by Germany and cleared the sale of the Argentine gold through the Federal Reserve.[11]

Chapter 17

RATLINES

'The Jews were said to have formed hit squads, and the Soviets set up military tribunals to eliminate Nazi perpetrators in occupied zones. The Poles wanted justice, and the Americans established themselves in Gmunden where the U.S. Army Intelligence Corps was leading the search for Nazi criminals.'[1]

Ratlines were a system of escape routes for Nazis and other fascist war criminals fleeing Europe after the German surrender. There were two distinct routes: one through Spain and the other through Italy, but both led to countries in South America. While a number of prominent Nazis were arrested and put on trial at Nuremberg, focus on those who remained at large became blurred as Cold War paranoia began to dominate the European political agenda. In this way, many Nazi war criminals were able to avoid detection for years, especially in the region of South Tyrol, where German, Austrian and Italian borders met in the high Alpine mountains. Here was a predominantly German-speaking population that had once been part of the Austro-Hungarian Empire and was annexed by Italy in 1922. Their new political masters did not endear themselves to the population, and strong pro-German and then pro-Nazi sympathies developed as a result. South Tyrolians agitated for incorporation into the Reich, but Hitler would not support it for fear of antagonising Mussolini, whom he privately despised but who he needed as a political ally in the 1930s.

In 1945, as the Allied forces withdrew, the territorial status of South Tyrol was unclear, but by then the province had become a bolthole for thousands of Nazi fugitives and their families. For months before the end of the war, the area had been seen by the Nazis as a place where they could make a last stand and hope to survive as the Western Allies faced up to the Soviets in an uneasy stand-off that, right from the moment of German surrender, deteriorated inexorably into the Cold War. Many had moved their families into the area towards the end of the war and it was not difficult to join them and hide out after May 1945. It should be noted that apart from a few high-ranking Nazis who had been in positions where they could get hold of and move significant quantities of currencies and valuables, the majority of fugitives had little money and had to rely on the generosity of the indigenous population for support. Meran (Merano) became the centre of refugee activity where Nazis found generous and cordial hospitality. The town, undamaged by the war, was on the Innsbruck-Brenner Pass escape route from southern Germany through to Genoa, and was an ideal place for escaping Nazis to stop and make the necessary arrangements for passage through Italy to their final destination of South America. It also had the advantage of a number of military hospitals.

Once ensconced in South Tyrol in relative safety, the fugitives could remain there under adopted identities, but if they had ambitions to emigrate, they would require documentation that would pass muster across customs barriers. The chaos that reigned in Europe after the war with its vast refugee populations and the many organisations working hard to alleviate their hardship saw many millions of displaced persons, many of whom were unable to provide proof of identity. One such organisation was the Zentralstelle für Deutsche in Italien (ZDI) (Central Office for Germans in Italy), run by Dr Willi Nix, who worked closely with Karl Heinemann, the deputy of Bishop Alois Hudal, who ran Santa Maria dell'Anima, the German Church in Rome. Hudal had been born in Graz in 1885 and had come to the attention of Pope Pius XI in 1923 on account of his study of the Serbo-Croat National Church. At this time, he became coadjutant of the Instituto Santa Maria dell'Anima. Later, in 1933, when the Nazis took control of the German state, he addressed a congregation of prominent Nazis in Rome when he welcomed the new Reich 'founded on loyalty to Christ and the Fatherland'.[2] The ZDI, meanwhile, was even used by the Allies to process truckloads of refugees 'of every race and religion' until the organisation's activities in issuing false papers could no longer be ignored and was closed down.[3] Among the Nazi war criminals known to have passed through Meran was Adolf Eichmann, later tried and hanged in Israel in 1962, whose new documents saw him become Ricardo Klement.

The biggest problem for fleeing Nazis was the acquisition of false identification papers of sufficiently high quality to allow them to obtain entry visas for South American countries. Normally identities would have to be confirmed after processing through the occupying forces in

Europe, but for ethnic Germans, the International Committee of the Red Cross (ICRC) were authorised to issue travel documents which were recognised by many countries as official identification papers. In 1947, however, the activities of the ICRC in the issuing of identity documents 'under the protection of the Vatican' were highlighted. These documents were secured 'without any identification on the part of the securer or any investigation [and] may be obtained under an alias or with false nationality'.[4] Proof of identity was an obvious problem for the ICRC and they were helped by the Pontificia Commissione Assistenza (PCA), the papal aid office in Rome, which issued identity cards to displaced and stateless persons with little or no examination of credentials. These papers did not have the authority of ICRC issue, but they did influence the ICRC when they came to process applications. The Croatian aid commission were particularly active in getting PCA support for their applications through the Ustaše colonel Father Dragonović, who noted the 'enormous importance of [the ICRC]'.[5]

By 1947, ICRC assistance to fleeing Nazis had become sufficiently well known for them to be called to account, but the pressure on the organisations still swamped by refugees allowed them to continue, albeit at a reduced level. When the ICRC delegations in Rome eventually stopped issuing travel papers on a large scale, the flow of Nazi refugees dried up, although by then most of the worst had left for foreign shores.

While the activities of the ICRC were of great significance in the facilitation of false documents, the U.S. Embassy in Rome reported on 15 May 1947 that 'The Vatican is, of course, the largest single organisation involved in the illegal movement of emigrants [who are] anti-communist and [of the catholic faith]'.[6] The Catholic Church had initially become involved in response to the humanitarian emergency created by the vast numbers of refugees in a small way, but the PCA expanded rapidly and was supported enthusiastically by Pope Pius XII, although it was run by Fernando Baldelli and Monsignor Giovanni Battista Montini.

During the war, the Catholic Church had been obsessed with supporting any and all forces opposing communism, which underpinned its moral justification for collaboration with the Nazis. This was reinforced by the Catholic Church's anti-Semitic prejudice, which had led it to adopt a sympathetic attitude towards National Socialism and allowed it to close its eyes to the excesses of the Nazis regime. Hudal, in particular, was a rabid anti-Semite and saw the possibility of a rapprochement between National Socialism and Christianity, and many of his actions should be viewed in this light. He had written a book in 1937 entitled *The Foundations of National Socialism* and had sent a copy to Hitler with the dedication 'to the Siegfried of German greatness'.[7] It was an open secret that at his Anima church at 20 Via della Pace in Rome, the headquarters of Hudal's Assistenza Austriaca organisation, 'four or five Nazi refugees were always hiding' with access to secret tunnels that took them into the church crypt.[8] Hudal furnished numerous Nazi refugees with ICRC papers that allowed them to stay in Italy legally while they negotiated passage to South America.

Chapter 18

THE ARGENTINE CONNECTION

'What better bargain could the Argentine Republic have made, than to bring these scientists and technicians here? All we paid for was their plane tickets, whereas Germany had invested millions of marks in their training.'

Juan Perón, President of Argentina

Deutsche Bank had been the lead bank in establishing economic authority over the banks and corporations of the occupied countries under a scheme called Neuordnung [New Order].[1] In Belgium, this meant establishing banking subsidiaries of the big German banks. These institutions also bought majority shareholdings of existing Belgian banks such as Banque Continental of Brussels and Antwerp; the Banque de l'Ouest and Banque Hanséatique of Brussels; and Dutch banks H. Albert de Bary & Co., Inc. In other acquisitions, the Berliner Handelsgesellschaft increased its holdings in the Hollandsche Koopmansbank, and the Bank der Deutschen Luftfahrt acquired all shares in N.V. Hollandsche Buitenland Bank. Meanwhile, several other German financial institutions secured majority shares in Rodius Koenig Handel Maatschappin, Bohmische Union Bank of Prague, Banca Commerciale Romana of Bucharest and Banque Générale de Luxembourg.[2] Once Martin Bormann had the German banks assume majority control of the fiscal apparatus of each overrun country and of the corporations of special worth to them, the German Four Year Plan was the next step in total administration,

I.G. Farben, the largest and most powerful chemical company in the world during the twelve years of the Third Reich, had connections with over 500 firms in 92 countries, including Standard Oil (New Jersey);

the Aluminum Company of America; E. I. du Pont de Nemours; Ethyl Export Corporation; Imperial Chemical Industries (Great Britain); the Dow Chemical Company; Rohm & Haas; Etablissements Kuhlmann (France); and the Mitsui interests of Japan. Hermann Schmitz, I.G. Farben's president, reported to Bormann that the 'measures of camouflage [of the true ownership of Farben assets]' had 'surpassed our expectations'. Other major German firms pursued the same complicated and devious course.[3]

The Samuel Klaus Mission to Spain in September 1944 looked into the possibility that Spanish banks were assisting the movement of German looted gold to Argentina. Klaus was special assistant to the General Counsel of the Treasury Department, attached to the U.S. Foreign Economic Administration, and he reported that Spain was 'the most discouraging as well as the most difficult' of all the neutral countries. Most worrying was the fact that U.S. Embassy officials had obstructed his investigations, even though Spain was 'beyond question the country in which the most damaging Safe Haven activities' were occurring.[4] Klaus noted that the governmental Instituto Española de Moneda Extranjera (Foreign Exchange Institute) coordinated all commercial transactions, allowing Germans to make personal deals with their friends and so bypass regulations. With this access, Klaus believed Germans could easily cloak their assets in Spanish enterprises, and he also believed that the Nazis were using Tangier as a conduit to move their assets from Spain and Portugal to Argentina, noting that many holding companies were being established there and that the Spanish government and citizens were buying local properties.[5] Where the German government preferred to transfer funds from Europe, it found no serious obstacle in any Argentine exchange control regulations, and that the availability of these funds made possible the subversive activities in which German organisations were known to have engaged, such as intervention in Argentine elections, press and propaganda subsidisation, and purchase for shipment of strategic materials for the German war machine.

In her book *The German Connection: The Laundering of Nazi Money in Argentina*, Gaby Weber looks at the links between the Peróns and two parallel but complementary money streams: the Nazi Party organisation and the companies who had no interest in financing a Nazi resurgence. Weber focuses largely on Mercedes-Benz. According to Argentine documents seized after the overthrow of Perón, about half of one large shipment of Mercedes sedans to Argentina went directly to the president's office. Perón appears to have kept four cars himself, but sent the others to judges and prosecutors, politicians, journalists and others whose support he was seeking. As for the Nazi connection, Weber claims that Adolf Eichmann was hired, initially under his own name but later under an alias, at the Mercedes-Benz plant in the suburbs of the capital. It is suggested that he may have functioned as a sort of paymaster, financing the movement and flight to Argentina of other fugitive Nazis.

During the 1930s, the pro-Nazi military regime of President José Félix Uriburu and of his successor Agustín Pedro Justo had welcomed a growing Nazi presence in Argentina. Up until 1938, there was an official figure of 1,400 members of the NSDAP/AO (the German National Socialist Party/Foreign Organisation), based in Argentina, with 12,000 supporting members of the cover-up 'Unión Alemana de Gremios' (the German Union of Syndicates) and an additional 8,000 affiliated to other Nazi organisations. In 1938, Justo had been replaced by anti-Nazi President Roberto Ortiz, who established the 'Special Commission to Research Anti-Argentine Activities', principally to de-Nazify Argentina.

Argentina pursued a policy of neutrality during the Second World War, but the government became increasingly dominated during the war by pro-Axis leaders, particularly after the overthrow of civilian authority and the establishment of a military regime in June 1943. The Argentine government did not sever diplomatic and commercial relations with Nazi Germany until January 1944. Up until this time, Argentina ignored Allied entreaties to end all financial interaction, direct or indirect, with the Nazis, and the Allies became particularly concerned about the operation within Argentina of subsidiaries of Germany's leading firms, including I.G. Farben, Staudt and Co., and Siemens Schuckert. These firms maintained links with Germany throughout the war and supported major Nazi espionage operations in Latin America. On the other hand, Argentine exports to the U.S. and especially Britain, which had strong pre-war ties with the country and depended on Argentine beef to help feed its population, rose dramatically during the war.

The Allies found it difficult to extend the Safehaven Programme to Argentina because the U.S. had refused to recognise its government and withdrew its ambassador in June 1944. They pressurised other countries to do likewise and froze $400 million of Argentine gold stocks. Consequently, the government of President Edelmiro Julián Farrell instructed the Argentine Central Bank to withhold cooperation to U.S. investigators in locating German assets, which led the U.S. to suspect that Argentina had been a repository of German gold. The Act of Chapultepec of 1945 recognised the right of each republic of the Western Hemisphere, including the United States, to dispose of German property within its own respective jurisdiction and retain the proceeds, meaning the Allies could not lawfully lay claim to German assets in Argentina. Instead, the U.S. worked out a replacement programme under which Argentina would, like other American republics, eliminate Axis firms by liquidation, expropriation, and forced sale, but despite agreement that the proceeds from Argentina's Replacement Programme would be deposited in accounts intended to reimburse wartime losses, no negotiations regarding the distribution of the proceeds of liquidated assets were undertaken.

In February 1946 the United States published its Argentine Blue Book, in which it sought to provide evidence of the pro-Axis policies pursued by Argentine governments during the war, including systematic attempts to distribute or dissipate assets of German firms in Argentina and to demonstrate the continuing potential for Argentina to become a base for a resurgent Nazism. The U.S. press picked up on the story and ran with headlines such as '90,000 Nazis creating a Fourth Reich in Argentina', creating the impression of a movement that was preparing for 'future aggression against the United States'.[6] Even the CIA reported on 'evidence of intention to carry on Nazi activities [and] belief in Nazi resurgence'. However, by the end of 1946, U.S. relations with Argentina had begun to improve as the Cold War with the Soviet Union broke out. A final Safehaven report in May 1946 estimated German assets in Argentina at $200 million but concluded that Argentina had not become a haven for looted gold or assets. A U.S. government examination in 1997 of selected records released by the Argentine Central Bank found no evidence that any gold was acquired by the Argentine Central Bank from Europe between August 1942 and the end of the war, but the records also contain no information about the origin of any gold the bank received prior to August 1942. The U.S. was clearly anxious to put the issue behind them and look to building its future relationship with Argentina.

Juan Perón admitted that while he was President of Argentina, he had given refuge to several thousand Nazis for what he called humanitarian reasons and had allowed the entry of 5,000 Croats whom Tito had threatened with death. Shortly before the start of the Second World War, Perón had been in the Argentine military and had been sent to observe Italy's northern Alpine battalions on exercise. During this time, he had also been able to make a clandestine visit to a Wehrmacht battle camp near Tannenberg, where he was introduced to and acquired admiration for the ideas of National Socialism as practised by the Nazis. In 1943, the U.S. had become frustrated by Argentina's reluctance to openly support the Allied cause against Germany and turned instead to Brazil, who received substantial U.S. funding for armaments. When President Ramirez of Argentina broke all ties with the Axis, it was Perón who organised the coup that brought General Farrell to power and gave Perón the War Ministry on 24 February 1944.

Soon afterwards, on 8 July 1944, Perón became de facto Vice President of Argentina, but after the war ended, the U.S. conducted an anti-Perón campaign in the press calling him and his new wife, Eva, 'Nazis'. Despite, or because of, the U.S. State Department's Blue Book, published in February 1946, suggesting that Nazis had been infiltrated into the executive chambers of the Argentine military government, on 4 June 1946 Perón won an election that elevated him to the presidency.

His pro-Nazi sympathies came to the fore and Argentinian policy turned openly towards encouraging German scientists and engineers to emigrate from a war-shattered Germany to build a new modern economy in Argentina. This became easier after 1946. Of course, most of those Germans who were welcomed had been Nazis and many were wanted war criminals on the run from justice. Perón did not want to invite international approbation for this policy and so exploited the chaotic refugee situation in Europe to bring these people into Argentina through links in Italy, where he set up recruitment agencies to make contact with what were now the second tier of German experts, after the U.S., Britain and the Soviet Union had creamed off the elite. They still had to compete with other states such as Syria and Egypt, who were also actively trawling for the same specialists to boost their own economies. The Italian press reported 'an absolute stampede to the labour exchange of people wanting to emigrate [to Argentina]'. The Austrian newspaper *Wiener Zeitung* called Argentina 'an ideal country of emigration [promising] affluence for all'. It was not all that easy for most would-be migrants, though. Only in Italy, where Argentina had diplomatic links, were the circumstances conducive to processing the required paperwork and even here the number of applications meant that some had to wait months or years until their documentation was complete. One of Germany's elite fighter pilots, Adolf Galland, who became a personal friend of President Perón, wrote of a 'feeling...of being treated fairly [by] a nation that approached them sympathetically'.[7]

Most Argentine support for German immigrants was targeted at the few experts who were quickly integrated into industry. Companies such as Siemens, Krupp, Volkswagen, Bayer, and Badische Anilin- und Sodafabrik (BASF) and Mercedes Benz had well established subsidiaries. Others were left very much to their own devices, but many thrived, especially doctors who, after a period of adjustment, went on to enjoy luxurious lifestyles.

Heinz Schneppen points out that of the many German technicians, engineers, and natural scientists who immigrated to Argentina after the war, few had political motives. Among those with Nazi credentials, he also comments on the very small number of war criminals, as defined by the Allied Control Council Law No. 10 of December 1945, who sought refuge in Argentina. He concludes that, while one could certainly consider Argentina's behaviour careless and morally questionable, the scholarly evidence refutes the notion of any concerted and calculated effort on the part of Perón's regime to help Nazi war criminals flee Europe.

A story from Brazil is of interest in relation to Nazi gold in South America. In 1983, Albert Blume died and was buried in a poor man's grave, but he left behind a $4 million fortune in luxury watches, rings, gold bars and gold teeth. This caught the attention of Brazil's first commission to investigate Nazi war criminals who fled there with looted Jewish property. Investigations uncovered that Blume had been a pawnbroker. One theory is that he fled to Brazil to escape Nazi persecution of homosexuals and that the gold was merely collateral for loans. Another has him arriving in Brazil in 1938 to work for E. Schlemm & Company, a concern that acted as an agent for German companies trading in Brazil and to act as a conduit for stolen gold.

The Brazilian commission, with the help of the World Jewish Congress, identified fourteen dormant Nazi accounts worth $15 million in 1997 and tried to determine whether Blume's fortune came from victims of the Holocaust. Among Blume's papers were identity documents and Gestapo promotions belonging to a Colonel Walter Blume, commander of Unit 7-A of Einsatzgruppe B, who was sentenced at Nuremberg to hang for killing Jews in Eastern Europe. It is conjectured that Albert Blume had received money from a colleague in Germany, presumably his namesake, for which he would serve as guardian. Colonel Blume's 1948 death sentence was commuted in 1951 to twenty-five years and was reduced further by German judges in 1955. After release, he is believed to have gone to Buenos Aires.[8]

Chapter 19

MARTIN BORMANN: CASUALTY OR FUGITIVE?

'There was at least one man in the bunker who thought only of living—Martin Bormann.'

Hugh Trevor-Roper, Historian

By September 1944, Hitler's authority in the Nazi Party was not what it had been, and Martin Bormann was becoming the power in the land. Bormann had been a member of the Nazi Party since the early 1920s and in 1933 had become chief of staff to the Deputy Führer, Rudolf Hess. He was described as a short, squat man in a badly fitting civil servant's uniform with his briefcase under his arm, always working to advance his own interests. Even among so many ruthless men, he stood out by his brutality and coarseness. The historian Louis L. Snyder called him a classic manipulator, an anonymous power seeker who worked in secrecy and outmanoeuvred all his rivals to gain Hitler's approval.[1] Bormann really came to prominence after Rudolf Hess had made his bizarre flight into Allied captivity on 10 May 1941, when he became head of the Party Chancellery responsible for strengthening the party against both the leaders of the German armed forces and the SS, and, later in 1943, was appointed Secretary to the Führer.

Bormann used his authority to claim a share of the Melmer plunder and instructed Puhl to surrender a portion to him on the pretext that it was required to meet party expenses. By early 1944, Bormann had expanded this into an operation now worthy of a code name: Aktion Feuerland. Heavily armoured trucks would take the loot across Germany and France down to Cadiz on the Spanish coast, where General Wilhelm Faupel and Captain Dietrich Niebuhr supervised the loading onto U-boats bound for South America. On 18 April, a special investigator of the Argentine Navy's Intelligence service, Niceforo Alarcón, submitted a report entitled 'German Disembarkation at San Clemente del Tuyu' (CF-OP-2315 Coordinación Federal). This report named Rudolf Eugen Ludwig Freude, a lieutenant in the Argentine Naval Reserve, who had made 'extensive deposits in various banks' including Banco Alemán, Banco Alemán Transatlántico, Banco Germánico and Banco Tornquist in the name of Maria Eva Duarte Iburguren.[2] A rare financial document was discovered in the files of the Argentine secret police's Central de Inteligencia, showing a joint bank account shared by Bormann and Iburguren dating from 1941, in the Deutsche Bank of Buenos Aires.[3] Martin Bormann had bank accounts in many cities, including Berlin, Zurich, Buenos Aires and New York, when he served Hitler and Germany as Reichsleiter. He had sent diplomats General Wilhelm Faupel and Gottfried Sandstede to Buenos Aries as early as 1943 to arrange all the details of receipt and storage of the looted treasure with Lieutenant Freude. For his part, Freude cemented his relationship with Iburguren by lavishing expensive jewellery on her, much of it looted from Holocaust victims. Born into poverty, Iburguren had pursued a career as a stage, radio, and film actress and would later marry Juan Perón on 18 October 1945 and become known to the world as Evita.

Alarcón reported that one particular German U-boat had arrived at the secluded Samboronbón Bay, off Punta Norte, and delivered 'shipment No. 1744' containing an unspecified number of bags and crates. These were loaded onto trucks and taken to a ranch owned by a man called Lahousen on 28 March 1945. From there the shipment was taken to Buenos Aries, where it was placed in bank vaults. Throughout 1944 and early 1945, U-boats were said to arrive at six to eight weekly intervals.[4]

An Argentinian documentary released in 2004 claimed that many millions of pounds of Nazi gold was sent across the Atlantic to the coast of Patagonia by submarine in the last days of the Second World War. The researchers obtained 'great evidence from staff at the U-boat museum at Laboe on the Baltic near Kiel'.[5] The film's producer, Rodolfo "Rolo" Pereyra, accused Pope Pius XII of telling various senior clergy to collaborate with the organisers of the gold shipments, notably Bishop Hudal and Monsignor Krunoslav Draganović, the Croat who ran the San Girolamo Institute where Ante Pavelić hid for a while (see Chapter 6). British Intelligence files show that Draganović specialised in forging documents for fascist Croats, helping some 7,250 Ustaše on their way to Argentina in 1946-1948. The charge was $1,000 per person, or $1,400 for VIPs. When Draganović assisted Klaus Barbie by providing false documents in the name of Altmann, after receiving him from the hands of U.S. Intelligence agents at Genoa railway station, he shepherded him on to an Argentine ship in March 1951, telling him, 'We must preserve a sort of reserve off which we can feed in the future'. Antonio Caggiano, archbishop of the Argentine city of Rosario and later of Buenos Aires, was the link between the fleeing Nazis and Perón.[6]

By early 1945, Bormann was ensconced in the Führerbunker, behind the old Reich Chancellery at Wilhelmstrasse 77 in Berlin, with several other leading Nazis. By this time Hitler presented what was described as a hideous and pitiful spectacle: half-blind with his body bent, dragging his feet and unable to stand unaided, his left arm hanging limp and useless. He had become almost totally dependent on Bormann, who was at his elbow still madly wheeling and dealing in what was left of the Nazi power game, but the end was nigh. When Soviet forces broke into the outskirts of Berlin, Hitler refused to leave the bunker to attempt escape, fearful of being captured. He committed suicide on 30 April and Bormann assumed command as his nominated successor.

He assembled the staff and high party officials to tell them of their escape plan. They would move in groups through underground passages to the underground station at Wilhelmsplatz, then exit into the street outside the ruins of the Hotel Kaiserhof and then on to Friedrichstrasse station. They would then make their way over the Weidendamm Bridge over the Spree to vanish among the general population. Under constant Soviet bombardment, Bormann then discussed his own plans for escape with his close confidant, Heinrich Müller, the SS chief group leader and senior general of the Waffen SS. Müller worked out of Gestapo headquarters in the Kurfuerstenstrasse building, which had a radio transmitting room whose signal was powerful enough to reach Buenos Aires.

It is accepted that Bormann left the Führerbunker at 11pm on the night of 1 May as one of a small group, including Generalleutnant Johann (Hans) Rattenhuber and SS Obersturmbannführer Peter Högl, his deputy, all of whom made their way to the Weidendammer Bridge. Here they came up against a Soviet anti-tank barrier on the far side and had to wait for German tanks to smash a way through. Rattenhuber was hit by shrapnel and left behind. What happened next is shrouded in mystery and controversy. Some claim that Bormann was killed on the bridge, while a mass of contradictory testimony also asserts that he survived and went on to live for many years in Argentina.

Erich Kempka was Hitler's chauffeur and had left the bunker with Bormann. His version of the events on that night is that he had reached the Friedrichstrasse ahead of Bormann and had taken refuge in the Admirals Palast building some 200 feet from the Weidendammer Bridge. From here, he claims to have seen Bormann and Werner Naumann, Goebbels' deputy, walking by the side of a tank, which was hit by Soviet bazooka fire and blew up as it crossed the bridge. At Nuremberg, Kempka claimed that the explosion had such force that 'it was impossible for [Bormann] to survive', even though he had been blinded by the explosion and did not actually see Bormann die.[7] Kempka's testimony must be treated with caution. It was dark at the time and identification of anyone at that distance was nigh on impossible. What is certain is that Obersturmbannführer Högl was killed on the Weidendammer Bridge that night, but an officer of Hitler's bodyguard, a man called Harry Mengershausen, claims that Bormann was not killed in the explosion. He says that although Bormann was riding in a tank, it was not his tank which was blown up. Furthermore, former SS Major Joachim Tiburtius made a statement to the Swiss newspaper *Der Bund*, on 17 February 1953, to the effect that he had seen Bormann after the explosion at the Hotel Atlas, where he had changed into civilian clothes and together they had gone on to the Schiffbauerdamm and the Albrechtstrasse.

Arthur Axmann, the one-armed former Hitler Youth leader, told the eminent historian Hugh Trevor-Roper that he was part of a group, along with Günther Schwägermann and Jochen von Lang, who had left with Bormann. At Lehrter station, they split up with Axmann and followed German tanks under fire from Soviet anti-tank bazookas towards the Ziegelstrasse, when one of the tanks was hit and exploded. Among the injured were Bormann and Ludwig Stumpfegger, Hitler's surgeon. Both were thrown to the ground, said Axmann, but escaped serious injury.[8] Bormann and Stumpfegger then made their way east, said Axmann, along the Invalidenstrasse, in the direction of Stettiner station. Following them, Axmann claimed that he later came across both men who were, in his words, 'outstretched on their backs, moonlight on their faces, both dead'. He went on to say, however, that he did not go close up to the bodies because of incoming fire from Soviet forces. Interviewed many years later, Axmann, who was the only witness to Bormann's death, said, 'He looked dead to me, but I couldn't swear that he was really dead'.[9]

In August 1945, Stumpfegger's wife, Gertrude, received a letter from a man called Berndt, who was the postmaster at Lehrter station. In it he says, 'On May 8 this year a soldier was found by employees of the post office on the railroad bridge crossing Invalidenstrasse...a military pass in his pocket identified him as Ludwig Stumpfegger. Your husband was buried with other dead soldiers on the grounds of the Alpendorf at 63 Invalidenstrasse.'[10] There was no mention of Bormann being among 'the other dead soldiers' but, of course, it may be that Bormann was not carrying any identification papers.

Hugh Trevor-Roper interviewed all known surviving members of the group which had consisted of Bormann, Stumpfegger (Hitler's surgeon), Kempka (Hitler's driver), Beetz (Hitler's second pilot), Axmann (Hitler's Youth leader), Naumann (Goebbels' assistant), Schwägermann (Goebbels' adjutant), and Rach (Goebbels' driver). Trevor-Roper concluded that Bormann had certainly survived the tank explosion but had possibly, though by no means certainly, been killed later that night.[11] Trevor-Roper was to interview a source in West Germany in 1953 who claims to have seen Bormann on 2 May looking dishevelled and with superficial injuries to his foot being attended to in a German military first aid station at Konigswurst Erhausen.

What follows is an account by Ladislas Farago of how Bormann escaped from Berlin and ended up in Bolzano, Italy. Hesse's attorney, Dr Fritz Bauer, investigated the disappearance of Bormann and began by speaking to Heinrich Lienau, who claimed to have seen Bormann on a train heading for Flensburg on the German-Danish border. Denmark would have been of interest to Bormann because of two organisations working there who enabled Nazi fugitives to flee from justice, one of which was working under cover of the International Red Cross and arranging transit routes through Bavaria to Argentina. Bormann stayed in Schleswig-Holstein until October 1945 before receiving word that his wife was seriously ill with abdominal cancer and had been admitted to a hospital in northern Italy. He was smuggled south as part of a group of Austrian POWs who were being repatriated. In a cabin high in the snowy Resia Pass, Bormann was taken to a monastery and from there monks escorted him to Meran, where his wife was now close to death. There is no evidence that Bormann ever visited his wife who was, by then, in a coma. She died in March 1946. Eight of Bormann's ten children were then taken into the care of the Reverend Theodor Schmitz. Assuming the name of Luigi Boglioli, Bormann then went to Bolzano where he is believed to have lived for two years in a Franciscan monastery. While there he was reputedly recognised by a number of people, including one Frau Thalheimer, whose husband, a doctor, had treated Bormann in Munich. Trevor-Roper interviewed Frau Thalheimer and said, 'As a witness, she gave the impression of being competent, judicious, and reliable. Her story seemed to me plausible'.[12]

At the end of his investigations in 1965, Bauer said, 'Martin Bormann succeeded in escaping from the Reich Chancellery and for some time thereafter lived in Schleswig-Holstein. We believe that Bormann stayed for some time in the Danish royal castle at Graasten near Sönderborg, which had been an SS hospital during the war. The castle was run by a man called Heyde and was reputed to have become a hideout for a number of high-ranking Nazis.'[13]

When the Nuremberg War Trials convened, Bormann was indicted and tried in absentia. Since he could not be found, his indictment was broadcast through the printing of 200,000 copies of a document accusing him of crimes against the peace, war crimes and crimes against humanity. The notice was also broadcast four times each week on the radio in Berlin, Halberstadt and Mecklenburg. Bormann's defence council pleaded that the case against Bormann should be thrown out on the grounds that he was already dead. The judges, however, dismissed this saying that, 'there is no convincing evidence that Bormann is dead'.[14] On 1 October 1946, Bormann, a man the world presumed to be dead, was found guilty and sentenced to death by hanging.

Another version has Bormann being helped by the ODESSA organisation (Organisation der ehemaligen SS-Angehörigen). After the collapse of the Third Reich and the beginning of the Cold War, a whole series of networks was set up by governments, both in the East and the West, who had an interest in helping SS war criminals. One such network was investigated by an international commission of eminent historians appointed by the Argentinian Foreign Ministry in 1990 to study the influx of Nazi war criminals into the country during the late 1940s.[15]

The path to South America led over the Brenner Pass into the North Tyrol region, which had been annexed by the Third Reich after the surrender of Italy in 1943. After the war it had become a sort of 'no-man's-land', both territorially and politically, where large numbers of SS men and Nazi war criminals found refuge. In April 1945, Bormann's family had moved there from the Obersalzberg and holed up in the town of Meran, which became 'a sort of El Dorado of big and small fish' who found a generous and warm-hearted hospitality and reception.[16] Those who were fleeing were not just fugitive Nazis and war criminals, but also exiles from the eastern German regions, collaborators, Red Army deserters, ex-prisoners of war, slave labourers, displaced persons, soldiers, and survivors of extermination camps and concentration camps. Simon Wiesenthal, the Nazi-hunter, wrote that from time-to-time in Meran illegal Nazi transports and illegal Jewish transports converged to spend the night under the same roof. The Jews would be hidden on the second floor and instructed not to stir; and the Nazis on the ground floor were urgently warned not to let themselves be seen.[17]

After the war, the elusive SS ODESSA organisation is reputed to have secretly moved several thousand SS men, many of them war criminals, out of Germany via Munich and over the Alps to Genoa. The former West German diplomat Heinz Schneppen however, vehemently challenges the idea that ODESSA ever actually existed at all.[18] Political motives, ideological bias, and outright disinformation, he says, often masquerade as fact but are accompanied by a shortage of verifiable data. What Schneppen considers to be largely myth evolved out of what he calls a profound spiritual vacuum within German at the end of the war, when diehard Nazis still clung to a belief in a timeless, indestructible Germany of eternal 'blood and soil'. ODESSA, he believes, was no more than a conspiracy theory existing beyond the empiricism of causes and contexts. He does concede, however, that with all their irrationality, such myths often demonstrate plausibility by referring to particular facts and events, whose truth cannot be denied. Schneppen argues that all serious historical inquiry refutes the existence of any such organisation due to the lack of evidence. No leading Nazi escapees who wrote biographies after the war made any reference to ODESSA.

The ODESSA organisation was supposedly formed in the vicinity of Odessa in 1947 to provide a well-connected, smoothly functioning network in which all Nazi escapees could rely on a contact point every 25 miles over the so-called cloister route to Genoa and Rome, with the assistance of the Vatican and Italian authorities, and from there to Perón's Argentina. While it is not disputed that the ICRC and Catholic Church did assist escapees, Schneppen says in his book, *Odessa und das Vierte Reich: Mythen der Zeitgeschichte,* that this did not amount to a coordinated or systemic planned operation. ODESSA, he says, is bound up with the Maison Rouge meeting of 10 August 1944, the evidence for which, he says, simply does not exist.

According to Schneppen, the persistence of the ODESSA theory is due to a number of factors associated with the political motivations of the proponents. One such was Simon Wiesenthal, a survivor of the Nazi death camps and an individual who dedicated his entire life to documenting Nazi crimes and hunting down perpetrators. This made him all too willing to believe that Nazis were lurking in secret, planning a resurgence through the solidification of a Fourth Reich. Another was U.S. Treasury Secretary Henry Morgenthau, who pointed to the existence of ODESSA and the supposed ever-present danger of a Nazi resurgence in order to bolster his case that the Allies needed to deindustrialise Germany to avoid a resurgence of militarism. Left-wing groups in the Federal Republic and communist organisations in general propagated the myth to agitate against the rise of neo-Nazi movements in West Germany, and finally, the theory served as a pretext for the U.S. to conduct its interventionist policy throughout Latin America.

However, in his book, *The Real Odessa: Smuggling the Nazis to Perón's Argentina*, the Argentine writer Uki Goñi argues that ODESSA was bigger even that Wiesenthal believed it to be, but it is hard to see how Goñi's idea of a movement including Vatican institutions, Allied intelligence agencies and secret Argentine organisations that overlapped at strategic points with French-speaking war criminals, with Croatian Fascists and even with the SS, could have avoided leaving some evidence of its existence after all this time.[19] Gitta Sereny's book *Into That Darkness* was based on many hours of interviews with Franz Stangl the commandant of Treblinka concentration camp, who escaped to Argentina after the war and concluded that there was no centralised organisation that funded and provided structure for the escape routes.[20]

Whatever the truth about ODESSA, there were certainly groups organising escape routes for Nazi war criminals who were confident they could spirit Bormann out of Europe. Using what was nicknamed the Monastery Route, one such means was run by Roman Catholic priests, especially Franciscans, who helped to move fugitives from one monastery to the next. Franciscans, like several other Catholic organisations, operated with a high level of independence within the Catholic Church. The main transit point was a particular Franciscan monastery, Via Sicilia in Rome, and the most active priest was Bishop Hudal in Graz. Safe houses were established along the route and the travellers always arrived and departed on time according to a strict schedule. An underground network called 'Die Spinne' (the Spider) supplied false papers and passports, safe houses, and contacts. The burly Otto 'Scarface' Skorzeny, a man who had been described as 'Hitler's favourite commando', ran the Die Spinne escape organisation, along with Reinhard Gehlen, for SS members after the war while both were working for the CIA.

After the first Nuremberg Trial had ended in early 1946, Bormann was moved to a safe house near Domstedt where the U.S. Army's *Stars & Stripes* newspaper for Europe was published. The late editions left by trucks just after midnight to be distributed by morning to all U.S. Army bases. It was a simple matter for Heinrich Müller to arrange for Bormann to be a casual passenger aboard such a truck, with a German driver, which went to Munich where it stopped to let Bormann out. Once there, Bormann went to the house of his brother, Albert. In his book *Martin Bormann: Nazi in Exile*, the noted American journalist Paul Manning says that Bormann left Munich in a car supplied by a German mayor, who managed to acquire rationed petrol and drive into the Bavarian hills, after which Bormann and a companion continued on foot to avoid U.S. patrols and became just one of thousands of refugees and displaced persons swarming all over Germany. They crossed the River Inn and found themselves in the Alpine village of Nauders, where the Austrian, Swiss, and Italian frontiers meet. The next stage of the journey took them through Val d'Adige and down towards Lake Garda, where they rested in a local monastery for a few days before pushing on to another Franciscan monastery in Genoa.

In Argentina, Perón and his new wife Eva were plotting to take control of Bormann's treasure that was sitting in the Buenos Aries banks under Bormann and Iburugen's name. It was obviously necessary for Bormann to travel to Argentina for the banks to release it and so Señora Perón made a trip to Rome in July 1947, where she introduced Bormann to the Vatican's Secretariat of State for displaced persons, Giovanni Montini, who would later become Pope Paul VI in 1963, and an Argentinian priest called Father Silva, in Genoa. The results of that meeting were described in a report submitted to the Argentine Central Intelligence Bureau by Reverend Egidio Esparza, a political opponent of Juan Perón, who worked for the Catholic Intelligence Service. This report states that Father Silva was 'the link between' the Bishop of Genoa, Monsignor Guiseppe Siri, Señora Perón and Bormann, who was introduced by Señora Perón as Luigi Boglilio despite his heavily Germanified Italian accent. Siri's agreement to help Bormann may have been influenced by the presence of two Italian Generals, Graziani and Cassiani. Siri provided Bormann with a Vatican passport in the name of Juan Gomez, a Jesuit priest.[21]

According to Manning, from Genoa Bormann boarded a small steamer, which took him to Tarragona, just south of Barcelona, where he was met by two of Müller's SS men. They drove him along the coast to El Vendrell and then on a long overland journey to Tudela, before heading for Logroño and their final destination of the Dominican monastery of San Domingo. After several weeks a freighter arrived at Vigo and took on a large number of fleeing SS men, including Bormann, and sailed for Buenos Aires in the winter of 1947.[22]

Farago, however, has Bormann sailing direct from Genoa to Buenos Aries on the *Giovann C*, arriving on 17 May 1948 where he was met by

Freude and General Juan Batista Sosa Molina, the Argentine Minister for War. Staying at a house at 120 Calle Salta in San Martin, Bormann then abandoned the Juan Gomez identity and registered as a stateless person, a geologist, born in Piotrkow on 20 August 1901 under 'Identity Certificate No. 073,909' in the name of Eliezer Goldstein. He was issued an identity card No. 1,361,642 by the federal police, and on 12 October 1946 was granted residential status.

Shortly afterwards he went into a conference with the Peróns to argue over apportionment of the looted treasure. With Juan Perón's powerful grip on Argentinian society, he was able to pressurise Bormann into accepting only a 25 per cent share, which was still an enormous fortune. This was not the sum total of Bormann's wealth, however, since Freude had also invested large sums in 175 financial, commercial and industrial enterprises, seventeen agricultural concerns and numerous other smaller companies. Bormann had a keen financial brain, which had been recognised by Hitler who had made him his personal financial adviser. Hitler had acquired substantial real estate thanks to Bormann, but it was all held in Bormann's name. He had also been able to extract 'voluntary' contributions from German industry to Nazi Party coffers in the Führer's name, funds over which Bormann had personal control. Much of these contributions were in the form of assets outside Germany. Once in Argentina, Bormann set about using his power of attorney to have these assets transferred to various holding companies he set up in South America.

Another source of Bormann's wealth was two sums of money he had been able to extract from two of Germany's wealthiest men. Fritz Thyssen, head of the United Steel Works, had been a contributor to the Nazi Party since 1923 but had fallen foul of Hitler in 1940 and was confined to a sanitorium in Berlin. Bormann had arranged for his escape to Switzerland, but in 1942 he was recaptured and thrown into Sachsenhausen then Dachau concentration camps. Again, Bormann interceded on his behalf, not to have him released but to ensure his survival. In return Thyssen handed over to Bormann the rights to his assets in South America. Bormann's other target was the Krupp family, who had pleaded with Bormann to petition Hitler to bypass a law that prevented Alfred Krupp from passing on his vast industrial empire to his son. Bormann was happy to help in return for control of considerable liquid assets in Argentinian banks and a massive ranch of 800,000 acres in Salta. It was this Rancho Grande that Bormann would call his home when he settled in Argentina.

Bormann's position stabilised. Few serious attempts were made by Nazi-hunters to locate him, and he was surrounded by ex-Nazis such as Rudel and Skorzeny and enjoyed the patronage of the Peróns. All was not well, however, as Freude and others who administered Bormann's holdings began to push for a bigger share. Bormann himself was a frugal man and expected the same from those who managed his affairs. One of Bormann's closest financial managers was Heinrich Dörge, a former aide of Hjalmar Schacht, who had been a consultant of the General Bank of Argentina since before the war. His body was discovered on a Buenos Aries street in 1949. Another, Ricardo von Leute, was found dead a year later and Ricardo Staudt, the general manager of the Lauhausen ranch, a few months afterwards. Freude was found dead in 1952 after drinking poisoned coffee. It should be remembered that Buenos Aries at this time was a 'hotbed of Nazism and fascism in exile'.[23] Many of these exiles, German, Italian and Croat were of the most brutal and vicious type and rivalries among the various groups was to be expected, so these deaths may have been the result of relationships with others rather than with Bormann.

In February 1973, Dr Alfonso Finot, a resident of Bolivia, approached the Hungarian historian and journalist Ladislas Faragó to edit a manuscript he had purporting to be a diary written by Bormann in exile in South America. Each page of the document was marked by Bormann's initials and thumbprint. In the diary, Bormann describes parties he attended at the home of Werner Haase and his family, joined by people such as ex-Luftwaffe pilots Hans-Ulrich Rudel, Adolf Galland and Werner Baumbach. While the last three were certainly in Argentina around 1950, Werner Haase, who had been one of Hitler's personal doctors and who had been in the Führerbunker with Bormann when Hitler died, had died in Soviet captivity in 1950. Of course, Bormann may have been referring to a different Haase since he only mentions him by his last name. In their writings, neither Galland nor Baumbach mentioned ever seeing Bormann after the war. Another strange entry in the diary that tends to discredit its authenticity is where Bormann writes things such as 'Nobody seemed to know who I really was, not even Eichmann'.[24] This seems unlikely. The Bormann diary has never been published.

Evidence for Bormann having lived for many years after the war can be found in Faragó's book, *Aftermath*, all the documentary evidence for which is held in the archives of Boston University. When Stewart Steven published an article in the *Daily Express* on 25 November 1972 claiming, on Faragó's evidence, that Bormann was alive and living in Argentina, it was accompanied by a photograph purporting to be a recent image of Bormann. The photograph was quickly proven not to be of Bormann but of Rodolfo Nicolás Siri, a 54-year-old teacher. On the strength of this error, Faragó's book was dismissed as fabrication. Furthermore, a man called Juan José Velasco, whom Faragó refers to as José F. Velasco and identifies as being the chief of the Buenos Aries Provincial Police, gave an interview to the *New York Times* on 7 December in which he described himself as 'a former intelligence agent'. Velasco went on to claim that 'the documents supporting the story were written to order, with official stamps cut from other papers and pasted onto them...The Argentine documents [Farago] has are false—at least the ones I've seen in the papers. I can prove they are false because I have the originals—in a safe place... You have only to see the originals to know they are false.' The article went on to say that 'Commissioner Osvaldo A. Messore of the Federal Police, was supplied earlier with a written list of the documents cited by number in Mr. Farago's series and with copies of the *Daily Express* in which the facsimiles of some documents were reproduced. Two days later, he said that the files had been searched and that he had been authorised by Brig. Gen. Alberto S. Cáceres, commander of the Federal Police, to say: "There is no sign of these documents in our archives".'[25]

Contradicting this is a letter written to the *New York Review* on 20 February 1975 by New York attorney Joel H. Weinberg, which stated:

> I am a New York attorney familiar with the rules of evidence. When in September 1972, Mr. Farago succeeded in obtaining certain documents from the files of the Argentine Secret Services, presenting apparently conclusive proof that former Reichsleiter Martin Bormann had managed to escape to and settle in Argentina, he immediately called upon me to join him in Buenos Aires to aid him in the authentication of the documents, and in his efforts to establish "beyond a reasonable doubt" that the documents were authoritative and authentic.
>
> I arrived in Buenos Aires on September 14, 1972, and proceeded with the execution of my commission as an attorney, conducting a professional investigation into the origins and authenticity of the Bormann documents. In this endeavor I was aided in Buenos Aires by Mr. Stewart Steven, then Foreign Editor of the *Daily Express*, who had flown from London also at Mr. Farago's invitation to assist him in the authentication of the documents; by three distinguished Argentinian attorneys, Dr. Jaime Joaquin Rodriguez, Dr. Guillermo Macia Ray and the last Dr. Silvio Frondizi of Buenos Aires; and by Dr. Horacio A. Perillo, a practicing attorney in Buenos Aires, formerly legal aid to President Arturo Frondizi.
>
> I personally interrogated several of the special agents whose names were mentioned in or whose signatures appeared on the documents,

including Inspector Hector Rodriguez Morguado of Coordination Federal, and Commissioner Alejandro Rafaelo of Policia Federal, and ascertained that the documents in Mr. Farago's possession bearing on the Bormann case were, indeed, genuine, and originated as claimed at the Seguridad Federal, formerly known as Coordination Federal, the central archives of the Argentine Secret Service Establishment.

Based upon my investigation and my questioning of the parties concerned in the acquisition of the documents, I have no hesitation to state that the classified documents are genuine and authentic, true copies of the originals on file at the agency until recently called Seguridad Federal in Buenos Aires.

Joel H. Weinberg

In 1965, a retired postal worker named Albert Krumnow stated that around 8 May 1945, the Soviets had ordered him and his colleagues to bury two bodies found near the railway bridge near Lehrter station in West Berlin. One was reputedly a member of the Wehrmacht and the other an SS doctor. Krumnow's colleague, Wagenpfuhl, is said to have found a paybook on the SS doctor's body identifying him as Dr Ludwig Zengger. He gave the paybook to his boss, postal chief Berndt, who turned it over to the Soviets. They in turn destroyed it. The Soviets allowed Berndt to notify Stumpfegger's wife. He wrote and told her that her husband's body was interred with the bodies of several other dead soldiers in the grounds of the Alpendorf in Berlin NW 40, Invalidenstrasse 63. In mid-1965, Berlin police excavated the alleged burial site looking for Bormann's remains but found nothing. Krumnow stated he could no longer remember exactly where he buried the bodies. Then, on 7 December 1972, just two weeks after the publication of the *Daily Express* articles, after a tip-off to *Stern* magazine, construction workers who were laying cables uncovered human remains near the Lehrter station, just 12 metres (39 feet) from the spot where Krumnow claimed he had buried them.

Dental records, reconstructed from memory in 1945 by Dr Hugo Blaschke, identified the skeleton as Bormann's, and damage to the collarbone was consistent with injuries Bormann's sons reported he had sustained in a riding accident in 1939. The second skeleton was deemed to be Stumpfegger's, since it was of similar height to his last known proportions. Fragments of glass in the jawbones of both skeletons suggested that Bormann and Stumpfegger had committed suicide by biting cyanide capsules to avoid capture (which in no way corresponds to the only known eye-witness account of Bormann's death). Soon afterwards, in a press conference held by the West German government, Bormann was declared dead; a statement condemned by the *Daily Express* as a whitewash perpetrated by the Brandt government. West German diplomatic officials were given official instruction that 'if anyone is arrested on suspicion that he is Bormann, we will be dealing with an innocent man'. The *Frankfurter Allgemeine Zeitung* newspaper announced on 12 April 1973 that 'Martin Bormann died on the night of 2 May 1945 between one and three o'clock on the railway bridge in Invalidenstrasse in Berlin'. The Bormann investigation file, file number Js 11/1961, was closed.

Hugh Thomas, the international forensic expert and author, wrote extensively about the Bormann forensics investigation, which precipitated a six-month Scotland Yard inquiry. The resulting report was suppressed and never exposed to scrutiny. Thomas confirms that the original Bormann medical reports in 1972 released only some and not all the information found under the microscope. While it is true the dentistry of the skull found was identified as Bormann, the official report failed to reveal to the public that there was dentistry performed in the skull, which could only have been done in the 1950s due to the technology used. Also, the skull 'found' in Berlin was encased in a 'red clay' type earth, exotic to Germany but local to a place in Paraguay.

One important witness, a former military ADC to Juan Perón, made a taped testimony on the understanding that it would only be revealed after his death to protect his family. He claims that he met Bormann frequently in Buenos Aires in late 1952 up until the end of 1953. He also testifies that on the instructions of Perón, he organised personal security for Bormann and escorted him to various meetings in Argentina. He tells of how Bormann had been installed in a luxury hotel in Buenos Aries throughout 1953, to which he was sent on a weekly basis to collect the Bormann bill from the hotel concierge, which he was then instructed to take directly to Perón, who paid the bill from his personal bank accounts.[26]

At the Hessian Ministry of Justice, the Frankfurt Attorney General Hans Christoph Schaefer arranged for another examination of the Bormann bones in 1997. Parts of the skeleton found in 1972 made their way through laboratories in Frankfurt, Bern and Munich and experts in Bavaria managed to compare the DNA of the bones and the blood of a Bormann descendant. The testing was led by Wolfgang Eisenmenger, Professor of Forensic Science at Ludwig Maximilian University of Munich. The result confirmed there was strong evidence to suggest that the two were related. The comparison of the sequence of HV1 and HV2 from the skeletal remains and a living maternal relative of Martin Bormann revealed no differences and this sequence was not found in

1,500 Caucasoid reference sequences. Based on this, the investigation concluded that 'we support the hypothesis that the skeletal remains are those of Martin Bormann'.[27] The prosecutors closed the file Js 11/1961 a second time, and the Berlin registry office registered the death of Bormann under the number 29223. There is no mention in the report of any of the injuries that might have been expected had Bormann been killed as a result of his proximity to an exploding German tank, as claimed by Axmann.

It is extremely surprising to discover that of this forensic analysis of the Bormann remains in 1998, only mitochondrial DNA was put on the record and the Bormann relation used to confirm the identity of the skeleton was a Bormann maternal relative, not Martin Bormann's son, who was easily available for such a procedure. Mitochondrial DNA can only be used to match a person or corpse to maternal blood relations. This means that the Martin Bormann DNA profile held on official documents is worthless for matching with any possible offspring or grandchildren. One would have thought that after going to such extraordinary lengths of opening a thorough investigation and having such remains available for research, the scientists and doctors would have taken every possible bit of data possible, particularly DNA. No further examination of the skeletal remains reputed to be Bormann's is possible since they were cremated and buried in the Baltic Sea on 16 August 1999. The question of when Bormann actually died remains open.

As a footnote to the Bormann – Perón saga, 400 tons of gold, worth $1.5 billion at 1973 prices, may have been sold on the gold black market in 1973 by a Chilean businessman living in Madrid, whose identity remains unknown. An account to handle the transaction was opened at the Swiss Credit Bank branch in Chiasso, on the Swiss-Italian border, under the name of Vitalita. The transfer agent was Professor Vincenzo de Nardo, an Inspector-General of the Italian Finance Ministry who claimed that he acted in a purely private capacity and that it had nothing to do with his official functions at the Italian Ministry of Finance. Despite this, he called the origin of the gold 'quite normal' since it came with a certificate of authenticity. He went on to say that the gold originated from a European country and that the transaction was done privately to avoid scrutiny of the government's finances.[28]

One report which appeared in the *Sunday Telegraph* suggested that the gold belonged to the former Argentine dictator, Juan Perón, and was sold to finance his return to power. Gold-trading houses in London and Zurich declined to confirm that any such mammoth transaction had taken place, but otherwise well-informed bankers in London said the sale did take place and that consortiums of banks had to be organised to handle the financial details because of the size of the deal.

The Spanish evening newspaper *Informaciones* reported that 'well informed circles' in Madrid speculated whether the gold might have belonged to Eva Perón, who was reported in 1947 to have had $800 million in gold (figured at the old price of $35 an ounce) in Swiss banks. Journalists and historians have long suspected that Eva Perón used her European tour in 1947 to deposit bribes from Nazi war criminals after she changed her itinerary to visit Swiss bankers in Geneva, Bern, Neuchâtel and Lucerne.[29] A spokesman for the Federal Reserve Bank of New York, when asked about a 400-ton gold sale, said, 'Our people have never heard of it'. Asked if it would be possible for them not to know of such a gigantic sale, he replied that it would be 'not likely, but possible'.[30]

Chapter 20

THE LONDON CONFERENCE OF 1997

'We are here to clarify one of the darkest episodes in human history.'
Robin Cook opening the London Conference, 2 December 1997

For many years the issue of Nazi gold and the involvement of Swiss banks in the handling of looted monetary gold faded from view, but on 2 May 1996, Swiss banking officials signed an agreement with the World Jewish Congress and the World Jewish Restitution Organization to investigate deposits of Holocaust victims in Swiss banks. The agreement provided for the creation a six-member commission, an 'Independent Committee of Eminent Persons', to carry out a thorough audit to identify and recover dormant accounts. The Contact Office for the Search of Dormant Accounts Administered by the Swiss Banks was established and handled all claims, but critics were unimpressed with the lack of scrutiny of its procedures. For their part, the banks contended that 'original amounts [of Jewish deposits] were peanuts'.[1] Frustrated claimants took their case to New York Senator Alfonse D'Amato, the 'brash, pit-bull' Republican chairman of the Senate Banking Committee, who saw political advantage in raising the issue in Washington.

On 12 January 1997, United Press International announced that D'Amato and other American Jewish leaders claimed to have documents that proved Swiss bankers had worked actively on behalf of the Nazis during the Second World War. D'Amato's committee was investigating the role of the Swiss government and banks in the loss of property taken from victims of the Holocaust and had come across a top-secret report to the director of the Office of Strategic Services claiming that between May 1943 and February 1944, up to $500 million in gold was shipped to Spain and Portugal in trucks bearing the national emblem of Switzerland. Documents in the committee's possession from the 1946 Conference on German External Assets and Looted Gold showed specific shipment amounts and recorded the license plate numbers of the Swiss trucks used to transport the wealth. This was supported by a transcript of the August 1945 interrogation of Karl Graupner, the man responsible for gold in the Foreign Exchange Department of the Nazi Reichsbank. Requests for an interview with Swiss banking officials at this time were ignored. D'Amato also wrote to the ambassadors of Portugal and Spain, asking if the gold sent to their countries remained in banks there, or was shipped on to South American nations.

The Swiss Economics Minister, Jean-Pascal Delamuraz, gave an interview to the French-language press in which he accused Jewish organisations of extortion and ransom demands, but the Swiss were forced to address the issue when the newly formed UBS (a merger of the Union Bank of Switzerland and the Swiss Bank Corporation) applied for access to U.S. markets. D'Amato, with huge public support, had previously called for a boycott of Swiss banks operating in the U.S. On 12 August 1998, after plaintiffs angrily rejected a Swiss offer of around $600 million to settle the claims, the Swiss banks Credit Suisse and UBS agreed to pay $1.25 billion to settle lawsuits filed by Holocaust survivors and their heirs, who claimed the banks illegally kept millions of dollars deposited by their relatives before and during the Second World War. The first $250 million of the settlement was payable within ninety days, and the rest was to be paid out over the following three years in annual payments of about $333 million. Despite this, the final payment was not made until 2013; fifteen years after the agreement was signed.[2]

U.S. Undersecretary of Commerce Stuart Eizenstat opened an inquiry into exactly what was done with the $60 million the Swiss had handed over to the Tripartite Gold Commission, and why the Allies were not more forceful in their negotiations with the Swiss. Speaking in Jerusalem in August 1996, he explained:

> We know that in 1946 the Swiss Government turned a significant amount of funds over to the U.S. Government, possibly looted money. We believe that the amount was distributed. Some was kept in the U.S. Treasury, some was distributed to the Allied powers. What we do know is that none of that money went into the hands of those from whom it was looted. Just as Switzerland may have to undergo some painful examination about its role, so too will the U.S. Government.

It was revealed that 2 tons of the gold turned over to the U.S. had been kept at the Federal Reserve Bank in New York City for close to fifty years.

An investigation was set up in Britain, despite the British initially denying that they had any knowledge of the matter. A question to the British Foreign Secretary Malcolm Rifkind in 1996 from Greville Janner MP resulted in the publication of a 24-page report that came to be known as the Rifkind Report, but was correctly called 'Nazi Gold: Information from the British Archives'. Central to the report were statements made by the SNB Vice President, Alfred Hirs, in 1946, in which he claimed that the volume of gold traded with the Nazis was so small as to be almost irrelevant. The report prompted the western press to re-open the issue of Swiss-Nazi gold transactions, and leading western politicians, including U.S. President Clinton, weighed in with promises to support a new investigation. According to *The Times* newspaper, the report was, 'a fascinating account of greed, deception and double dealing. It does not admit to any British conspiracy to hide ill-gotten ingots in the Bank of England, but it does point to an almost unconscionable delay in overcoming the legal and bureaucratic obstacles that stood between the Nazis' victims, or their heirs and representatives, and the money plundered from them to fund Hitler's war machine.' It went on to call the Swiss banks 'immoral, selfish and unworthy of a democracy'.[3]

As a result of the furore caused by the D'Amato investigation, on 2 December 1997 British Foreign Secretary Robin Cook opened the London Conference, with representatives of forty-one nations present. The conference represented 'everyone with an interest in resolving the question of Nazi gold' and expressed the hope that they might 'clarify one of the darkest episodes in human history…to look for compensation for a suffering that can never be expiated'.[4] The conference addressed the questions of how much gold was stolen, where it went, and what should be done about it, including using assets of the Tripartite Gold Commission. There were 5.5 tons of gold left in the Bank of England and the U.S. Federal Reserve which, according to the Paris Agreement of 1946, should be distributed to the countries that had been looted by the Nazis, stipulating that some or all of it should be given to the survivors either in their own countries or through an international fund set up at the Federal Reserve Bank of New York under an account of the British Government. Cook admitted that there would be a limit to what could be achieved and conceded that, while the Allies had made genuine efforts in good faith to 'do the right thing in the midst of post-war chaos' in relation to the needs of survivors, with hindsight, things might have been done differently.

The Argentinian delegation used the conference to lay out its approach to establishing the facts about Nazis in the country after the war. The Argentine ambassador to Britain, Rogelio Pfurter, said that in 1992 previously secret documents had been released. Then in May 1997, the Commission of Enquiry into the Activities of Nazism in the Argentine Republic (CEANA, created by Decree No. 390/97) was set up to 'get to the full facts concerning those illegal activities'. Pfurter went on to say that the Argentine government would make a contribution to the compensation fund for survivors of the Holocaust. CEANA investigations would be conducted in eight areas:

1. Quantification of Nazi war criminals according to Argentine government documents.
2. Quantification of Nazi war criminals according to German and Austrian sources.
3. Spain as a possible stepping stone for Nazi war criminals and loot aimed at Argentina.
4. Italy as country of transit for Nazis and other war criminals arrived in Argentina.
5. German U-boats and the arrival in Argentina of Nazi war criminals, hierarchies and assets.
6. Central bank transactions in gold and hard currency with Axis and neutral countries and Argentina's international economic exchanges.
7. Nazi investments in Argentina through third parties.
8. The impact of war criminals and other Nazi arrivals on Argentine politics and society.

In September 1997, an article written by Nick Durey and Peter Rodgers for the Bank of England recounted the story of two bars of Nazi gold that found their way into the bank's vaults. These were part of shipment of gold looted from Belgium that had been re-smelted and sent from the Reichsbank to Bavaria on 19 April 1945. When the shipment was inventoried on arrival it was found to be short of two bars. There was little time for an investigation and the rest of the loot was buried in Mittenwald (see Chapter 13). However, two days later they were discovered having been concealed in a chimney and were handed over to Walther Funk, who took them with him to Berchtesgaden where they were eventually passed over to the U.S. authorities. The bars were again overlooked as they sat in a corner of the Munich Land Bank until they were discovered in 1949, but they remained there until 1996 when they turned up in the possession of the Tripartite Gold Commission (TGC). The bars were handed over to the U.S. authorities, who promptly gave them back to the TGC for them to deposit in the vaults of the Bank of England. A Bank of England press release of 8 May 1997 stated that:

> The Bank of England has been authorised by the Tripartite Commission for the Restitution of Monetary Gold to state that it holds a total of 114,637.213 troy ounces of fine gold (=about 3,565.615 kilograms) on behalf of the Tripartite Commission. Almost all of this, 113,839.674 ounces, has recently been placed on interest-bearing fixed term deposit. When the Tripartite Commission's gold was first received in the Bank many years ago, it was the Bank's policy not to store specific gold for specific customers: customers were given credit for quantities of gold, not specific bars. The bars which were recently placed on deposit were not, therefore, the bars originally credited to the Tripartite Commission's account. Similarly, when the gold is retrieved from the fixed term deposit, it will not be the same bars which are returned.
>
> The origins of the gold deposited with the Bank of England on behalf of the Tripartite Commission have been described in detail in the documents published recently by the Foreign and Commonwealth Office.
>
> In addition to the gold mentioned above, the Bank also holds on behalf of the Tripartite Commission a further two bars, totalling some 797 ounces, which were transferred from the Deutsche Bundesbank in September 1996. These bars bear the refining stamp of both the Prussian State Mint (1938) and Degussa (1958).

A further press release on 29 January 2016 stated that, 'The bank no longer holds these bars'.

Chapter 21

TREASURE HUNTERS

'Buddy, I'm going to get you a bottle of wine so you'll enjoy the rest of the trip to Salzburg. When they get their hands on you at divisional headquarters, they're going to string you up feet first.'
Custody sergeant to Otto Skorzeny, 16 May 1945

According to figures supplied by the Reichsbank and the Allied authorities, the total amount of gold looted by the Germans between 1938 and 1945 was $621,847,038, while the total amount either recovered or sold to Swiss banks is $640,213,000. This obviously suggests that most of the looted monetary gold was accounted for, but, of course, it does not consider gold looted from private citizens and all gold that passed through the Melmer account. It is much more difficult to find a total value for non-monetary gold looted and this has therefore allowed for a number of stories about hidden Nazi gold to emerge over the years.

Globocnik and the Weissensee Hoard
One of the most famous stories about hidden Nazi gold is the one told by Gregory Douglas about the Weissensee hoard. It is included here so that the reader might have sufficient information to make up their own minds about its authenticity. The story begins with a convoy of five trucks, all painted the medium camouflage yellow of the later war German Wehrmacht, and one staff car bearing license plates of the SS, which supposedly left the German-occupied Italian city of Muggia on the Adriatic Sea and drove north through Udine and then north-east to Villach, which is now in Austria, in late April 1945. In the car was SS Gruppenführer Odlio Globocnik, Senior SS and Police Commander of the Adriatic Region. The trucks each carried two armed Ukrainian guards and dozens of heavy wooden German ammunition boxes. It is claimed that the boxes contained English currency, millions of dollars'

worth of gold coins, religious medals, gold jewellery, platinum, silver, antique coins, gold pencils, containers of dental gold and bridgework, and wedding rings, much of which had been looted from concentration camp victims at Belzec and Treblinka.

Turning off just before Villach, the convoy arrived at the shores of the deep Lake Weissensee, where the wooden crates were buried. Globocnik was captured in late May 1945 in the Weissensee area and unverified U.S. Intelligence reports indicate very clearly that Globocnik was taken into custody and ended up working in Syria for the CIA-controlled Gehlen Organization. Globocnik is supposed to have handed over a map overlay which he claimed showed the exact locations of each burial spot, with a brief notation of the contents. Several different searches of the area were made at different times up until the year 2000 and each time considerable quantities of gold, jewellery and other valuables were discovered.[1]

In 2005, the writer Kenneth D. Alford received a 4-page fax from a Florida-based treasure hunter. The pages concerned SS generals Heinrich Müller and Odlio Globocnik, who, according to the documents, survived the Second World War and worked for U.S. Intelligence. If true, Halford says, it would be 'front page news for every major newspaper and TV broadcast in the world. Public outcry would demand that Cold War history be rewritten and everyone involved be held accountable from former President Harry S. Truman through to the top military officials of the late 1940s.'[2] Faxed documents describe the full extent of the Müller and Globocnik treasure: 2,100 kg gold bars; 1,375 kg gold jewellery; 217 kg scrap platinum; 15,381 British gold sovereigns; 6,113 French 20-franc gold Napoleons; 4,659 French 10-franc gold Napoleons; 2,554 U.S. $20-gold coins; 23,459 German 100-Reichsmark notes and much more, including thousands of carats of diamonds.

Alford's research told him that after his capture in southern Austria, Globocnik had taken cyanide and died. A document in The National Archives, dated 15 November 1963, states: 'Globocnik did not survive the war, he was killed or committed suicide in northern Italy in early 1945'. Alford inquired about the authenticity of the documents and was told that they were supplied by Gregory Douglas, who was also known as Peter Stahl. Robert Wolfe, the retired director of the Military Branch of The National Archives, told Alford that he had studied the documents in the mid-1990s and examined them for more than two years. The author Gitta Serney had also seen the documents as early as 1983. Both Wolfe and Serney had concluded that the Peter Stahl documents were fake.

Richard Raiber, a treasure hunter, posted a comment on a blog in 1996 pertaining to one Peter Stahl, aka Gregory Douglas aka Yetta

Schwarz – yet another pseudonym. Stahl, he says, had sent him a copy of a map which he had apparently found in a German officer's map case he had purchased. The map was a plan of the Wolfschanze (Wolf's Lair), Hitler's Eastern Front military headquarters, and was dated spring/ summer 1944, thus making it a significant find. However, says Raiber, who had visited the Wolfschanze near Ketrzyn/Rastenburg several times, Stahl's plan showed features which had been eliminated in the spring/summer 1944 reconstruction and could not have appeared on any plan drawn in that period. It also did not show a new, concrete-surfaced road built in 1943. Raiber claims that Stahl had reproduced the genuine, autumn 1942 plan and made his own alterations to it. It was after this that Stahl changed his name to Douglas.

The following is a copy of a letter written by W.K. Hedley, a soldier of the 4th Queen's Own Hussars:

> When the war ended the 4th Queen's Own Hussars were ordered to move to Paternion in the Drau Valley. The officers were quartered in the Castle at Paternion with the lock-up 100 yards away.
>
> As the only officer who spoke German reasonably fluently, I was detailed to deal with all matters which could affect the local population. This assignment sounded rather drab, but became more exciting when it became apparent that Dr Friedrich Rainer, the *Gauleiter* was hiding in the neighbouring mountains and was thought to be the figurehead around whom a Werewolf Resistance Group was forming.
>
> In the course of my duties I arrested a number of SS officers and lodged them in a local lock-up. They were given minimum rations of water in the hope that hunger would loosen their tongues. This proved to be the case as on the night of the 30th of May, when a party was given in the officers' mess [and] one of the captured SS officers stated he wished to make a statement.
>
> This was to the effect that *SS-Obergruppenführer* Globocnik and certain members of his staff were hiding in a hut above the Weissensee. He had been acting as a food carrier and stated they could not be taken by day as they withdrew to a vantage point above the hut from which they could watch troops bathing in the lake below and any approach to the hut.
>
> A party of troops was organised and was accompanied by a number of special service officers of the parachute regiment who were attending the party in the officers' mess. The hut was surrounded (after an arduous climb) shortly before 4 am, 31st May. It was locked and after both doors had eventually been opened a number of men and women were hustled out of the rather dim interior. Some were rather reluctant "to get a move on" and were encouraged with a kick in the pants.
>
> One of them said in German "Don't treat me like that, I am the *Gauleiter*". Rainer was known to have a duelling scar on his cheek and was easily identified from this and his circulated description.

His presence tended to distract attention from the others in the hut, approximately seven men and three women. After a preliminary search of the building I decided to escort Rainer to Paternion and arrange for more vehicles to go to the bottom of the mountain as our bag had greatly exceeded expectations. I handed over to Major Ramsay of the Parachute Regiment, a fluent German speaker.

During the search Rainer was found to have a metal phial containing a suicide capsule as issued to all senior members of the Nazi hierarchy. Little attention was, at the time, attached to a similar empty phial found on the floor of one of the rooms.

Rainer was lodged in the local lock-up and the main body of prisoners arrived in Paternion at about 11 am. The SS informer had identified all the prisoners by name and gave details of their duties in Trieste. With one exception they were all locked up, the exception stated he was, "a poor merchant from Klagenfurt frightened by the possible Yugoslav invasion". He had almost convinced Major Ramsay of his innocence [and] was walking up and down in the castle yard, very coolly, escorted by the regimental provost sergeant until his Klagenfurt references could be checked.

The informer insisted he was Globocnik. Major Ramsay and I decided that he (Ramsey) should sharply shout out the name Globocnik while I watched the captive's reaction very closely. When the name was called Globocnik's step never faltered, but his head moved fractionally. I shouted to him (in German) "You have given yourself away, you moved your head very slightly", and ordered Sowler to add him to the gang in the lock-up. I then started to go to my room to have a bath only to hear shouts of "he's dead, he's dying". I ran downstairs to find Globocnik lying on the ground between the castle yard and the lock-up. He had held his suicide capsule under his tongue continually since his arrest until using it about 11.25. We had noticed at the time that he refused any form of food or drink.

Captain M.M. Leigh RAMC, the Regimental Medical Officer, was quickly on the scene and he gave Globocnik two inoculations in the arm and one in the heart, but to no avail. As soon as they saw his corpse, Lerch, Hofle, Michaelsen and Helletsberger, who had denied their identities, admitted who they were and identified the corpse as their former commanding officer Globocnik. Rainer also identified the corpse as Globocnik.

Globocnik was subsequently buried by the regimental police in the presence of Captain G.P.M.C. Wheeler.

Signed
W.K. Hedley[3]

The Walbrzych Gold Train

In August 2015, a law firm in south-west Poland was contacted by two men who claimed to have found a Nazi train rumoured to be full of gold, gems and guns that had disappeared in the Second World War near what is now the Polish city of Wrocław. The place was close to the one near Książ Castle, which for years had been rumoured to be the location of such a train. The two men, Piotr Koper, a Polish owner of a construction company, and Andreas Richter, a German geologist, together with officials in the city, formed an emergency committee led by the mayor to investigate the claims.

The train was reputed to be hidden within up to 5 miles of tunnels dug between 1943 and 1945 by Nazi prisoners of war near Wałbrzych and were apparently to be used as factories. A KS-700 Ground Penetrating Radar system was used, and Polish Deputy Culture Minister Piotr Żuchowski said that the images appeared to confirm the claim, leading to parts of the mountain being sealed off to keep amateur treasure hunters from hurting themselves.

Polish authorities sectioned off woodland in the area and deployed police and other guards to prevent access to the numerous treasure hunters who had arrived armed with detection equipment. In late September, the Polish military, acting at the request of the regional governor, began to clear the surface of trees and search for booby traps and mines. They confirmed that no explosives or other dangers existed down to a depth of 1 metre.

Ever since the end of the war, people had been motivated by an account of a German miner who claimed to have seen a group of German soldiers wheel a train loaded with gold, jewels and other looted valuables into a tunnel leading into the Owl Mountains in south-west Poland. Koper and Richter were just the latest in a long line of treasure hunters.

At a press conference, Koper and Richter presented findings gathered by their own research team, which they said was even more proof that they had found the lost train. 'We carried out similar examinations in many other locations, but we have never encountered anything like this', Koper said at the press conference, pointing to a series of round, rectangular and oval shapes seen in images taken with ground-penetrating radar. In mid-November, two different teams, including specialists from the Kraków Mining Academy, were cleared by city authorities to make a non-invasive assessment of the site. By 15 December, however, no actual evidence of the train had come to light, although there was some evidence of a collapsed tunnel.

In the following year a group of thirty-five volunteer explorers, including engineers, geologists, chemists, archaeologists and a specialist in military demolitions, all led by Koper and Richter, obtained the necessary permits from Polish State Railways and began digging with heavy machinery. After ten days, however, nothing was found and the search was wound up. Nevertheless, local residents had benefitted significantly, with the hunt for the Nazi train bringing a multi-million-pound tourism boost to the town of Wałbrzych.

At the beginning of December 2016, Koper and Richter created a foundation to raise money to drill down to 20 metres in 2017, and during the this search the excavation team encountered seven cavities, which were suspected to be a railway tunnel. The find made deep drilling necessary, which required further finance, but another dig was scheduled for the spring or summer of 2018.

Although a great deal of this story is speculative, in 2019 Koper made a completely accidental discovery while helping renovate a baroque dome in a palace located in the village of Struga, near the city of Wrocław. Two dozen priceless Renaissance paintings were discovered in the walls of the building, which had previously been transformed into a headquarters for Hitler. The renovators deduced that the paintings were at least 500 years old. The owner of the palace where the paintings were found believes that there may be many other valuable objects still to discover there, all linked to the lost Nazi gold train.[4]

Minkowskie Palace

A group of treasure hunters calling itself the Silesian Bridge Foundation were given permission in 2022 to begin digging for buried Nazi gold in an old orangery in the grounds of an eighteenth-century palace, built by the Prussian general Friedrich Wilhelm von Seydlitz in the village of Minkowskie. In 2008, researchers from the foundation came into possession of a cache of documents, including a wartime diary, given to them by the secretive Quedlinburg Lodge, a mysterious group that dates back to the time of the first German king Henry the Fowler in the early tenth century. Over the centuries, the organisation has been connected to prominent figures in religion, high society, science, and the arts, and during the Nazi rule in Germany formed an uncomfortable alliance with Hitler under which they became part of the cultural elite in the Third Reich. The deal protected its own status and gave Hitler an air of respectability and a sense of historical legitimacy. Its members could be found in top positions in many Nazi-era institutions, most notably the fearsome Waffen SS. Many were close to Hitler. It was members of this shadowy Christian organisation who had passed on the diary to the Silesian Bridge Foundation, supposedly as a gift to the Polish nation as an apology for its suffering during the war.

The war diary, written by a Waffen SS officer under the pseudonym Michaelis, describes an operation under the leadership of Günther Grundmann, the heritage conservator for the Germans in Lower Silesia, to hide the vast art holdings of Reich museums, institutions, and also private collections before and during the war. Grundmann compiled a detailed list of all the treasures and their seventy-four hiding places in Lower Silesia. He was also tasked with hiding all the treasures under the control of SS chief Heinrich Himmler at the end of the Second World War. It was Michaelis who, along with many other Waffen SS officers, was a member of the Quedlinburg Lodge, and was in charge of all the transport available to the Waffen SS in Lower Silesia. The diary describes eleven locations across Lower Silesia and Opole where valuables are said to be located.

One page in the diary gives soldiers ID numbers 453 and 219 and gives thanks to Mr Grundmann, who had opened an ancient well in the palace of the Hochberg family. According to the diary, once the treasure had been placed in the well, it was filled in. Among the bundle of documents was a letter from a senior SS officer called Carl von Stein to one of the girls who worked at the palace in Minkowskie, and who later became his lover. The officer wrote: 'My dear Inge, I will fulfil my assignment, with God's will. Some transports were successful. The remaining 48 heavy Reichsbank's chests and all the family chests [were hidden, very well covered with earth and camouflaged with plants]. I hereby entrust [them] to you. Only you know where they are located. May God help you and help me, fulfil my assignment.' The head of the Silesian Bridge Foundation, Roman Furmaniak, said that the foundation had taken a long-term lease on the property and was given permission to begin searching by the Opole Heritage Conservator.

In May 2022, the treasure hunters detected a metal canister 3 metres below the surface. At the time of writing, they are waiting for permission to raise the canister to the surface.

Hochberg Palace

Roztoka, in southern Poland, is said to hold gold deposits of the Reichsbank in Breslau (Wrocław) and valuables looted from civilians in Lower Silesia, all which had been in the possession of the SS in 1945. On 25 May 2020, Roman Furmaniak revealed the location in Roztoka, which he claims to be the first of eleven hiding places detailed in the diary mentioned previously. The palace in Roztoka, now under new ownership, was the family seat of the famous Hochberg family, owners of numerous estates in the area since the early thirteenth century. One of their estates was Książ Castle, which was built by the Piast Duke of Świdnica-Jawor Bolko I Surowy in the thirteenth century. The new owners enthusiastically supported the searches and installed perimeter surveillance to monitor tourists and treasure hunters. A map accompanying the diary was said to show the location of a well in the grounds of the palace where treasure had been buried. Another document asserted that witnesses to the burial were killed and dumped in the well before it was backfilled. On 3 September 2022, Furmaniak reported that his team had found a scattering of wartime German Reichsbank pfennigs clearly marked with Swastikas and dated 1942, 1944, and 1945.

Secrets hidden in a Music Score?
Dutch musician and composer Cyril Whistler was a 53-year-old music teacher, violinist and violin maker from Arnhem, who claimed in 2015 to have found the exact spot where Adolf Hitler's treasure, worth £50 million, was buried after cracking a code hidden in a sheet of wartime music. He stated that he had spent two years studying the music sheet titled 'Marsch Impromptu' by composer Gottfried Federlein. The score is believed to be the key to a cache of lost gold and diamonds belonging to the Nazi leader and is buried somewhere in Mitten. Whistler declared that the treasure is buried behind the barbed wire of a German army depot in Mittenwald. Dutch filmmaker Leon Giesen made three excavations around the town, but Whistler believed he had now located the exact spot.

Whistler studied the score and claimed to have discovered a typical number that returns over and over again between the bars, as well as being encrypted throughout the score. It is thought the marks and typewritten comments above each line of music were added by Hitler's private secretary, Martin Bormann, as clues to the whereabouts of the so-called 'Tears of the Wolf'. Wolf was Hitler's nickname among his inner circle, with tears referring to his diamonds. 'The more I studied the piece, the more I discovered. The letters, the number and the signs reveal a route,' Whistler said. 'I am sure beyond reasonable doubt to have found the exact location which the score leads to.' The haul is believed to contain 100 gold bars and a huge stash of Hitler's diamonds.[5]

On 13 March 2022, Whistler released a music CD called 'Tears of the Wolf', and it cannot be discounted that his story about hidden gold was little more than an advertising stunt.

Hans Glueck and the Arrach Treasure

Himmler's deputy Ernst Kaltenbrunner and his paymaster, SS Oberführer Josef Spacil, had looted the new Reichsbank headquarters in Berlin in April 1945, taking jewels, securities and the last remaining foreign exchange assets held in the vault, valued altogether at 23 million gold Reichsmarks. It had been Spacil's administration which had looted in the death camps, and his skills in disguising the origins of looted assets had convinced Kaltenbrunner and then Himmler that he was the man to be trusted to remove the SS's remaining liquid assets from Berlin and transport them into hiding in Austria. So, in one of the last aircraft to leave Berlin, Spacil headed south to Salzburg. There the loot was loaded onto a lorry and driven to the town of Burgwies. With Allied troops closing in, it was soon clear that he could go no further so he arranged to bury the treasure on a steep slope close to the road between Taxenbach and Rauris, but he did not bury it all. Some of the remaining hoard was handed out to other surviving Gestapo officers such as Franz Conrad and Captain Karl Radl, adjutant to Otto Skorzeny. Radl received a large sum of gold coins, Swedish crowns and a quantity of mixed currencies. Radl, Skorzeny and a few SS officers then took the treasure up into the mountains and hid it.

Spacil was eventually captured by U.S. forces and taken to Ebersburg POW camp, where he disguised himself as a lowly Wehrmacht sergeant named Aue in order to avoid detection, arrest, or worse.[6] Once there, he tried to obtain the cooperation of another German officer, Obersturmführer Walter Hirschfeld, to effect an escape in return for a share of the treasure, but Hirschfeld was not convinced that Spacil was telling the truth and did not want to risk a heavy sentence for helping him. Afraid that Spacil might cause trouble, on 5 June Hirschfeld told U.S. Intelligence officer John E. Alter and CIC field agent U.S. Lieutenant Claus Nacke about Spacil's plan. Nacke told Hirschfeld to discuss the plan with Spacil and he would record the conversation. Hirschfeld told Spacil that Nacke was willing to create false documents for him in return for information about the hidden treasure. On 9 June 1945, Alter, Nacke, and Hirschfeld went to Taxenbach, where at the home of a man called Urschunger, under the floor of a barn, they found a cache of nineteen bags of gold coins and 10.5 kg of gold bullion, along with $117,752 in currency in bags with Reichsbank seals.[7]

When Skorzeny was taken into captivity, however, he did not reveal the location of the treasure he had hidden during the three years he was in captivity at Nuremberg and at Dachau internment camp, nor during his trial on war crimes charges. Only when he was a free man in Spain five years after the war and living in a large villa in Madrid where he entertained lavishly with his countess wife, and was actively engaged in lucrative arms sales, was it clear that he had recovered his hoard.

Ernst Kaltenbrunner instructed his deputy, Arthur Scheidler, to take his portion of the loot, $100,000 American dollars and thousands of gold coins stuffed into six large cloth sacks each weighing 30kg to Altausee.[8] It was loaded onto a special train that formerly belonged to Reinhard Heydrich, which was also jammed full of expensive furniture, food, liquor, artwork, and other valuables and set off for Fürsteneck on the German-Austrian border. The train, however, was attacked and destroyed by Allied aircraft and Kaltenbrunner's treasure was transferred to a truck and taken to Gmunden in Austria, under the protection of SS Sturmbannführers Reinhard Eimers and Lothar Kuhne. Once at Gmunden, the load was split, with gold and currency destined for Altausee and the rest for Schloss Glanek, near Salzburg. It seems, however, that orders were confused, and the gold went to Schloss Glanek instead of Altausee.

Scheidler chose not to tell Kaltenbrunner about the mix-up immediately and was relieved of the need to do so after a couple of days when the two men were forced to flee ahead of approaching Allied forces. They were captured on 12 May in the Wildensee region of the Totes Gebirge range of the Austrian Alps. A search of the Schloss Glanek found no trace of any gold and it has never been recovered.[9]

Hans Glueck, from Heidelberg, had been a keen treasure hunter for twenty years when he claimed to have found the location of a hidden cache of Nazi gold in 2015 in the Bavarian woods. This, he claimed, was the looted SS treasure hidden by Himmler's deputy Ernst Kaltenbrunner that he took from the Berlin Reichsbank in 1945. Glueck said that the train was heading for Passau on the German-Austria border, but Allied air attacks and advancing Russians forced it to hide for three days in a tunnel at Tittling in Bavaria, then ended up in Arrach close to the border with what is now the Czech Republic; in the opposite direction from Passau. In 1995 Glueck gave an interview to Bavaria TV about his various worldwide treasure hunts and was subsequently contacted by a man who said he had an old map that had reputedly belonged to an SS officer captured by the Russians and imprisoned in Siberia. This officer is said to have handed the map with the details of the Arrach treasure on it to Willi Jahnke, a Wehrmacht soldier and prisoner of war. Jahnke survived captivity to return to his home in East Germany.

When Jahnke went to Arrach in 1990, he was told by the locals of how they had been forced to stay indoors while twenty heavy crates were offloaded from a train by Polish POWs onto carts and taken into the forest. The Poles were shot in Arrach three days later. Jahnke died in 1995 following an operation and handed the SS treasure map to the owner of the forest before his death. Over two weekends in May 1995, after being contacted by the landowner, Glueck went to Arrach and claimed to have discovered a metal box containing part of a map annotated with additional notes and markers. The markings were a cross, a few dots, lines, and the numbers 600, 900 and 750.

Over the next two decades he drove to Arrach many times searching for the treasure, which he claimed to have found the location of. Using ground-penetrating radar, he believed that he obtained readings indicating metal under the ground. He later stated that the landowner had refused permission for him to dig and wanted to claim the treasure for himself, but Glueck still has the map.[10]

The remaining valuables in the Berlin Reichsbank were removed some time after May 1945. On 15 May a Russian officer, Major Feodor Novikov of Red Army Intelligence, opened the Reichsbank vaults in Berlin and found ninety gold bars and over 4.5 million gold coins, as well as $400 million in negotiable bonds technically payable in gold or dollars. Within days the vaults were emptied. The gold was never seen again, but the bonds started turning up in 1951 at intervals in West Germany, the Netherlands, Israel, USA, Switzerland, Canada and Great Britain, and later in Central America.

POSTSCRIPT

The story of Hitler's gold has been long and complicated and there is still much that has yet to come to light. The full story may never be told, but that which is known is a guide to what remains hidden.

During the Second World War, Swiss banks handled 80 per cent of the estimated $1.7 billion of all gold looted by the Nazis, with the vast bulk of that going through the Swiss National Bank. Just how much the Swiss knew or wanted to know about the origin of this gold, especially that taken from Holocaust victims, remains uncertain. How much remains in their vaults is also impossible to determine.

Swiss banking practices, in this regard, seem to have changed little. In his 2019 book *Gold Laundering: The Dirty Secrets of the Gold Trade and How to Clean Up*, Mark Pieth, Professor of Criminal Law at the University of Basel, believes that Swiss refineries still process gold from places such as eastern Congo, where genocide has killed as many as six million people.[1]

Credit Suisse aided fleeing Nazis who escaped to South America, and even honoured the bank accounts they left behind. According to a report by Aaron Reich published in the *Jerusalem Post* on 7 March 2020, the Argentinian investigator Pedro Filipuzzi found that at least 12,000 Nazis in Argentina maintained accounts at Credit Suisse. The issue of how much money has been transferred from Swiss banks to escaped Nazis may never be known entirely, but a 1990's investigation called it 'unprecedented'.[2]

In August 2022, Switzerland banned imports of Russian gold and gold products, in line with similar moves by the European Union and the United States following Russia's illegal invasion of Ukraine in February of that year. The Federal Council, the Swiss government's seven-member executive board, said in a statement that the gold ban aligned with the European Union's latest sanctions on Russia and that Switzerland was 'implementing the most urgent measures in terms of time and substance'.

More recently, the American writer Paige Baschuk reported that a mysterious shipment of Russian gold worth $200 million showed up in Switzerland months after sanctions were imposed on the country for its invasion of Ukraine. In January 2023 the website swissinfo.ch reported on Russian gold entering Switzerland from the UK, which seems to have evaded sanctions since it had been in British vaults since before sanctions were imposed.[3] Anna Golubova of Kitco News says that various reports point out that investors have likely been using the opportunity to remelt their old Russian gold at one of Switzerland's refineries, which could make it easier for them to sell their bullion without any stigma attached to it. Russia is the world's second-largest gold miner and Switzerland is home to four major gold refineries, which together handle two-thirds of the world's gold.[4]

The Swiss Association of Manufacturers and Traders in Precious Metals (ASFCMP), which represents the refineries, said in a statement none of their members is responsible for these imports. The ASFCMP pointed out that dubious gold has no place in Switzerland and that it expects its members to act with the utmost caution and to refrain from buying in case of doubt. Moreover, it asserts that none of the major Swiss refineries has accepted this gold.

Appendix 1

US MILITARY INTELLIGENCE REPORT EW-Pa 128

US Military Intelligence Report EW-Pa 128
Enclosure No. 1 to despatch No. 19,489 of Nov. 27, 1944, from the Embassy at London, England.

S E C R E T
SUPREME HEADQUARTERS
ALLIED EXPEDITIONARY FORCE
Office of Assistant Chief of Staff, G-2
7 November 1944
INTELLIGENCE REPORT NO. EW-Pa 128

SUBJECT: Plans of German industrialists to engage in underground activity after Germany's defeat; flow of capital to neutral countries.

SOURCE: Agent of French Deuxieme Bureau, recommended by Commandant Zindel. This agent is regarded as reliable and has worked for the French on German problems since 1916. He was in close contact with the Germans, particularly industrialists, during the occupation of France and he visited Germany as late as August 1944.

1. A meeting of the principal German industrialists with interests in France was held on August 10, 1944, in the Hotel Rotes Haus in Strasbourg, France, and attended by the informant indicated above as the source. Among those present were the following:
   Dr. Scheid, who presided, holding the rank of S.S. Obergruppenfuhrer and Director of the Heche (Hermandorff & Schonburg) Company

US MILITARY INTELLIGENCE REPORT EW-PA 128

Dr. Kaspar, representing Krupp
Dr. Tolle, representing Rochling
Dr. Sinderen, representing Messerschmitt
Drs. Kopp, Vier and Beerwanger, representing Rheinmetall
Captain Haberkorn and Dr. Ruhe, representing Bussing
Drs. Ellenmayer and Kardos, representing Volkswagenwerk
Engineers Drose, Yanchew and Koppshem, representing various factories in Posen, Poland (Drose, Yanchew and Co., Brown-Boveri, Herkuleswerke, Buschwerke, and Stadtwerke)
Captain Dornbuach, head of the Industrial Inspection Section at Posen
Dr. Meyer, an official of the German Naval Ministry in Paris
Dr. Strossner, of the Ministry of Armament, Paris.

2. Dr. Scheid stated that all industrial material in France was to be evacuated to Germany immediately. The battle of France was lost for Germany and now the defense of the Siegfried Line was the main problem. From now on also German industry must realize that the war cannot be won and that it must take steps in preparation for a post-war commercial campaign. Each industrialist must make contacts and alliances with foreign firms, but this must be done individually and without attracting any suspicion. Moreover, the ground would have to be laid on the financial level for borrowing considerable sums from foreign countries after the war. As examples of the kind of penetration which had been most useful in the past, Dr. Scheid cited the fact that patents for stainless steel belonged to the Chemical Foundation, Inc., New York, and the Krupp company of Germany jointly and that the U.S. Steel Corporation, Carnegie, Illinois, American Steel and Wire, and national Tube, etc. were thereby under an obligation to work with the Krupp concern. He also cited the Zeiss Company, the Leisa Company and the Hamburg-American Line as firms which had been especially effective in protecting German interests abroad and gave their New York addresses to the industrialists at this meeting.

3. Following this meeting a smaller one was held presided over by Dr. Bosse of the German Armaments Ministry and attended only by representatives of Hecho, Krupp and Rochling. At this second meeting it was stated that the Nazi Party had informed the industrialists that the war was practically lost but that it would continue until a guarantee of the unity of Germany could be obtained. German industrialists must, it was said, through their exports increase the strength of

Germany. They must also prepare themselves to finance the Nazi Party which would be forced to go underground as Maquis (in Gebirgaverteidigungastellen gehen). From now on the government would allocate large sums to industrialists so that each could establish a secure post-war foundation in foreign countries. Existing financial reserves in foreign countries must be placed at the disposal of the Party so that a strong German Empire can be created after the defeat. It is also immediately required that the large factories in Germany create small technical offices or research bureaus which would be absolutely independent and have no known connection with the factory. These bureaus will receive plans and drawings of new weapons as well as documents which they need to continue their research and which must not be allowed to fall into the hands of the enemy. These offices are to be established in large cities where they can be most successfully hidden as well as in little villages near sources of hydro-electric power where they can pretend to be studying the development of water resources. The existence of these is to be known only by very few people in each industry and by chiefs of the Nazi Party. Each office will have a liaison agent with the Party. As soon as the Party becomes strong enough to re-establish its control over Germany the industrialists will be paid for their effort and cooperation by concessions and orders.

4. These meetings seem to indicate that the prohibition against the export of capital which was rigorously enforced until now has been completely withdrawn and replaced by a new Nazi policy whereby industrialists with government assistance will export as much of their capital as possible. Previously exports of capital by German industrialists to neutral countries had to be accomplished rather surreptitiously and by means of special influence. Now the Nazi Party stands behind the industrialists and urges them to save themselves by getting funds outside Germany and at the same time to advance the Party's plans for its post-war operation. This freedom given to the industrialists further cements their relations with the Party by giving them a measure of protection.

5. The German industrialists are not only buying agricultural property in Germany but are placing their funds abroad, particularly in neutral countries. Two main banks through which this export of capital operates are the Basler Handelsbank and the Schweizerische Kreditanstalt of Zurich. Also there are a number of agencies in Switzerland which for a 5 per cent commission buy property in Switzerland, using a Swiss cloak.

6. After the defeat of Germany the Nazi Party recognizes that certain of its best known leaders will be condemned as war criminals. However, in cooperation with the industrialists it is arranging to place its less conspicuous but most important members in positions with various German factories as technical experts or members of its research and designing offices.

For the A.C. of S., G-2.
WALTER K. SCHWINN
G-2, Economic Section
Prepared by
MELVIN M. FAGEN
Distribution:
Same as EW-Pa 1,
U.S. Political Adviser, SHAEF
British Political Adviser, SHAEF

Appendix 2

PART III OF THE PARIS REPARATIONS AGREEMENT

RESTITUTION OF MONETARY GOLD
Single Article

A. All the monetary gold found in Germany by the Allied Forces and that referred to in paragraph G below (including gold coins, except those of numismatic or historical value, which shall be restored directly if identifiable) shall be pooled for distribution as restitution among the countries participating in the pool in proportion to their respective losses of gold through looting or by wrongful removal to Germany.

B. Without prejudice to claims by way of reparation for unrestored gold, the portion of monetary gold thus accruing to each country participating in the pool shall be accepted by that country in full satisfaction of all claims against Germany for restitution of monetary gold.

C. A proportional share of the gold shall be allocated to each country concerned which adheres to this arrangement for the restitution of monetary gold and which can establish that a definite amount of monetary gold belonging to it was looted by Germany or, at any time after March 12th, 1938, was wrongfully removed into German territory.

D. The question of the eventual participation of countries not represented at the Conference (other than Germany but including Austria and Italy) in the above mentioned distribution shall be reserved, and the equivalent of the total shares which these countries would receive, if they were eventually admitted to participate, shall be set aside to be disposed of at a later date in such manner as may be decided by the Allied Governments concerned.

E. The various countries participating in the pool shall supply to the Governments of the United States of America, France and the United Kingdom, as the occupying Powers concerned, detailed and verifiable

data regarding the gold losses suffered through looting by, or removal to, Germany.
F. The Governments of the United States of America, France and the United Kingdom shall take appropriate steps within the Zones of Germany occupied by them respectively to implement distribution in accordance with the foregoing provisions.
G. Any monetary gold which may be recovered from a third country to which it was transferred from Germany shall be distributed in accordance with this arrangement for the restitution of monetary gold.

ALLOCATION OF A REPARATION SHARE TO NONREPATRIABLE VICTIMS OF GERMAN ACTION

In recognition of the fact that large numbers of persons have suffered heavily at the hands of the Nazis and now stand in dire need of aid to promote their rehabilitation but will be unable to claim the assistance of any Government receiving reparations from Germany, the Governments of the United States of America, France, the United Kingdom, Czechoslovakia and Yugoslavia, in consultation with the Inter-Governmental Committee on Refugees, shall as soon as possible work out in common agreement a plan on the following general lines:

A. A share of reparation consisting of all the non-monetary gold found by the Allied Armed Forces in Germany and in addition a sum not exceeding 25 million dollars shall be allocated for the rehabilitation and resettlement of non-repatriable victims of German action.
B. The sum of 25 million dollars shall be met from a portion of the proceeds of German assets in neutral countries which are available for reparation.
C. Governments of neutral countries shall be requested to make available for this purpose (in addition to the sum of 25 million dollars) assets in such countries of victims of Nazi action who have since died and left no heirs.
D. The persons eligible for aid under the plan in question shall be restricted to true victims of Nazi persecution and to their immediate families and dependents, in the following classes:

(i) Refugees from Nazi Germany or Austria who require aid and cannot be returned to their countries within a reasonable time because of prevailing conditions;
(ii) German and Austrian nationals now resident in Germany or Austria in exceptional cases in which it is reasonable on grounds of humanity to assist such persons to emigrate and providing they emigrate to other countries within a reasonable period;

(iii) Nationals of countries formerly occupied by the Germans who cannot be repatriated or are not in a position to be repatriated within a reasonable time. In order to concentrate aid on the most needy and deserving refugees and to exclude persons whose loyalty to the United Nations is or was doubtful, aid shall be restricted to nationals or former nationals of previously occupied countries who were victims of German concentration camps or of concentration camps established by regimes under Nazi influence but not including persons who have been confined only in prisoners of war camps.

E. The sums made available under paragraphs A and B above shall be administered by the Inter-Governmental Committee on Refugees or by a United Nations Agency to which appropriate functions of the Inter-Governmental Committee may in the future be transferred. The sums made available under paragraph C above shall be administered for the general purposes referred to in this Article under a program of administration to be formulated by the five Governments named above.

F. The non-monetary gold found in Germany shall be placed at the disposal of the Inter-Governmental Committee on Refugees as soon as a plan has been worked out as provided above.

G. The Inter-Governmental Committee on Refugees shall have power to carry out the purposes of the fund through appropriate public and private field organisations.

H. The fund shall be used, not for the compensation of individual victims, but to further the rehabilitation or resettlement of persons in the eligible classes.

I. Nothing in this Article shall be considered to prejudice the claims which individual refugees may have against a future German Government, except to the amount of the benefits that such refugees may have received from the sources referred to in paragraph A and C above.

SOURCES

Alford, Kenneth and Savas, Theodore P., *The Allied Search for Hidden SS Gold* (Casemate, 2002)

Alford, Kenneth, *Monetary Men: The Allies' Struggle to Recover and Restore Nazi Gold, Silver and Diamonds* (Schiffer Publishing, 2015)

Allen, Robert W. Jnr., *Britain and the Belgian Exiles* (University College London, 1997)

Aubion, Roger, *The Bank for International Settlements, 1930-1955* (Princeton University, 1955)

Auboin, Roger, *Essays in International Finance: The Bank for International Settlements* (Princeton University, 1955)

Banken, Ralph, *National Socialist Robbery of Precious Metals, 1933-1945: The Role of Degussa and the Case of Poland* (escholarship.org, 2006)

Baschuck, Paige, 'Tracing Nazi Gold through Switzerland', *The Swiss Times*, 4 July 2022

Blaazer, David, 'Finance and the End of Appeasement: The Bank of England, the National Government and the Czech Gold', *Journal of Contemporary History*, Jan., 2005, Vol. 40, No. 1

Bradsher, Greg, 'Nazi Gold: The Merkers Mine Treasure', *Prologue Magazine*, Spring 1999

Cain, P. J. and Hopkins A.G., *British Imperialism: Vol. 1, Innovation and Expansion, 1688-1914, Vol. 2, Crisis and Deconstruction, 1914-19* (Addison-Wesley Longman Ltd; 1993)

Cardarelli, Sergio and Martano Renata, *I Nazisti e l'Oro della Banci d''Italia; Sottrazioni e recupero 1943-1958* (Editori Laterza, 2003)

Clark, Margaret, *Safehaven Study: Records of the Federal Economic Administration* (RG 169)

Comstock, Alzada, 'German Reparations: the Potsdam Plan' *Current History* 9, No. 49, 1945

Davies, Glynn, *A History of Money* (University of Wales Press, 2016)

d'Erizans, Alexander Peter, *Odessa und das Vierte Reich: Mythen der Zeitgeschichte Review* (Oregon State University, 2011)

Farago, Ladislas, *Aftermath: Martin Bormann and the Fourth Reich* (Hodder and Stoughton, 1974)

Farnsworth, Clyde H., 'Mystery shrouds gold sale report', *New York Times*, 11 September 1973

Fotich, Constantin, *The War We Lost: Yugoslavia's Tragedy and the Failure of the West* (Literary Licensing, 2012)

Golson, Eric Bernard, *The Economics of Neutrality: Spain, Sweden and Switzerland in the Second World War* (The London School of Economics and Political Science, 2011)

Golubova, Anna, 'Switzerland's Russian Gold Imports Climb in 2022', kitco.com 26 January 2023

Hale, William, 'Turkey and Britain in World War II: Origins and Results of the Tripartite Alliance, 1935-40', *Journal of Balkan and Near Eastern Studies*, Vol. 23, No. 6, 2021

Higham, Charles, *Trading With the Enemy: The Nazi-American Money Plot 1933-1949* (Barnes and Noble, 1995)

Hutchison, Robert, *Their Kingdom Come* (Transworld, Kindle Edition)

Kirkpatrick, Sidney, *Hitler's Holy Relics* (Simon & Schuster UK, Kindle Edition)

Labord, Larry, *French Gold In World War II*, (321gold.com, 2019)

Lacey, James, *Gold, Blood, and Power: Finance and War through the ages* (Strategic Studies Institute and U.S. Army War College P, May 2015)

LeBor, Adam, *Hitler's Secret Bankers* (Head of Zeus, 2020)

LeBor, Adam, *Meet the American Banker Who Helped Hitler Loot Jewish Gold—While Spying for the OSS* (tabletmag.com, 2013)

LeBor, Adam, *The secret report that shows how the Nazis planned a Fourth Reich ...in the EU* (Mailonline, 9 May 2009)

Leitz, Christian, *Economic Relations Between Nazi Germany and Franco's Spain 1936-1945* (Clarendon Press, 1996)

Louça, Antonio and Schäfer Ansgar, 'Portugal and the Nazi Gold: The "Lisbon Connection" in the Sales of Looted Gold by the Third Reich', *Yad Vashem Studies*, Vol. 27, 1999

Manning, Paul, 'Martin Bormann and the Future of Germany', *New York Times*, 3 March 1973

Manning, Paul, *Martin Bormann: Nazi in Exile* (Kindle Edition)

Mello, Laurence de, (goldeneyepublishingltd.wordpress.com, 24 August 2016)

Milward, Alan S., 'Could Sweden Have Stopped the Second World War?', *Scandinavian Economic Historical Review*, 1967

Morley, John F., *Vatican Diplomacy and the Jews During the Holocaust* (Ktav Inc, 1980)

Nicholas, Lynn H., *The Rape of Europa: The Fate of Europe's Treasures in the Third Reich and the Second World War* (Vintage Books, 1995)

Novitski, Joseph, *Never Saw Bormann, Argentinian Declares* (nytimes.com)

O'Shaughnessy, Hugh, 'Nazi gold "shipped by U-boat" to Argentina', *The Independent*, 7 Nov 2004

Packard, Jerrold Michael, *The European Neutrals in World War II (1989). Dissertations and Theses. Paper 3984* (Portland State University, 1989)

Pieth, Mark, *Gold Laundering: The Dirty Secrets of the Gold Trade and how to Clean Up* (Salis Verlag, 2019)

Prouty, L. Fletcher, *The Secret Team* (Skyhorse; 2nd edition, 2011)

Pruska, Anna, 'U.S.-Swiss Relations in the Context of Swiss Banking Secrecy', *Journal of American Studies* No. 16, 2015

Reich, Aaron, 'List found of 12,000 Nazis in Argentina with money in Swiss bank', *Jerusalem Post*, 7 March 2020

Riaud, Xavier, 'History of Nazi Dental Gold: From Dead Bodies to Swiss Bank', *SAJ Forensic Science* Vol. 1, 2015

Rosenfeld, Gavriel David, *The Fourth Reich: The Specter of Nazism from World War II to the Present* (Cambridge University Press, 2019)

Rubin, Seymour J., 'The Washington Accord Fifty Years Later: Neutrality, Morality, and International Law', *American University International Law Review,* 14, No. 1, 1998

Sands, Philippe, *The Ratline; Love Lies and Justice on the Trail of a Nazi Fugitive* (Wiedenfeld and Nicolson, 2020)

Savas, Theodore P., *Nazi Millionaires: The Allied Search for Hidden SS Gold* (Casemate Publishers, Kindle Edition)

Schacht, Hjalmar, *Account Settled* (Duckworth, 1948)

Schemo, Diana Jean, 'A Nazi's Trail Leads to a Gold Cache in Brazil', *New York Times*, 23 September 1997

Schloss, Henry H., *The Bank for International Settlements* (North Holland Publishing Co., 1958)

Schweitzer, Arthur, 'The Role of Foreign Trade in the Nazi War Economy', *Journal of Political Economy* Vol. 51, No. 4, August 1943

Sereny, Gitta, *Into that Darkness* (Vintage Books, 1974)

Shirer, William L., *The Rise and Fall of the Third Reich: A History of Nazi Germany* (Ballantine Books, 1992)

Singer, Kurt D., 'How Norway's Gold was Saved', *Browsing Dalhousie Review,* Vol. 23, 1943

Slany, William S., *U.S. and Allied Efforts to Recover and Restore Gold and Other Assets Stolen or Hidden by Germany During World War II; Preliminary Study* (U.S. State Department, 1997)

Smith, Arthur L., *Hitler's Gold: The Story of the Nazi War Loot* (Berg, 1989)

Steinacher, Gerald, *Nazis on the Run* (Oxford University Press, 2010)

Steinacher, Gerald, 'The Cape of Last Hope': The Postwar Flight of Nazi War Criminals through South Tyrol/Italy to SouthAmerica (Faculty Publications, Department of History University of Nebraska, 2006)

Steinberg, Jonathan, *The Deutsche Bank and Its Gold Transactions During the Second World War* (C. H. Beck, 1999)

Taber, George M., *Chasing Gold: The Incredible Story of how the Nazis stole Europe's Bullion* (Pegasus Books, 2014)

Tanner, Jakob, 'How the Swiss Banks Deal was Brokered', www.swissinfo.ch

Tooze, Adam, *The Wages of Destruction* (Penguin Books, Kindle Edition)

Uki, Goñi, *The Real Odessa: Smuggling the Nazis to Perón's Argentina* (Granta Books, 2002)

Van der Wee, Herman & Monique Verbreyt, *A Small Nation in the Turmoil of the Second World War Money, Finance and Occupation (Belgium, its Enemies, its Friends, 1939-1945)* (Leuven University Press, 2009)

Vincent, Isabel, *Swiss Banks, Nazi Gold and the Pursuit of Justice* (William Morrow and Company Inc, 1997)

Wahlbäck, Krister, 'Neutrality and Morality: The Swedish Experience', *American University International Law Review,* Vol. 14, Issue 1, 1996

Weinberg, Gerhard L., 'German Plans and Policies regarding Neutral Nations in World War II with Special Reference to Switzerland', *German Studies Review,* Feb., Vol. 22, No. 1, 1999

Weitz, John, *Hitler's Banker: Hjalmar Horace Greeley Schacht* (Little, Brown and Company, 1997)

White, Elizabeth, 'The Disposition of SS-Looted Victim Gold During and After World War II' *American University International Law Review,* Vol. 14, Issue 1, 1998

Wiesenthal, Simon, *Doch die Mörder leben* (Munich, Droemer Knaur, 1967)

Woods, John, *Have you ever heard about the Hungarian Gold Train that was captured by the USA?* (dailynewshungary.com, 3 May 2020)

Zabludoff, Sidney, 'Movements of Nazi Gold: Uncovering the Trail', *Institute of the World Jewish Congress Policy Study,* No. 10, 1997

Ziegler, Jean, *The Swiss, the Gold and the Dead: How Swiss bankers helped finance the Nazi war machine* (Harcourt Brace & Company, 1997)

1971 Report of the Tripartite Gold Commission, vol. I, (US Department of State, 1971)

British Public Records Office, War Office Files, WO 204/11574

Cable of General Marshall to the U.S. Legation to Budapest, July 27, 1948, (NARA, RG 84, POLAD- USCOA Records, Papers of the U.S. Legation to Austria, Box 106)

Diplomatic Documents of Switzerland dodis.ch/48220

Diplomatic Documents of Switzerland dodis.ch/65

Diplomatic Documents of Switzerland dodis.ch/68

Documents on German Foreign Policy, 1918-1943, from the Archives of the German Foreign Ministry, (British Foreign Office and the U.S. Department of State, Series D, 1949-1956., v. IX)

'Dr. Schacht's Dismissal and the German Economic Situation', *Bulletin of International News* Vol. 16, No. 2, 28 Jan 1939

'Germans Admit Losing Files on Gold That Nazis Stole From Jews', *New York Times,* 24 July 1998

Gold Transactions in the Second World War: Statistical Review with Commentary: A contribution to the Conference on Nazi Gold London, 2 – 4 December 1997 (December 1997)

Identification of the skeletal remains of Martin Bormann by mtDNA analysis (National Library of Medicine, 2001)

Indiscriminate Issuing and use of Identity Documents of the International Red Cross (US National Archives and Record Administration RG84 entry 2057 box 2, 20 January 1947)

Information Report, Subject: "Croatian Gold Question," (CIA Reference Files, 1951)

Information Report, Subject: "Jugoslavia: Present Whereabouts of Former Ustaši Officials" (CIA Reference Files, 1946)

Information Report, Subject: "Transfer of Croatian Gold to Argentina" (CIA Reference Files, 1952)

kenalford.blogspot.com, June 2005

Klaus Report to Currie, Coe, and Cox, Franklin D. Roosevelt Library, Franklin D. Roosevelt Papers (1945)

l'Eldofildo dui tolhiborazlonis (Alto Adige, 22 May 1947)

SOURCES

Letter of the Central Board of Jews in Hungary and the Autonomous Orthodox Israelitic Religious Bodies in Hungary to the U.S. Legation in Budapest (NARA, RG 84, Papers of the U.S. Legation in Budapest, Box 4, 26 February 1947)

Memorandum from Klaus to Currie, Coe, and Cox (Franklin D. Roosevelt Library, Cox Papers, Lend Lease File, Box 104, 21 October 1944)

Memorandum to Walter Surrey, (attorney, Division Chief, Office of Economic Policy, Department of State, 1946-1947) (General Records of the Department of State RG 59, Decimal Files 1945-49 800.515/1-1046, 10 January 1946)

Nazi Gold; The London Conference (Foreign and Commonwealth Office, London, 1997)

'Nazi-Hunter thinks Evita hid gold in Swiss Banks', *Orlando Sentinel*, 27 June 1997

Odessa und das Vierte Reich: Mythen der Zeitgeschichte (Berlin: Metropol Verlag, 2007)

romanjews.com/gold-of-rome-incredible-story-nazi-occupation downloaded 09/11/2022

Rugs removed from Military Government Warehouse MAXGLAN, Salzburg by order of Maj. Gen. Harry J. Collins for use in his villa MARIA THERESIEN SCHLOSS (NARA, RG 260, Box 77, USACA Records, RD & R Division, Property Control Branch)

The Role of Swiss Financial Institutions in the Plunder of European Jewry (Institute of the World Jewish Congress, 1996)

Treaty of Friendship Between Germany and Turkey June 18, 1941 (Lillian Goldman Law Library, 2008)

US National Archives and Record Administration RG84 entry 2057 box 2.20, 15 May 1947

NOTES

Chapter 1

1. Lacey, James, *Gold, Blood, and Power: Finance and War through the Ages* (Strategic Studies Institute and U.S. Army War College, May 2015), p.77.
2. Ibid., p.v.
3. Ibid., p.36.
4. Schweitzer, Arthur, 'The Role of Foreign Trade in the Nazi War Economy', *Journal of Political Economy*, Vol. 51, No. 4, August 1943, p.330.

Chapter 2

1. Tooze, Adam, *The Wages of Destruction* (Penguin Books, Kindle Edition), p.214.
2. *Gold Transactions in the Second World War: Statistical Review with Commentary: A contribution to the Conference on Nazi Gold London, 2-4 December 1997*, December 1997.
3. Shirer, William L., *The Rise and Fall of the Third Reich: A History of Nazi Germany* (Ballantine Books, 1992), p.477.
4. Smith, Arthur L., *Hitler's Gold: The Story of the Nazi War Loot* (Berg, 1989), p.2.
5. Ziegler, Jean, *The Swiss, the Gold and the Dead: How Swiss bankers helped finance the Nazi war machine* (Harcourt Brace & Company, 1997), p.40.
6. Taber, George M., *Chasing Gold; The Incredible Story of How the Nazis Stole Europe's Bullion* (Pegasus Books, 2014), p.119.
7. Ibid., p.121.
8. Ziegler, p.37.
9. Schacht, Hjalmar, *Account Settled* (Duckworth, 1948), p.134.
10. Ziegler, p.41.
11. Ibid., p.40.
12. 'Dr. Schacht's Dismissal and the German Economic Situation', *Bulletin of International News*, Vol. 16, No. 2, 28 Jan 1939.
13. Smith, p.4.
14. Blaazer, David, 'Finance and the End of Appeasement: The Bank of England, the National Government and the Czech Gold', *Journal of Contemporary History*, Vol. 40, No. 1, Jan. 2005, p.32.
15. *Nazi Gold: The London Conference* (Foreign and Commonwealth Office, London, 1997), p.247.
16. Blaazer, p.29.
17. Taber, p.115.
18. Blaazer, p.28.
19. Ibid., p.33.

NOTES

20 *Nazi Gold: The London Conference*, p.247.
21 Smith, p.56.
22 Cain, P.J. and Hopkins A.G., *British Imperialism: vol. 1, Innovation and Expansion, 1688-1914 vol. 2, Crisis and Deconstruction, 1914-19* (Addison-Wesley Longman Ltd., 1993), p.104.
23 Blaazer, p.37.
24 Taber, p.137.
25 Ibid., p.41.
26 Ibid., p.143.
27 Ibid., p.146.
28 Singer, Kurt D., 'How Norway's Gold was Saved', *Browsing Dalhousie Review*, Vol. 23, 1943, p.347.
29 Allen, Robert W. Jnr., *Britain and the Belgian Exiles* (University College London, 1997), p.60.
30 Taber, p.235.
31 Ibid., p.275.
32 Van der Wee, Herman & Monique Verbreyt, *A Small Nation in the Turmoil of the Second World War Money, Finance and Occupation (Belgium, its Enemies, its Friends, 1939-1945)* (Leuven University Press, 2009), p.65.
33 Smith, p.12.
34 Ibid., p.23.
35 Taber, p.322.
36 Labord, Larry, *French Gold In World War II* (321gold.com, 2019).
37 Smith, p.28.
38 *Nazi Gold; The London Conference*, p.324.
39 romanjews.com/gold-of-rome-incredible-story-nazi-occupation downloaded 09/11/2022.

Chapter 3

1 Golson, Eric Bernard, *The Economics of Neutrality: Spain, Sweden and Switzerland in the Second World War* (The London School of Economics and Political Science, 2011), p.31.
2 Ibid.
3 *Documents on German Foreign Policy, 1918-1943, from the Archives of the German Foreign Ministry* (British Foreign Office and the U.S. Department of State, Series D, 1949-1956., v. IX,), p.142.
4 Packard, Jerrold Michael, 'The European Neutrals in World War II', *Dissertations and Theses. Paper 3984* (Portland State University, 1989), p.80.
5 Wahlbäck, Krister, 'Neutrality and Morality: The Swedish Experience', *American University International Law Review* Vol. 14, Issue 1, 1996, p.106.
6 Milward, Alan S., 'Could Sweden Have Stopped the Second World War?', *Scandinavian Economic Historical Review*, 1967, p.127.
7 Hale, William, 'Turkey and Britain in World War II: Origins and Results of the Tripartite Alliance, 1935-40', *Journal of Balkan and Near Eastern Studies*, Vol. 23, No. 6, 2021, p.824.
8 *Treaty of Friendship Between Germany and Turkey June 18, 1941* (Lillian Goldman Law Library, 2008).
9 Slany, William S., *U.S. and Allied Efforts to Recover and Restore Gold and Other Assets Stolen or Hidden by Germany During World War II; Preliminary Study* (U.S. State Department, 1997), p.142.
10 Manning, Paul, *Martin Bormann: Nazi in Exile* (Kindle edition), p.82.
11 Leitz, Christian, *Economic Relations Between Nazi Germany and Franco's Spain 1936-1945* (Clarendon Press, 1996), p.205.

12. Louça, Antonio and Schäfer Ansgar, 'Portugal and the Nazi Gold: The "Lisbon Connection" in the Sales of Looted Gold by the Third Reich', *Yad Vashem Studies*, Vol. 27, 1999, p.105.
13. Slany, p.25.

Chapter 4

1. Ziegler, p.xi.
2. Ibid., p.76.
3. LeBor, Adam, *Hitler's Secret Bankers* (Head of Zeus, 2020), p.10.
4. Taber, p.377.
5. Smith, pp.60-1.
6. LeBor, *Hitler's Secret Bankers*, p.81.
7. Ziegler, p.58.
8. Weinberg, Gerhard L., 'German Plans and Policies Regarding Neutral Nations in World War II with Special Reference to Switzerland', *German Studies Review*, Vol. 22, No. 1, Feb. 1999, p.101.
9. LeBor, *Hitler's Secret Bankers*, p.81.
10. Ziegler, p.70.
11. Slany, pp.6-7.
12. LeBor, *Hitler's Secret Bankers*, p.77.
13. Ziegler, p.48.
14. Smith, p.65.
15. Taber, p.419.
16. Ziegler, p.22.

Chapter 5

1. LeBor, *Hitler's Secret Bankers*, pp.99-100.
2. Smith, p.58.
3. LeBor, *Hitler's Secret Bankers*, p.101.
4. *Nazi Gold: The London Conference*, p.45.
5. Smith p.54.
6. LeBor, Adam, *Meet the American Banker Who Helped Hitler Loot Jewish Gold—While Spying for the OSS* (tabletmag.com, 2013).
7. Ibid.
8. LeBor, *Hitler's Secret Bankers*, p.104.
9. Smith, p.53.
10. *Nazi Gold: The London Conference*, p.58.

Chapter 6

1. Taber, p.415.
2. Fotich, Constantin, *The War We Lost: Yugoslavia's Tragedy and the Failure of the West* (Literary Licensing, 2012), pp.117-18.
3. Morley, John F., *Vatican Diplomacy and the Jews During the Holocaust* (Ktav Inc, 1980), p.147.
4. *1971 Report of the Tripartite Gold Commission, vol. I* (US Department of State, 1971), p.64.
5. *Information Report, Subject: "Croatian Gold Question"*, (CIA Reference Files, 1951).
6. *Information Report, Subject: "Transfer of Croatian Gold to Argentina"*, (CIA Reference Files, 1952).

NOTES

7 *British Public Records Office, War Office Files*, WO 204/11574.
8 *Information Report, Subject: "Jugoslavia: Present Whereabouts of Former Ustaši Officials"*, (CIA Reference Files, 1946).

Chapter 7

1 Clark, Margaret, *Safehaven Study: Records of the Federal Economic Administration* (RG 169).
2 Ibid., p.22.
3 *Klaus Report to Currie, Coe, and Cox, Franklin D. Roosevelt Library, Franklin D. Roosevelt Papers*, 1945.
4 Smith, p.69.
5 Slany, p.21.
6 Clark, p.189.
7 Smith, p.74.
8 Ibid., p.75.
9 Ibid., p.78.

Chapter 8

1 Rosenfeld, Gavriel David, *The Fourth Reich: The Specter of Nazism from World War II to the Present.* (Cambridge University Press, 2019), p.2.
2 LeBor, *Hitler's Secret Bankers*, p.124.
3 Steinacher, Gerald, *Nazis on the Run* (Oxford University Press, 2010), p. xvii.
4 d'Erizans, Alexander Peter, *Odessa und das Vierte Reich: Mythen der Zeitgeschichte. Review* (Oregon State University, 2011).
5 Enclosure No. 1 to dispatch No. 19,489 of 27 November 1944 from the London Embassy. Intelligence Report No. EW-Pa 128, 7 November 1944.
6 Ibid.
7 Slany, p.50.
8 LeBor, Adam, *The secret report that shows how the Nazis planned a Fourth Reich ...in the EU* (Mailonline, 9 May 2009).

Chapter 9

1 Taber, p.406.
2 Bradsher, Greg, 'Nazi Gold: The Merkers Mine Treasure', *Prologue Magazine*, Spring 1999.
3 Taber, p.407.
4 Bradsher, 'Nazi Gold'.
5 Smith, p.94.

Chapter 10

1 Taber, p.356.
2 Ibid.
3 White, Elizabeth, 'The Disposition of SS-Looted Victim Gold During and After World War II', *American University International Law Review*, Vol. 14, Issue 1, 1998, p.216.
4 Steinberg, Jonathan, *The Deutsche Bank and Its Gold Transactions During the Second World War* (C.H. Beck, 1999).
5 'Germans Admit Losing Files on Gold That Nazis Stole From Jews', *New York Times*, 24 July 1998.

6. state.gov/regions/eur/rpt_9806_ng_reichsbank.pdf
7. Riaud, Xavier, 'History of Nazi Dental Gold: From Dead Bodies to Swiss Bank', *SAJ Forensic Science*, Vol. 1, 2015, p.3.
8. Ibid.

Chapter 11

1. Banken, Ralph, *National Socialist Robbery of Precious Metals, 1933-1945: The Role of Degussa and the Case of Poland* (escholarship.org, 2006), p.11.
2. Ibid., p14.
3. Ibid., p16.
4. Taber, p.386.

Chapter 12

1. Woods, John, *Have you ever heard about the Hungarian Gold Train that was captured by the USA?* (dailynewshungary.com, 3 May 2020).
2. NARA, RG 84, Papers of the U.S. Legation to Budapest, Box 4, Letter of the Central Board of Jews in Hungary to the Department of State, July 28, 1947.
3. *Letter of the Central Board of Jews in Hungary and the Autonomous Orthodox Israelitic Religious Bodies in Hungary to the U.S. Legation in Budapest* (NARA, RG 84, Papers of the U.S. Legation in Budapest, Box 4, 26 February 1947).
4. *Cable of General Marshall to the U.S. Legation to Budapest, July 27, 1948* (NARA, RG 84, POLAD- USCOA Records, Papers of the U.S. Legation to Austria, Box 106).
5. *Rugs removed from Military Government Warehouse MAXGLAN, Salzburg by order of Maj. Gen. Harry J. Collins for use in his villa MARIA THERESIEN SCHLOSS* (NARA, RG 260, Box 77, USACA Records, RD & R Division, Property Control Branch).

Chapter 13

1. Taber, p.421.
2. Ibid., p.423.

Chapter 14

1. Smith, p.103.
2. Slany, p.55.
3. Smith, p.105.
4. Slany, p.57.
5. Smith, p.106.
6. Vincent, Isabel, *Swiss Banks, Nazi Gold and the Pursuit of Justice* (William Morrow and Company Inc, 1997), p.205.
7. *Diplomatic Documents of Switzerland dodis.ch/65.*
8. Ziegler, p.189.
9. *Diplomatic Documents of Switzerland dodis.ch/68.*
10. Rubin, Seymour J., 'The Washington Accord Fifty Years Later: Neutrality, Morality, and International Law', *American University International Law Review 14*, No. 1, 1998, p.61.
11. *Diplomatic Documents of Switzerland dodis.ch/48220.*
12. Ziegler, p.184.
13. Slany, p.xxvi.
14. Ziegler, p.194.

NOTES

Chapter 15

1. Smith, p.132.
2. *Nazi Gold: The London Conference*, p.547.
3. Smith, p.133.
4. Ibid., p.141.
5. Alford, Kenneth D., *Monetary Men* (Sciffer Publishing, 2015), p.184.
6. Ibid., p.185
7. Ibid., P.186.
8. Ibid.
9. Ibid.
10. Ibid., p.187.
11. Ibid., p.182.
12. Ibid., p.188.
13. Ibid., p.189.
14. Ibid., p.190.
15. Ibid., p.189.
16. Dissolution of the Tripartite Gold Commission (*US Department of State*)

Chapter 16

1. Smith, p.151.
2. Slany p.121.
3. Ibid., p.129.
4. Ibid.
5. Ibid., p.137.
6. Ibid., p.138.
7. *Memorandum to Walter Surrey, (attorney, Division Chief, Office of Economic Policy, Department of State, 1946-1947)* (General Records of the Department of State RG 59, Decimal Files 1945-49 800.515/1-1046, 10 January 1946).
8. Smith, p.151.
9. Slany, p.141.
10. Ibid., p.144.
11. Ibid., p.145.

Chapter 17

1. Sands, Philippe, *The Ratline: Love Lies and Justice on the Trail of a Nazi Fugitive* (Wiedenfeld and Nicolson, 2020), p.159.
2. Farago, Ladislas, *Aftermath; Martin Bormann and the Fourth Reich* (Hodder and Stoughton, 1974), p.188.
3. Steinacher, *Nazis on the Run*, p.44.
4. *Indiscriminate Issuing and use of Identity Documents of the International Red Cross* (US National Archives and Record Administration RG84 entry 2057 box 2, 20 January 1947).
5. Steinacher, *Nazis on the Run*, p.81.
6. U.S. National Archives and Record Administration RG84 entry 2057 box 2.20, 15 May 1947.
7. Steinacher, *Nazis on the Run*, p.119.
8. Ibid., p.121.

Chapter 18

1. Manning, *Martin Bormann: Nazi in Exile*, p.65.
2. Manning, Paul, 'Martin Bormann and the Future of Germany', *New York Times*, 3 March 1973.
3. *Memorandum from Klaus to Currie, Coe, and Cox* (Franklin D. Roosevelt Library, Cox Papers, Lend Lease File, Box 104, 21 October 1944).
4. Ibid.
5. Manning, *Martin Bormann: Nazi in Exile*, p.65.
6. Steinacher, *Nazis on the Run*, pp.217-19.
7. Ibid.
8. Schemo, Diana Jean, 'A Nazi's Trail Leads to a Gold Cache in Brazil', *New York Times*, 23 September 1997.

Chapter 19

1. Spartacuseducational.com/GERbormann.htm
2. Farago, p.205.
3. Manning, *Martin Bormann: Nazi in Exile*, p.216.
4. Farago, p.209.
5. O'Shaughnessy, Hugh, 'Nazi gold "shipped by U-boat" to Argentina', *The Independent*, 7 Nov 2004.
6. Ibid.
7. Farago, p.145.
8. Manning, pp.190-1.
9. Farago, p.355.
10. Ibid., p357.
11. Manning, pp.191-2.
12. Farago, p.213.
13. Ibid., p.157.
14. Ibid., p.152.
15. Steinacher, Gerald, *'The Cape of Last Hope': The Postwar Flight of Nazi War Criminals through South Tyrol/Italy to South America* (Faculty Publications, Department of History University of Nebraska, 2006).
16. *l'Eldofildo dui tolhiborazlonis* (Alto Adige, 22 May 1947), pp. 2-3.
17. Wiesenthal, Simon, *Doch die Mörder leben* (Droemer Knaur, Munich,1967), p.109.
18. *Odessa und das Vierte Reich: Mythen der Zeitgeschichte* (Metropol Verlag, Berlin, 2007).
19. Uki, Goñi, *The Real Odessa: Smuggling the Nazis to Perón's Argentina* (Granta Books, 2002).
20. Sereny, Gitta, *Into that Darkness* (Vintage Books, 1974).
21. Farago, p.215.
22. Manning, pp.224-5.
23. Farago, p.223.
24. Ibid., p.229.
25. Novitski, Joseph, *Never Saw Bormann, Argentinian Declares* (nytimes.com).
26. Mello, Laurence de, (goldeneyepublishingltd.wordpress.com, 24 August 2016).
27. *Identification of the skeletal remains of Martin Bormann by mtDNA analysis* (National Library of Medicine, 2001).
28. Hutchison, Robert, *Their Kingdom Come* (Transworld, Kindle Edition), pp.211-12.
29. 'Nazi-Hunter thinks Evita hid gold in Swiss Banks', *Orlando Sentinel*, 27 June 1997.
30. Farnsworth, Clyde H., 'Mystery shrouds gold sale report', *New York Times*, 11 September 1973.

NOTES

Chapter 20
1. Vincent, p 195.
2. Tanner, Jakob, 'How the Swiss Banks Deal was Brokered', www.swissinfo.ch
3. *The Role of Swiss Financial Institutions in the Plunder of European Jewry* (Institute of the World Jewish Congress, 1996).
4. *Nazi Gold: The London Conference*, p.5.

Chapter 21
1. www.istrianet.org/istria/history/1800-present/camps/globocnik/gold.htm
2. kenalford.blogspot.com, June 2005.
3. The National Archives FO 371/ 179969 q
4. mailonline.co.uk 3 April 20193
5. tearsofthewolf.com/mittenwald
6. Savas, Theodore P., *Nazi Millionaires: The Allied Search for Hidden SS Gold* (Casemate Publishers, Kindle Edition), p.188.
7. Kirkpatrick, Sidney, *Hitler's Holy Relics* (Simon & Schuster UK, Kindle Edition).
8. Savas, p.316.
9. Ibid., p.318.
10. *Treasure hunter who found £500million of Nazi treasure in a Bavarian wood says landowner won't let him dig it up 'because he wants it for himself'*, (Mailonline, 30 July 2017).

Postscript
1. Pieth, Mark, *Gold Laundering: The Dirty Secrets of the Gold Trade and how to Clean Up* (Salis Verlag, 2019).
2. Reich, Aaron, 'List found of 12,000 Nazis in Argentina with money in Swiss bank', *Jerusalem Post*, 7 March 2020.
3. Baschuck, Paige, 'Tracing Nazi Gold through Switzerland', *The Swiss Times*, 4 July 2022.
4. Golubova, Anna, 'Switzerland's Russian gold imports climb in 2022', kitco.com 26 January 2023.

INDEX

Abs, Hermann, 80, 81
Adenauer, Konrad, 81
Ahnenerbe, 101
Alarcón, Niceforo, 149
Allied Control Council, 117
Allied Control Council Law No. 10, 146
Allied-Swiss Washington Accord, 59
Almansi, Dante, 39
Alter, John E., 177
Aluminum Company of America, 143
Ansiaux, Herbert, 25, 26–28, 30
Argentine Blue Book, 145
Atlee, Clement, 113
Austrian National Bank, 11
Axmann, Arthur, 151

Badische Anilin und Sodafabrik, 145
Badoglio, Pietro, 35
Banca d'Italia, 35–37, 39, 97
Banco Alemán, 149
Banco Alemán Transatlántico, 149
Banco Commerciale Italiana, 97
Banco de Portugal, 50, 51, 66
banco Germánico, 149
Banco Tornquist, 149
Bangesellschaft, 73
Bank Deutscher Lander, 95
Bank for International Settlements, BIS, 11, 15–19, 37, 50, 57, 58, 60–66, 74
Bank of Canada, 30
Bank of England, 5, 11, 12, 15–19, 25, 30, 34, 51, 60, 64, 66, 67, 88, 89, 90, 116, 125, 166–168
Bank of France, 21, 25–28, 30–33, 60
Bankaufsichtamt, 30
Bankers' Trust, 64
Bankverin, 73
Banque Continental of Brussels and Antwerp, 142

Banque d'Athens, 94
Banque de l'Ouest, 142
Banque Générale de Luxembourg, 142
Banque Hanséatique, 142
Barbie, Klaus, 70
Basler Handelsbank, 73
Bauer, Fritz, 152, 153
Bayer Ltd., 46, 50, 146
Bearn, 33
Becker, Hans von, 30
Beograd, 67
Bergier, Jean François, 121
Bergier Commission, 96, 121
Berlin Pawn Institute, Berliner Zentrale Pfandleihe, 11, 93, 96, 101
Bernstein, Bernard D., 85, 87, 88, 115
Blaschke, Hugo, 160
Blume, Albert, 147
Blume, Walter, 147
Bohemian Discount Bank of Prague, 94
Bohmische Union Bank of Prague, 142
Boisson, Pierre, 30
Bormann, Martin (aka Luigi Boglilio, aka Juan Gomez, aka Eliezer Goldstein), 142, 143, 148–163, 176
Breart de Boisanger, Yves, 28, 29, 32
Brecken, Brendan, 17
Brett, Robert E., 21
Bretton Woods Resolution VI, 71, 72, 73, 133, 136
Brown Brothers Harriman, 64
Bruggmann, Charles, 120

Cáceres, Alberto S., 159
Caggiano, Antonio, 150
Canaris, Wilhelm, 53
Cembran, Allesandro, 36
CF-OP-2315 Coordinación Federal, 149
Chamberlain, Neville, 12, 19, 33

INDEX

Charqueraud, Paul, 118
Chase National Bank of New York, 135
Churchill, Winston, 17, 27, 29, 46
Citibank, 135
Clodius, Karl, 45, 58
Cobbold, Cameron, 16
College of San Girolamo degli Illirici, 69
Collins, Harry J., 106
Conrad, Franz, 177
Contact Office for the Search of Dormant Accounts, 164
Cook, Robin, 166
Cragon, Henry D., 86
Crédit Suisse, 76, 79, 165, 180
Croatian State Bank, 68, 69
Cunningham, John, 29
Currie, Lauchlin, 117
Czechoslovakian National Bank, Česká Národní Banka, 15, 17

D'Amato, Alfonse, 164, 165, 166
De Gaulle, Charles, 29
Debenedetti, Giacomo, 39
Declaration on Gold Purchases, 51
Degussa, 83
Delamuraz, Jean-Pascal, 165
Deutsche Bank, 46, 47, 94, 102, 149
Deutsche Orient Bank, 46
Deutsche Reichsbank, 11
Devisenfahndungsamt, 91
Devisenschutzkommando, 101
Dörge, Heinrich, 158
Douglas, Gregory (aka Peter Stahl, aka Yetta schwarz), 169, 170
Dow Chemical Company, 143
Draganović, Krunoslav, 69, 70, 111, 149
Dresdner Bank, 47, 94
DuBois, Herbert G., 88
Dulles, Allen, 53, 63
Dulles, John Foster, 63
Durey, Nick, 167
Dutch National Bank, 23

E. I. du Pont de Nemours, 143
E. Schlemm & Company, 147
Eden, Anthony, 46
Eichmann, Adolf (aka Ricardo Klement), 139, 144, 158
Eidgenössiche Bank, 73
Eimers, Reinhard, 178
Einsatzgruppen, 101
Eisenhower, Dwight D., 85

Eizenstat, Stuart, 40, 60, 121, 165
Emile Bertin, 21, 33,
Epervier, 21
Esparza, Egidio, 156
Etablissements Kuhlmann, 143
Ethyl Export Corporation, 143

Farago, Ladislas, 152
Farrell, Edelmiro Julián, 144, 146
Faupel, Wilhelm, 148
Federal Reserve Bank of New York, 23, 25, 116, 135, 163, 166
Finance Office in the Troop Administration Department, 92
Finot, Alfonso, 158
First National Bank of Chicago, 60
First National Bank of Manhattan, 65
First National Bank of New York, 60
Fisher, Joel H., 88, 89
Five Power Agreement, 106
Floyar-Rajchman, Henryk, 20
Foà, Ugo, 39
Fournier, Pierre, 28
Franco, Francisco, 47, 49
Frankfurt Exchange Depository, 123
Franzesi Brothers, 4
Fraser, Leon, 65
Frick, Wilhelm, 11
Friedrich Roessler Söhne, 93
Friends of the New Germany, 76
Frondizi, Arturo, 159
Frondizi, Silvio, 149
Funk, Walther, 8, 14, 35, 57, 63, 74, 82–83, 92, 97, 109, 110, 167
Furmaniak, Roman, 175 176

Galland, Adolf, 145
General Electric, 64
General Motors, 64
General Trustee for Securing German Cultural Property, 102
German American Bund, 76
German External Property Commission, 117
German-Turkish Treaty of Friendship, 45
Giampietro, Pellegrini, 37, 38
Giesen, Leon, 176
Giovann C, 156
Gisevius, Hans Bend, 12, 53
Globocnik, Odilo, 95, 96, 109, 169
Gluek, Hans, 178

Goñi, Uki, 155
Göring, Hermann, 8, 10, 11, 12, 14, 32, 35–37, 101
Gottfriedsen, Bernd, 38
Groger, Helmuth, 111
Grotius, Hugo, 40

Haakon VII, 22
Hague Agreements, 62
Halifax, Lord, 17, 26, 33
Handels-und-Kreditbank of Riga, 94
Hansson, Per Albin, 43
Haslund, Frederik, 22
Haupttreuhandstelle Ost, 101
Hechler, Paul, 63
Hedley, W. K., 172
Heinemann, Karl, 139
Hemmen, Johannes, 28, 29, 30, 32
Hess, Rudolf, 148
Heydrich, Reinhard, 10, 14, 92, 100
Himmler, Heinrich, 67, 89, 92, 97, 109, 175, 177
Hirs, Alfred, 166
Hirschfeld, Walter, 177
Hitler, Adolf, 7, 8, 10, 12, 26, 29, 33, 35, 40, 45, 47, 50, 55, 78, 80, 82, 108–109, 118
HMS Arethusa, 23
HMS Ark Royal, 29
HMS Barham, 29
HMS Boreas, 23
HMS Enterprise, 23
HMS Glasgow, 23
HMS Keith, 23
HMS Resolution, 30
Högl, Peter, 150
Hollandsche Koopmansbank, 142
Howard Report, 90
Hudal, Alois, 139, 140, 141, 149
Hull, Cordell, 52

I.G. Farben, 46, 48, 50, 72, 80, 142, 143, 144
Iburguren, Maria Eva Duarte (aka Eva Perón), 143, 149, 156, 163
Imperial Chemical Industries, 143
Independent Committee of Eminent Persons, 164
Independent Committee of Experts, 121
Instituto Santa Maria dell'Anima, 139
Inter Allied Reparation Agency, 114
Inter-Allied Declaration Against Acts of Dispossession, 57

Intergovernmental Committee for Refugees, 105
International Committee of the Red Cross, ICRC, 140, 141, 154

J.P. Morgan and Co., 60
Janssen, Édouard, 30
Jost, Hans Ulrich, 59
Justo, Agustín Pedro, 144

Kaltenbrunner, Ernst, 107, 177, 178
Kappler, Herbert, 35, 39
Karpiński, Zygmunt, 20
Kauffmann, Henrik, 22
Kempka, Erich, 150
Kirdorf, Emil, 77
Klaus, Samuel, 72
Knights Templars, 4
Koc, Colonel Adam, 20
Kontinentale Bank of Brussels, 94
Koper, Piotr, 172
Kreditansalt, 73
Krosigk, Lutz von, 13, 92, 97
Krüger, George, 109
Krumnow, Albert, 160
Krupp Industries, 46, 77–80, 146, 157
Kubu, Edouard, 16
Kuhne, Lothar, 178

Lammers, Hans, 108, 109
Lamoureux, Lucien, 33
Lang, Jochen von, 151
Leopold III, 26
Leute, Ricardo von, 158
Lienau, Heinrich, 152
Loeb, Kuhn, 64
Luxembourg Savings Bank, 25

Madjerec, Juraj, 69
Maison Rouge Hotel, 76
Malik, Josef, 15, 16
Manning, Paul, 156
Masson, Roger, 53
Matuszewski, Ignacy, 20
Max Heileger' account, 92
Mayer, Gerry, 53
Mazzolini, Serafino, 37
McCombe, F.W., 118
McKittrick, Thomas, 58, 63, 64
Melmer Gold, 92, 93, 94, 95, 97, 99, 115, 148, 169
Mengershausen, Harry, 151
Mercedes Benz, 145

INDEX

Messore, Osvaldo A., 159
Michalski, Stephan, 26, 27
Mieg, Dolfuss, 88
Miesen, Bernard, 109
Moellhausen, Eitel Friedrich, 36
Moevus, 26, 27
Molina, Juan Batista Sosa, 157
Montini, Giovanni (Pope Paul VI), 140, 156
Morgenthau, Henry, 20, 64, 73, 74, 80, 154
Morguado, Hector Rodriguez, 160
MS Bomma, 23
Mühlmann, Kai, 102
Müller, Dr. Friedrich, 15, 155, 170
Müller, Heinrich, 150, 170
Municipal Pawnshop, 92, 93, 101
Mussolini, Benito, 29, 35, 36, 37, 138

N.V. Hollandsche Buitenland Bank, 142
Nacke, Claus, 177
Nardo, Vincenzo de, 162
National Bank for Bohemia and Moravia, Národní banka pro Čechy a Moravu, 15
National Bank of Belgium, 25, 30, 31, 60
National Bank of Greece, 34
National Bank of the Kingdom of Yugoslavia, 67, 68, 127
National City Bank, 64, 135
Naumann, Werner, 151
Neuhauser, Hans, 110, 111
New York Federal Reserve, 19, 22, 64, 67
Niebuhr, Dietrich, 148
Niemeyer, Otto, 16, 63
Nix, Willi, 139
Norges Bank, 22
Norman, Montagu, 12, 16, 18, 19
Novikov, Feodor, 179
Nyaradi, Nikolaus, 105

Office of Strategic Services, 53
Ohlendorf, Otto, 80
Onslow, Richard, 27
Operation Menace, 29
Operation Tannenbaum, 55
Orczykowski, Stanisław, 32
Ortiz, Roberto, 144

Papen, Franz von, 136
Paris Repatriation Agreement, 106
Parke-Bernet Galleries, 107

Patton, George, 84
Paul, Randolph, 118
Pavelić, Ante, 68, 69, 70, 149
Pererya, Rodolfo "Rolo", 149
Perillo, Horacio A., 159
Perón, Juan, 142, 143, 145–147, 149, 154–158, 161–163
Peroutka, Frantisek, 15, 16
Pfeiffer, Franz Wilhelm, 110
Pfurter, Rogelio, 167
Pilet-Golaz, Marcel, 54
Pohl, Oswald, 92
Polish National Bank, 20, 28
Pompey, 2
Pontificia Commissione Assistenza, 140
Pook, Hermann, 98
Pope Pius XII, 70, 140
Preparatory Commission for the International Refugee Organisation, 106
Primauguet, 34
Public Law No. 5, 74, 117
Puhl, Emil, 8, 12, 14, 32, 54, 57–58, 63, 73–75, 89, 92, 112, 148
Puk, Mirko, 69

Quedlinburg Lodge, 174
Quimica Commercial y Farmaceutica S.A. Farben Unicolor S.A., 48

Radl, Karl, 176
Rafaelo, Alejandro, 160
Rahn, Rudolf, 35–37
Raiber, Richard, 170
Rainer, Friedrich, 171
Rašín, Alois, 15
Rattenhuber, Johann (Hans), 150
Rauch, Friedrich Josef (aka José Federico Rauch), 108
Rave, Paul Ortwin, 84
Ray, Guillermo Macia, 149
Reichsbank's Precious Metals Department, 90, 97
Reichsbankhauptkasse, 102
Reichshauptkasse, 92, 94, 95, 102
Reichshauptkasse Beutestelle, 102
Reichssicherheitshauptamt, 102
Reichsstelle für Edelmetalle, 102
Ribbentrop, Joachim von, 32, 35, 36, 38, 58, 90, 107
Ribbentrop Gold, 90
Ricardi of Lucca, 4
Richter, Andreas, 172

Rifkind, Malcolm, 166
Rodgers, Peter, 167
Rodius Koenig Handel Maatschappin, 142
Rodriguez, Jaime Joaquin, 159
Rohm & Haas, 143
Roosevelt, Theodore, 20, 46, 52
Rosenberg-Lipinsky, Alfred von, 109, 110
Russel, William A., 84

Salazar, António de Oliveira, 48, 50
Sandstede, Gottfried, 149
Schacht, Hjalmar, 8, 10, 11, 12, 14, 18, 19, 158
Schaefer, Hans Christoph, 161
Scheid, Johann Friedrich, 77, 78, 79, 190
Scheidler, Arthur, 178
Schellenberg, Walter, 53
Schmitz, Hermann, 143
Schneppen, Heinz, 154
Schnitzler, Georg von, 77
Schroeder, Kurt von, 77
Schwägermann, Günther, 151
Schwedler, August, 109, 110
Schwerin, Johann, 11, 97
Sereny, Gitta, 155
Sestrire, 70
Shirer, William, 11
Siemens Companhia de Electricidad S.A.R.L, 51
Siemens Schuckert, 144
Simon, Sir John, 15, 16, 18
Siri, Guiseppe, 156 159
Skorzeny, Otto 'Scarface', 155, 158, 169, 177
Slany, William, 121
Sociedad Electro-Quimica de Flix, 48
Societa Bancara Romana of Bucharest, 94
Speer, Albert, 45, 77
SS Eocene, 21
SS Galatea, 22
SS Iris, 23
SS Randsford, 22
SS Titus, 23
SS Trafalgar, 22
Stalin, Josef, 113
Standard Oil, 64, 142
Staudt, Ricardo, 158
Stein, Carl von, 175
Steinacher, Gerald, 77, 191
Stimson, Henry, 73

Stucki, Walter, 75, 118, 119, 120
Stumpfegger, Gertrude, 151
Stumpfegger, Ludwig, 151
Styburski, Wiktor, 32
Swiss American Corporation, 76
Swiss Bank Corporation, 76, 165
Swiss Federal Council, 53, 117
Swiss National Bank, 37, 49–51, 57–58, 61, 65, 66, 68, 74, 97, 121, 131, 134, 135, 166
Szálasi, Ferenc, 104, 105

Task Force Fisher, 88
Task Force Hansen, 88
Task Force Whitney, 86
Temporary Managing Committee of the Central Bureau of Hungarian Jews, 105
Thalheimer, Frau, 152
Thomas, Hugh, 160
Thoms, Albert, 14, 83–85, 88, 90–93
Thyssen, Fritz, 77, 157
Tiburtius, Joachim, 151
Tomlienović, Josip, 69
Torp, Oscar, 22
Tripartite Commission for the Restitution of Monetary Gold, Tripartite Gold Commission, 39, 59, 66, 88, 111, 114, 122–129, 131, 132, 133, 137, 165, 166, 168
Truman, Harry, 113
Trustee Administration with the Government, 102

UBS, 121, 165
Unión Alemana de Gremios, 144
Unit 7-A of Einsatzgruppe B, 147
United Nations Monetary and Financial Conference, 71
Uriburu, José Félix, 144
USS Breeman, 33
USS Bronstein, 33
USS Vincennes, 33
Utilization and Management Company, 102

Van Vaerenbergh, 25
Vaubin, 21
Veick, Werner, 83, 84
Velasco, Juan José, 159
Victor Schoelcher, 26, 27, 34
Vienna Reichsbank, 11

INDEX

Wallenberg, Marcus, 63
Walsingham, Sir Francis, 5
Washington Accord, 120
Weber, Ernsy, 54
Weber, Gaby, 143
Wehrerfassungskommandos, 101
Wehrwirtschaftsrüstungsamt, 102
Weinberg, Joel H., 159
Whistler, Cyril, 176
White, Harry Dexter, 64
Wiesbaden Convention, 31
Wiesenthal, Simon, 153, 154, 155
Wifo and Roges, 102
Winkler, Max, 102

Wirtschaftsverwaltungshauptamt of the SS, 102
World Jewish Congress, 147, 164
World Jewish Restitution Organization, 164

Young Plan, 61

Zahngold, 97
Zengger, Ludwig, 160
Zentralstelle für Deutsche in Italien, 139
Ziller, Alois, 38
Żuchowski, Piotr, 173